Sunshine at Madinah

Studies in the Life of the Prophet Muḥammad

(ṣallā Allāhu ʻalayhi wa sallam)

ZAKARIA BASHIER

The Islamic Foundation

Published by the Islamic Foundation
Markfield Conference Centre, Ratby Lane,
Markfield, Leicester LE67 9SY, UK
Tel. (01530) 244944/5, Fax: (01530) 244946
E-Mail: i.foundation@islamic-foundation.org.uk

British Library Cataloguing in Publication Data
Bashir, Zakaria
Sunshine at Madinah.
1. Islam. Muhammad (Prophet)
I. Title
297'.63

ISBN 0-86037-197-2
ISBN 0-86037-196-4 pbk

Printed in Great Britain by The Cromwell Press Ltd.
Trowbridge, Wiltshire.

بسم الله الرحمن الرحيم

Contents

Chapter 4: The Socio-Economic Dimensions of the Prophet's State 175

Foreword

God's greatest blessing on mankind is divine guidance. This guidance has come through two channels – the Book and the Prophet. The uniqueness of this strategy lies in the fact that the Book and the Prophet represent two facets of the same reality. Though not a substitute for each other, they represent an integrated and indispensable source for human guidance.

The Book represents the Will of the Lord, in its sublime purity, the Word of God, the revelation with all its divine grandeur. The Prophet is the person through whom this guidance is revealed. He is the trusted receptacle, the one who receives the divine message, preserves it and communicates it to mankind without tampering or interpolation. But he is not a mere clearing-house for guidance. He unlinks that guidance in a manner that his life and character become the noblest personification of that guidance.

He is also not a mere communicator. He is assigned the responsibility of teaching, explaining and reconstructing individual life and social order in accordance with this guidance. He initiates a movement, a process of change and leads it in the desired direction. His life is a chronicle of the historic process of *da'wah* and the consequent transformation of individuals and society.

The Prophet Muḥammad, peace and blessings be upon him, is the last of the Prophets and the Qur'ān is the final book revealed by God. Ever since the advent of Islam, the *Sīrah* of the Prophet has remained a fascinating subject and a major instrument of *da'wah*. This has been such a favourite theme for Muslim writers and scholars in all periods of Muslim history and in all parts of the Islamic realm that it can be claimed that the largest number of books in Islamic history have been produced on the *Sīrah* of the Prophet, peace be upon him. Yet the topic remains unexhausted, perhaps even unexhaustible, one of the miracles of Islam.

My brother and colleague, Dr. Zakaria Bashier, joined the galaxy of writers on *Sīrah* by producing, almost a decade ago, a pioneering work: *The Meccan Crucible.* He breathed a new freshness into a subject, the story of an era, covered a thousand times. His approach was unique. He looked upon the life of the Prophet through the prism of the Qur'ān. His was not a chronicle of events. It represented the study of the life of a man who brought about the greatest revolution in human history, a study that focused on the man in the context of the mission. It was not a book of history either. It not only portrayed the major events of an era, it tried to peep behind the curtain of history, in an effort to understand its whys and hows. The focus moved beautifully and meaningfully from man to mission, from individual to movement, from past to the present and the future, from chronicle of events to ethos of society and history. This was new to the methodology of *Sīrah,* and a contribution which must not go unacknowledged.

I had the pleasure of requesting Brother Zakaria Bashier to continue his studies on the *Sīrah* and cover other aspects of the life of the Prophet to complete the picture. I am happy he has continued this valuable work. A small volume, *Hijra: Story and Significance,* has already been published by the Islamic Foundation. Now I am happy that a third study is seeing the light of day: *Sunshine at Madinah.* This contains four major studies: Pillars of the Prophet Muḥammad's Society; Two Documents of the Prophet's State; The House of the Prophet Muḥammad, and The Socio-Economic Dimensions of the Prophet's State. A fifth and very valuable study on an approach to the study of *Sīrah* has been added as an introduction to these studies. In fact this is an introduction to the entire series, beginning with *The Meccan Crucible,* going through *Hijra* and *Sunshine at Madinah,* and hopefully to be concluded by a fourth volume on War and Peace in the Life of the Prophet. I hope and pray that Brother Zakaria Bashier will be able to produce this final volume in the near future.

Every age has its own needs. The Islamic *Ummah* is today engaged in a struggle to re-establish its true ideological identity in a world steeped in secularism and worship of wealth, technology and power. Islam is not averse to wealth, technology or power; but it refuses to pursue these as goals and objects of human life. They are useful only as long as they remain means and instruments in the service of sublime goals and objectives of life – the pursuit of Godliness and the establishment of a social order based on justice and brotherhood. When these means begin to be looked upon as ends, that paves the way for disaster. Such is the predicament of mankind today. In this context, Islamic resurgence represents a movement to rebuild human society on values of *Tawḥīd, Taqwā* and *'Adl*. The inspiration for this historic struggle cannot come but from the life of the Prophet, peace be upon him. But his life has to be looked upon from a new perspective. Brother Zakaria Bashier's trio, in my humble opinion, provides one such source, not as a study that comprehends all important aspects of the life of the man who alone can provide the model for today and tomorrow, but at least as an approach to that rich and revolutionary life which is to be looked upon as a beacon for our own times.

I am grateful to all who helped in the production of the book, especially Dr. M. Manazir Ahsan, the Director General of the Foundation and Mawlana Iqbal Azami who read the manuscript and suggested numerous changes and improvements. Dr. Jamil Qureshi and Mr. Eric R. Fox deserve special thanks for meticulous editing and seeing the book through the press. Finally I would like to thank Mrs. Barratt for typing the manuscript more than once.

May Allah, *subḥānahū wa ta'ālā*, accept our humble effort and make it a source of inspiration and guidance for all.

Leicester, **Khurshid Ahmad**
Rabīʿ al-Awwal, 1410 A.H.
October 1989

بِسْمِ اللَّهِ الرَّحْمَٰنِ الرَّحِيمِ

إِنَّ ٱللَّهَ وَمَلَٰٓئِكَتَهُۥ يُصَلُّونَ عَلَى ٱلنَّبِيِّ يَٰٓأَيُّهَا ٱلَّذِينَ
ءَامَنُواْ صَلُّواْ عَلَيْهِ وَسَلِّمُواْ تَسْلِيمًا ٥٦

Allah and His Angels send blessings on the Prophet.
O you who believe! Send your blessings on him, and
salute him with all respect.

(*al-Aḥzāb* 33: 56)

اللهم صل على محمد وعلى آل محمد، كما صليت على إبراهيم
وعلى آل إبراهيم، إنك حميد مجيد

O Allah, send blessings upon Muḥammad, and his
family, as You blessed Ibrahim, and the family of
Ibrahim, You art indeed Praiseworthy and Glorious.

Introduction

In the Name of Allah, the Compassionate, the Most Merciful

AN APPROACH TO UNDERSTANDING *SĪRAH*

1. **Prologue**

To begin, we may ask a seemingly straightforward question: What is *Sīrah*? The straightforward answer is that it is the study of the life and career of the Prophet Muḥammad, *ṣallā Allāhu 'alayhi wa sallam,* as it happened in history. However, at a deeper level, *Sīrah* is the science that attempts to explain the reality of Muḥammad in all its dimensions and ramifications, its whole, profound impact not only during the Prophet's life-time and the era that immediately followed, but in all time since and to come.

The scope of *Sīrah* is thus very wide indeed. We may begin to appreciate the widening horizons of our conception of *Sīrah* if we take a close look at the rich variety of sources on which a rigorous study of the subject must strive to draw.

2. **The Sources of *Sīrah***

2.1 **The Glorious Qur'ān**

Information drawn from the Qur'ān is vital to a proper understanding of the life of the Prophet Muḥammad. Hardly a chapter of the Qur'ān is without some reference, direct or indirect, to him. Books on *Asbāb an-Nuzūl* (occasions of Qur'ānic revelation) by such authorities as al-Wāḥidī and others, go a long way towards projecting the dynamic career of the Prophet. As the Qur'ānic evidence is infallible, it affords a unique possibility of checking the authenticity of accounts of the *Sīrah* given in lesser sources such as the *Ḥadīth* books or indeed the standard specialized books on the *Sīrah,* such as Ibn Hishām or Ibn Sa'd.

Thus, if an incident of the *Sīrah* is given in a verse of the Qur'ān which has not been subsequently abrogated, then the Qur'ānic account of it is final. The Qur'ānic interpretation of the *Sīrah* is indeed its most proper interpretation, since the Prophet strove so wholeheartedly to live up to the ideals and imperatives of the Qur'ān. Attesting to his miraculous achievements in these endeavours, 'Ā'ishah said of him that his manners and conduct were the Qur'ān exemplified.

The life of the Prophet was the practical embodiment of the Qur'ān. It was educated, shaped and matured by the successive Qur'ānic revelations continuously received, pertaining to every facet and turn in that life. The relationship, the parallel, between the Qur'ān and the life of the Prophet is a very intimate one. His motives, aspirations and attitudes were primordially Qur'ānic, and his actions the manifestation of the norms and values of the Qur'ān. Thus the phenomenon of Muḥammad was to a very great extent a Qur'ānic phenomenon, the Qur'ānic modes of reasoning and of perceptions being the very essence of his life.

A unique feature of that life as depicted in the Qur'ān is that the Prophet's inward states of mind, the musings of his soul, his doubts, misgivings, hesitations and anxieties, are clearly disclosed. In the Qur'ānic accounts of the various battles which the Prophet and the Muslims fought against the Quraysh and their allies – battles such as Badr, Uḥud, al-Aḥzāb and Ḥunayn – the Prophet's thoughts and feelings as he engaged the enemy are depicted accurately and in close detail. These disclosures were such a surprise to the Prophet himself that he was, at times, visibly shaken and frightened by them. In some of these disclosures certain actions of the Prophet are questioned and criticized. In some indeed, he is even reproached in the Qur'ān. This is the case in *Sūrah 'Abasa* 80, (He frowned . . .); and again in relation to his hesitation to marry his cousin Zaynab bint Jaḥsh.

When the Prophet received the first visit of the Archangel Gabriel at Ḥirā, he experienced a severe depression brought on by a wave of doubts as to the reality of his Prophethood. That depression turned into a profound grief following the cessation of the Archangel's visits. The Qur'ān vividly portrays the inward state of the Prophet, and *Sūrah al-Ḍuḥā* (The Morning Hours) was revealed in which he is consoled and affectionately reassured. The Qur'ānic criticisms of the Prophet, the human quality of the portraits of him, effectively checked the usual human tendency to accord a divine status to Prophets. It is the Qur'ān's emphasis on the human side of the Prophet that made it possible for ordinary men and women to strive to emulate him as their personal ideal. If Muḥammad had been portrayed as some sort of supernatural person or being, how could ordinary, frail mortals have been expected to follow his example in their daily lives? Thus we find this ever-repeated emphasis, in the Qur'ān that Muḥammad, *ṣallā Allāhu 'alayhi wa sallam,* was only a human being entrusted with a divine mission to mankind – nothing but a faithful servant of his Lord, a messenger the essence of whose message is mercy to mankind.

Following the Qur'ānic approach to the *Sīrah* (if we may so put it) entails that while the Prophetic aspect of Muḥammad is fully acknowledged and revered, no effort should be made to conceal his ordinary human side: Muḥammad was the supreme example of human excellence and accomplishment, whose life demonstrated that there is no contradiction between leading a normal human life and total devotion and commitment to the service of God. It is his highest achievement that even when he had managed to obtain uncontested rule over Arabia, the hustle and bustle of affairs of state, in war as well as peace, did not distract him from the fullest devotion to his Lord, from being ever conscious of Him.

The life of the Prophet Muḥammad should therefore be portrayed just as it was, without exaggeration or diminution. He should not be turned into a supernatural being. He never claimed to be such. He was always at great pains to look and act human, he ate and worked and slept, and he married. He was involved in business, war, politics and the wide range of affairs that suited his sublime and noble temperament. There should be no myths or legends, no fanciful imaginings, woven into the salient factual happenings of his life. Fortunately, the diverse moments of that life, private as well as public, are recorded in abundant detail. No Prophet or great man before the Prophet enjoyed this privilege and burden. His gracious life is an open book, even his intimate, bedroom life is known and recorded, his moments of sadness as well as of joy, of frustration and disappointment as well as success and triumph. Also his physical appearance and his personal manners, in the smallest detail, are recorded. He is the only Prophet to have been born and lived in the full light of history.

Since he was the Prophet, the nobility of the events of his life and his greatness of character speak for themselves. They compel a reverent treatment from anyone, whether Muslim or otherwise, who approaches these accounts of his life with an objective mind. The Qur'ān, the first source of the *Sīrah*, could not have been written by him, an unlettered person, and moreover himself the subject, within its verses, of searching criticism, of psychological analysis, of warning and blame. Similarly, the Companions of the Prophet were quite often criticized in the Qur'ān, admonished to adhere to, or avoid and renounce, certain modes of speech or action.

3. The *Ḥadīth* and *Sunnah* as a Source of *Sīrah*

The Prophet lived for twenty-three years after the commencement of his mission. Those years were the busiest and most fruitful any man could have lived. He accomplished his mission of calling mankind to the worship of the One True God, Allah, *subḥānahū wa ta'ālā*. Throughout this period, he struggled against arrogance and unbelief, confronted unswervingly the forces of ungodliness and evil, and taught and educated those who believed. Further, he succeeded in establishing his faith in the world and built a state on the basis of it. In doing so, he remained entirely faithful to the ideas he preached, to the convictions of his religion. The political order he helped set up in Madinah was a practical embodiment of the spiritual and moral values he had advocated in Makkah. That state was in no way like a modern city-state or nation-state dedicated to a limited human vision of national pride or even of community welfare. It was, in actual fact, the seed of a world order and civilization, based on the principles of the worship of the One True God and brotherhood among men. *Sīrah* is the science that must systematically study these developments, how they came about, the ideas involved, the strategies and the mechanism.

Beyond that, a methodology must be devised to distinguish those practices of the Prophet which are meant to be emulated and followed and those that are not.

In this study, all the six collections of authentic *Ḥadīth* are accepted as essential sources (3.1). Thereafter, certain other well-known collections could also be accepted as sources of the *Sīrah,* where they do not contradict the Qur'ān, or any of the authentic *Ḥadīth*. The books of *Aḥādīth* that need to be consulted in writing the *Sīrah* are the following:

3.1 Bukhārī, Muslim, at-Tirmidhī, Abū Dāwūd, an-Nasā'ī and Ibn Mājah – the six authentic books of *Ḥadīth.* This is the first category. The second category consists of the following books:

3.2 *Musnad* of Aḥmad ibn Ḥanbal, *Muwaṭṭa'* of Mālik ibn Anas, *Musnad* of ad-Dārimī, *Ṣaḥīḥ* of Ibn Khuzaymah, *Mustadrak* of al-Ḥākim, *Sunan* of ad-Dāraquṭnī and the *Sunan* of Sa'īd ibn Manṣūr.

4. The Third Major Source of *Sīrah*: The Specialized Books on *Sīrah* and *Maghāzī*

A common but inadequate approach to writing the *Sīrah,* is to concentrate on the recognized, standard books of the *Sīrah,* and write out the life of the Prophet as a moving, chronological narrative of the main events. Obviously, however, the life of the Prophet Muḥammad is not merely a story to be told, or a biography to be outlined and characterized. Though his life was manifested in history, and therein constitutes *aẓ-Ẓāhirah al-Muḥammadīyah* (the phenomenon of Muḥammad) with its two elements of the human and the Prophetic, its meaning goes further, touches a realm far wider, than that. As we said at the opening of this introduction, the definition of the life of Muḥammad as only a manifestation in history is not adequate.

In addition to depicting the phenomenon, *aẓ-Ẓāhirah al-Muḥammadīyah,* an adequate *Sīrah* must strive also to capture *al-Ḥaqīqah al-Muḥammadīyah* (the reality of Muḥammad), a reality that though manifested in history, was never totally contained or limited by it. It is a profound, spiritual reality that greatly transcends its spatial and temporal manifestation, indeed its metaphysical dimensions were integral to its occasion in history. It would be naive to suppose that such a reality could be properly expressed simply by putting together an authoritative version of *Sīrah* based on the original traditional sources of the *Sīrah* books in Arabic, and the books of *al-Maghāzī.* These remarks must not, of course, be understood to detract from the great importance of these materials: they are intended only to stress the importance of the first two sources, namely, the Qur'ān, and the *Ḥadīth* and *Sunnah,*[1] as decisive and final. Thus if the accounts in the *Sīrah* and *Maghāzī* literature contradict either the Qur'ānic account or that of the *Ḥadīth* and *Sunnah,* the former must be discarded. The principal source books of *Sīrah* and *Maghāzī* are the following:

4.1 Ibn Hishām. His abridgement of the last pioneering work, *Sīrat Rasūl Allāh,* by Muḥammad ibn Isḥāq, is invaluable. As we said earlier, portions of Ibn Isḥāq have recently been recovered and published. Muḥammad Ibn Isḥāq (who died in 150 or 151 A.H.), is unquestionably the principal authority on the *Sīrah* and *Maghāzī* literature. Every writing after him has depended on his work, which though lost in its entirety, has been immortalized in the wonderful, extant abridgement of it, by Ibn Hishām. Ibn Isḥāq was one of *at-Tābi'īn,* a contemporary of Imām Mālik ibn Anas, who was, it is reported, jealous of the academic and scientific standing Ibn Isḥāq had achieved despite his humble beginning as a *Mawālī* (former slave). Perhaps for this reason, Mālik ibn Anas, it is reported, said rather unkind words about Ibn Isḥāq. But Mālik's negative remarks, if indeed they are correctly reported, were almost universally rejected by authorities[2] on *Ḥadīth, Sunnah, Sīrah* and *Maghāzī.* Ibn Isḥāq's work is notable for its excellent, rigorous methodology and its literary style is of the highest standard of elegance and beauty. This is hardly surprising when we recall that Ibn Isḥāq was an accomplished scholar not only in Arabic language but also in the science of *Ḥadīth*. For this reason, most of the *Isnād* that he gives in his *Sīrah* are also to be found in the authentic books of the *Ḥadīth*. Ibn Isḥāq, like Bukhārī and Muslim travelled very widely in the Muslim world in order to authenticate the *Isnād* of his *Ḥadīth*. It is reported that Ibn Isḥāq saw and heard Sa'īd ibn al-Musayyib, Abān ibn 'Uthmān ibn 'Affān, az-Zuhrī, Abū Salamah ibn 'Abd ar-Raḥmān ibn 'Awf and 'Abd ar-Raḥmān ibn Hurmuz al-A'raj. It is also reported that Ibn Isḥāq was the teacher of the following outstanding authorities among others:

(a) Yaḥyā ibn Sa'īd al-Anṣārī.
(b) Sufyān ath-Thawrī.
(c) Ibn Jurayḥ.
(d) Shu'bah ibn al-Ḥajjāj.
(e) Sufyān ibn 'Uyaynah.[3]
(f) Ḥammād ibn Zayd.

4.2 The second book on *Sīrah* is that of *Al-Maghāzī* by Muḥammad Ibn 'Umar al-Wāqidī al-Aslamī (who lived from 130 to 207 and is buried in Baghdad). This book was widely read in various parts of the Muslim world. While some authorities accused the author of having promulgated some exaggerations and inaccuracies, others commended him very highly. As to inaccuracies, even Ibn Isḥāq is not immune from them. A number of such inaccuracies occur in Ibn Isḥāq (and consequently Ibn Hishām). For instance:[4]

(a) Ibn Isḥāq put the number of Muslim companions of the Prophet participating in Ḥudaybiyyah as 700 men and women. But Bukhārī put the number as 1400, double the number of Ibn Isḥāq. Bukhārī's version is more correct.
(b) The men of ar-Rajī', according to Ibn Isḥāq, were six, but Bukhārī says they were ten men.
(c) The number of men of Bi'r Ma'ūnah were 40, according to Ibn Isḥāq, but al-Bukhārī and others give the figure as 70; etc.

4.3 The third authoritative work on *Sīrah* is Ibn Sa'd's[5] *aṭ-Ṭabaqāt al-Kubrā* (9 volumes). Ibn Sa'd was both the student, and the scribe/secretary of al-Wāqidī. The quality and scholarly excellence of the *at-Ṭabaqāt* of Ibn Sa'd say a great deal about the academic competence of his teacher and patron.

5. **Universal History and the History of Arabia**

The general history of mankind and, within it, the history of pre-Islamic Arabia, are an important background source of the life of the Prophet. These make up the fourth source coming directly after the specialized *Sīrah* works mentioned above. Although these *Sīrah* works do give some account of the universal history of mankind, from the descent of Adam to the beginning of the mission of the Prophet, their accounts are very sparse, being more of the nature of introductory chapters.

The spiritual history of mankind is particularly relevant. By 'spiritual history' we mean the history of the major revealed religions, especially those with special links to Arabia, therefore the history of the Scriptures previous to the revelation of the Qur'ān. Their importance can be inferred from the Qur'ān itself which alludes to them many times. The Qur'ān repeatedly draws the attention of the 'People of the Book' to the fact that the coming of the Prophet Muḥammad (the *Aḥmad* or the Praised One) has indeed been mentioned and foretold in their Scriptures.

Also of special interest to the study of the *Sīrah* are those aspects of universal history that depict the status of pre-Islamic Arabia, and especially the region of Ḥijāz. It seems many great ancient civilizations flourished, in Arabia 'Felix' and Ḥijāz, especially around the valley of Bakkah: 'Ād, Thamūd, Iram, Madyan, Tubā', etc. The civilizations and cultures of these peoples need to be studied, and their achievements and their failures, together with their ultimate doom, thoroughly understood.

Outstanding among the authorities who gave special attention to the *Sīrah* as a chapter of universal history of mankind are the following:

5.1 *Aṭ-Ṭabarī* (Ibn Jarīr died in 310 A.H.) in his monumental world history: *Ta'rīkh al-Umam wa ar-Rusul wa al-Mulūk.* Aṭ-Ṭabarī was not merely a historian, but also an unrivalled authority on Arabic language and grammar, on *Ḥadīth* and *fiqh,* and on the exegesis and interpretation of the Qur'ān. Evidence of the excellence of his scholarship, his prodigious and untiring intellectual genius, is provided by his major works which run into many lengthy volumes each.

5.2 *Khalīfah ibn Khayyāṭ al-'Uṣfurī* (died in 240 A.H.). Al-'Uṣfurī's book on universal history has recently been edited by Akram al-'Amrī (of the Islamic University of al-Madīnah al-Munawwarah).

5.3 *Ibn Ṭāhir al-Maqdisī* (died in 355 A.H.). Al-Maqdisī's book (*Al-Bad' wa at-Ta'rīkh*) is important for its inclusion with the *Sīrah* of an account of the history of pre-Islamic Arabia.

5.4 Al-Balādhurī (*Futūḥ al-Buldān*). Al-Balādhurī (Aḥmad ibn Yaḥyā ibn Jābir) died in 279 A.H. The work of this early historian is valuable for the texts it contains of certain important agreements which the Prophet concluded with some groups and individuals – among others, the texts of his agreement with the Christians of Najrān; his agreement with the people of Maqnā, his 'book' to al-Mundhir ibn Sāwī; and to Akaydar Dawmah.

Al-Balādhurī added an anecdote commenting on the Qur'ānic verse:

> And they favoured others over themselves even though they were in dire need.

that it was revealed about the *Anṣār,* when they agreed that their share of *Fay'* from the Banū an-Naḍīr should be distributed exclusively among the *Muhājirūn.*

5.5 Al-Ya'qūbī (Aḥmad ibn Ja'far ibn Wahb, d. 292 A.H.). Al-Ya'qūbī's work is unique for its examples of the Prophet's sermons, not to be found elsewhere, especially those containing instruction and admonition.

5.6 Al-Mas'ūdī (Abū al-Ḥasan 'Alī Ibn al-Ḥusain ibn 'Alī al-Mas'ūdī, d. 346 A.H.) is a well-known Arab historian, a descendant of one of the Companions of the Prophet, 'Abdūllah ibn Mas'ūd, author of two books on history including long sections on *Sīrah*: (i) *Murūj adh-Dhahab wa Ma'ādin al-Jawhar; (ii) al-Tanbīh wa al-Ishrāf.*

5.7 Ibn Kathīr (Abū al-Fidā' Ismā'īl 'Umar ad-Dimashqī, d. 774 A.H.). Though a much later authority, Ibn Kathīr's *Sīrat an-Nabī*, and his universal history *Al-Bidāyah wa an-Nihāyah* have received much acclaim and recognition. He was methodologically a most rigorous scholar. He gives various different chains of *Isnād* for the events he reports, sometimes comparing those *Isnād* and assessing which he regards as more reliable.

6. Books on *Ad-Dalā'il* (Proofs of Prophethood)

The books of *ad-Dalā'il* are concerned with giving proofs for the authenticity of the Prophethood of Muḥammad, *ṣallā Allāhu 'alayhi wa sallam.* They are principally collections of accounts of the miracles of the Prophet advanced as proofs. The most well-known amongst such books, usually entitled *Dalā'il an-Nubūwwah*, are by:

6.1 Abū al-Ḥasan al-Ḥarbī (d. 255 A.H.).
6.2 Abū Zur'ah ar-Rāzī (d. 264 A.H.).
6.3 Aḥmad ibn al-Ḥusain al-Bayhaqī (d. 458 A.H.).
6.4 Abū Nu'aym al-Iṣfahānī.

7. Books on *Ash-Shamā'il* (Character Traits)

These books deal with the character and virtues of the Prophet, his renowned courtesy during the day and the night. There are many works on this subject, but the two most important, sufficient for our purpose, are:

7.1 Muḥammad ibn 'Īsā at-Tirmidhī (d. 279 A.H.). He is more famous for his *Sunan*, but his *Kitāb ash-Shamā'il* is widely read, and a subject of many commentaries and epitomes.

7.2 Abū Muḥammad ‘Abdullāh ibn Muḥammad ibn Ja‘far al-Iṣfahānī (d. 369 A.H.). His book is entitled *Akhlāq an-Nabī (ṣallā Allāhu ‘alayhi wa sallam) wa Ādābuhū.*

8. **Books on the History of Makkah and Madinah**

The history of Makkah and Madinah before and after the advent of Islam is an important source of the *Sīrah*. The relevant history of Makkah before the inception of Islam concerns the Ancient House (al-Ka‘bah), and the narratives relating to its origin and initial building. Knowledge of the network of Arabian tribes that inhabited the Ḥijāz area at the time of the Prophetic mission is also relevant. They influenced greatly the course of events that shaped the vital formative years of the first Muslim community. Indeed, the history of pre-Islamic Arabia in general is important, not least because the Qur’ān itself commands Muslims to study the fate of those Arabian tribes who gave the lie to their Prophets and were consequently destroyed:

> Is it not a guidance for them (to observe) how many generations We destroyed before them, amid whose dwelling places they do walk? Lo, therein surely are portents! Will they not then take heed?[6]

The Qur’ān refers to itself as an ‘Arabic recitation’ – *‘qur’ānan ‘arabīyan’* – and points to the Arab element in the life and mission of the Prophet Muḥammad, calling him the Arabian Prophet, *‘an-nabī al-‘Arabī’*.

The Prophet’s being born and brought up in the most ancient valley of Bakkah in the Western Ḥijāz makes the history of pre-Islamic Arabia, especially the Ḥijāz, an integral part of the *Sīrah,* a fact widely acknowledged in the early Arabic sources. The lost pioneering work of Muḥammad ibn Isḥāq[7] is believed to have comprised three parts: the first being devoted to the history of pre-Islamic Arabia, and the universal history of man (*Al-Mubtada’*), the second to the mission of the Prophet Muḥammad (*Al-Mab‘ath*), and the third to his military actions (*al-Maghāzī*). A comprehensive, factual history of Arabia is a vital prerequisite to understanding the *Sīrah*. The monumental works of the Rev. W. Montgomery Watt[8] have greatly enriched this field, but much more work is needed if the Arabian factor in the life of the Prophet Muḥammad is to be fully appreciated. As well as a conventional historical account of the people of Arabia, we need to know of their society and culture generally – their social structures (including the structure and genealogy of the main tribes, clans and families), their linguistic and religious habits, their economic relations, etc. The Qur'ān, as we noted, refers to Muḥammad as the 'Arabian Prophet' a number of times, and the Prophet himself spoke highly of his pure Arabian descent on a number of occasions. He had the most consummate knowledge of the Arabian society of his times, rarely needing to be briefed if he chanced to meet or hear of any pre-Islamic Arabian dignitary – he would seem to have at his fingertips the most comprehensive and up-to-date information. In particular, he had a most thorough knowledge of the ruling houses of the vast network of the major Arabian tribes and clans, and their chief poets, saints and learned authorities. He likewise had an impressive knowledge of the people of the Scriptures, their views and their learned men, and he also knew quite well the neighbouring lands of Bahrain, Haḍramaut, Yemen (Arabia Felix), Abyssinia, Coptic Egypt, Syria, Mesopotamia, Byzantium and Persia.

The annals of the Quraysh, the poetry of pre-Islamic Arabia and the history of Makkah are essential background material and, related to them, the history of the whole Ḥijāz region as well as of Yathrib, Ṭā'if and Yemen.

There are significant allusions in the Qur'ān to Bakkah,[9] the Ancient House, Wādī al-Qurā, to Abraham and Ismā'il, and to the Quraysh. Early Arab historians wrote extensively on the early history of Makkah and the Ḥijāz. Their claims about the genealogy of the Arabs and the evolution of their languages are based in part on information contained in the Qur'ān and the *Ḥadīth,* and in part on the ancient books and materials which the Arabs inherited and procured from the ancient cultures and civilizations they conquered – Indian, Chinese, Persian, Egyptian, Syriac Greek and Byzantine. Ibn Hishām, aṭ-Ṭabarī, and Ibn Kathīr give a universal account of the genealogy of man, going back to Adam, progenitor of mankind – his descent from Paradise, his arrival in Bakkah, where the Ancient House (the Ka'bah) was originally built by the Angels, the foundation stone being of Green granite, not to be found anywhere in the vicinity of Bakkah. Ancient Arabic historical sources, on which Ibn Hishām was drawing, even assert not only that Adam and Eve actually visited Bakkah (Beccah), but also that Noah whirled the Ka'bah, in his Ark, on the occasion of the Great Flood (meaning either that the Ancient House was elevated or, that if it was immersed, the Ark merely encircled the spot under which it was immersed). According to these same sources, it would appear that Bakkah was perhaps the very first township or colony that man established on this earth, and the Ḥijāz region was thus the very first site of human settlement, the names of the holy landmarks of Ḥijāz ('Arafāt, Minā, Muzdalifah and the Ḥaram sanctuary and even the name 'Jeddah' of the main Arabian port on the Red Sea to the west of Makkah) date to periods long before the advent of Hagar and Ishmael referred to in the Bible and the Qur'ān. Certain of the sources claim that Eve is buried in Jeddah, which means 'grandmother' in Arabic.

The late 'Abbās Maḥmūd Al-'Aqqād,[10] the well-known Egyptian writer and twentieth-century literary critic claimed that the culture of Arabia Felix in some of its early stages is much older than both Greek and Hebrew cultures. Some older ancestral versions of Arabic must then be considered very ancient indeed. Yet the Qur'ān has described the pre-Islamic Arabs as *Ummīyīn* (unlettered) and characterized their age as *Jāhiliyyah.* As to the first description, it can only mean that literacy was not widespread, that among the pre-Islamic Arabs, the unlettered were the vast majority. As to the term *Jāhiliyyah*, it could mean, among other things, that the Arabs lacked moral guidance. However that may be, the Arabs of the time of Muḥammad, *ṣallā Allāhu 'alayhi wa sallam*, were not uncultured simpletons. Their elaborate poetry, and the rich and intricate grammar, phraseology and idioms of their language, attest to a very complex linguistic and conceptual framework. Not only that, the famous

Mu'allaqāt (so called because they were hung on the walls of the Ancient House), the best of the poems of pre-Islamic Arabia, make reference to a highly developed system of moral values, and their literary excellence argues a tradition of considerable complexity and refinement. These poets were heirs to a long tradition that goes back beyond Ishmael, the son of Abraham, to the poets of Kindah and other tribes of Southern Arabia. The Quraysh and Adnanite Arabs of Bakkah and Northern Arabia were called the Arabized Arabs, because their ancestor, Ishmael, was not an Arab himself. He married Arab women from the Yamani tribes of Jurhum and Khuzā'ah and settled in Bakkah, developing a new species of the Arabic language, the pure accent of the Quraysh. As Ishmael was older than Isaac, the Arabized Arabs were at least as old as their Israelite cousins (Ishmael being the uncle of Jacob who was the first to be called Israel).

Of course, Arabic language and culture go back to the much older Southern pure Arabs of Ḥimyar, Lukham and Kindah of Arabia Felix. The beginnings of these pure Arabs *(al-'Arab al-'Āribah)* are shrouded in the mists of pre-history. From what is known now of their language(s) and monuments they definitely pre-date the Hebrew, the Greek and the Ancient Egyptian, hence Al-'Aqqād's theory about the precedence of Arabic culture (some evidence for this may be obtained from philological speculation – names like Adam, Hawwā' (Eve), Sam, etc. have Arabic roots). Further evidence for the antiquity of Arabia comes from the Qur'ān itself:

(a) Bakkah or Makkah is referred to as the 'mother of the townships' (Umm al-Qurā).
(b) The Ancient House of Makkah is pronounced 'the first House ever built for the worship of the One, True God, Allah, *subḥānahū wa ta'ālā.*
(c) Muslim historical sources claim that the Ancient House was built by Angels originally, and merely rebuilt by Abraham and Ishmael. It may have been rebuilt also by Noah, after the Great Flood.

9. **The Arabic Factor**

The Arabic factor in the life and personality of the Prophet Muḥammad, *ṣallā Allāhu 'alayhi wa sallam*, is important. It comprises the following elements:

9.1 The ancient heritage of the Arabs, linguistic/conceptual, genealogical and cultural.

9.2 From Adam and Eve, Noah and Abraham and his son Ishmael, a heritage in spiritual and moral excellence is derived. The fortitude and perseverance of Abraham, his submission and obedience to Almighty God, his courage and his generosity – it is reported in Muslim sources (see Ibn Kathīr's commentary on the Qur'ān) that he would not eat unless he found some guest to share his meal – were all phenomenal. His moral character was such that the Qur'ān has described him as the equal of a whole *Ummah* (a whole people):

> Surely Abraham was (the model of) an *Ummah* (nation) most devout unto Allah, most truthful, upright and monotheistic and was never of the polytheists.[11]

The teachings and moral values, and the practical example, of Abraham and Ishmael influenced and to some extent shaped the culture of the Quraysh, in particular, and of the Arabs in general. Moreover, the existence of Jewish colonies in Yathrib and in the Northern Hijaz townships of Khaybar, Fadak, and Wādī al-Qurā was a significant element in the conversion of the population of Yathrib to Islam.[12] In Makkah itself there were few Christians, Waraqah ibn Nawfal, Khadījah's cousin, being one of them. But in South Arabia, there was a whole community of Christians – the Christians of Najrān – and a lesser Christian Arab community existed among the northern Arabs of Banū Taghlib.

9.3 The pure genealogical descent of the Arabs of the Quraysh, wedlock being very closely observed in typical, respectable Arab families, is well known. The Prophet Muḥammad, a Hashimite and a Qurayshi, cherished and proclaimed his pure Arabic descent (being the best of the best of the best, no boasting was entertained – *'fa-anā*

Khiyārun min Khiyārin min Khiyārin walā fakhr'). It is a well-known fact recorded in the Qur'ān[13] itself, that the pre-Islamic Arabs were not 'a lot of drunken licentious people' as some writers of the *Sīrah* would like us to believe.[14] The pre-Islamic Arabs had developed the values of *'Irḍ* (sexual chastity, purity, virginity, integrity and honour) – developed them perhaps to the point of obsession: *'Irḍ* may have contributed to the practice of burying infant daughters alive. 'Umar ibn al-Khaṭṭāb, himself sobbingly narrates how he in fact had buried one of his daughters alive, in his *Jāhiliyyah* days.

9.4 Allah, *subḥānahū wa ta'ālā,* in His infinite wisdom has made the Qur'ān 'an *Arabic* recitation'. All the major languages of the world have suffered change in their syntactical and semantical aspects, but not Arabic. Thus Allah planned and carried out His promise that He Himself will preserve the Qur'ān intact from all attempts at distortion and alteration.

9.5 Part of the Arabic factor was the role of the Hashimite clan in the protection of the Prophet Muḥammad in the Makkan period, their experience in the world, their financial and mercantile expertise. Important too is the fact that the first Muslim elite (the Companions) were, with the exception of a few individuals, overwhelmingly of Arabic stock.

9.6 Finally we must include, within the Arabic factor, the influence of the desert and of the positive aspects of the bedouin way of life – the virtues of enthusiasm, courage, chivalry, generosity, *najdah* and *muruwwah.* The bedouins were renowned for their courage and fortitude. They had a marshal tradition acquired by the young men of the Quraysh, who were often brought up in the desert with the bedouins. Their marshal virtues served well the cause of Islam when the Muslim Arabs met the much superior forces of the Romans and the Persians. Had Islam been first revealed to a feeble, primitive people, with no physical aptitude, no cultural depth, such as exist even today among the primitive tribes of Asia, Africa and the Americas, then it would have stood no chance of spreading across the known civilized world in less than a quarter of a century. Much of what we have said about the Arabic factor is designed to show that the pre-Islamic Arabs, not as a race, but as a community with a profound moral heritage, possessed those sociological prerequisites that made it possible for them to be the bearers of a divine mission.

10. **Later Sources**

Some of the later authorities and writers on the *Sīrah* are also important, either on account of their special merits, or because they follow a chain of narrations significantly different from that followed by Ibn Isḥāq, Ibn Sa'd, al-Wāqidī, Ibn Kathīr or aṭ-Ṭabarī. To say that they followed chains of narrations other than those followed in the well-known books on *Sīrah*, in effect acknowledges the existence of sources of *Sīrah* earlier than Ibn Isḥāq. These earlier works are mostly lost, but reference to them exists in Ibn Sa'd, al-Wāqidī, Ibn Kathīr, aṭ-Ṭabarī and in the books of authentic *Ḥadīth*. Most significant among these lost early works on the *Sīrah*, are the following:

10.1 The *Sīrah* by Abān Ibn 'Uthmān ibn 'Affān (died between 86–96 A.H.).

10.2 The *Sīrah* by 'Urwah ibn az-Zubayr ibn al-'Awwām (died in 94 A.H.).

10.3 The *Sīrah* by Shuraḥbīl ibn Sa'd (died 124 A.H.). He was reported to be particularly excellent in his knowledge of *al-Maghāzī* and the information concerning the people of Badr.

10.4 Among these early writers on the *Sīrah*, that went before Ibn Isḥāq, belongs Wahab ibn Munabbih a converted scripturist, widely versed in the lore of both Christians and Jews.

11. There are other books on the *Sīrah*, written by later authorities, indeed too many to be counted. On the whole, however, these are summaries and manuals for the teaching of *Sīrah* to pupils of the *Madrasah*. Some of them have

proved very popular, and some have enough intrinsic value to have established a special, permanent place in the curricula of those traditional Islamic schools.

11.1 One of these is the commentary of Imām as-Suhaylī (died 581 A.H.) on Ibn Hishām. As-Suhaylī's book, *al-Rawḍ al-Unf* became famous as a manual on Ibn Hishām, for a freshman's course on the *Sīrah*. But it has the very important advantage that it contains a refutation of the Emanation (or Light) theory of the nature of Muḥammad, *ṣallā Allāhu ʿalayhi wa sallam*. The *Nūr* or Light theory argued that the Prophet's nature is of pure illumination, non-substantial, without any opaque quality. As illumination, he existed before the creation of the world, even before the creation of Adam and Eve. It is for his sake that the world was created, and so were Adam and indeed all the Prophets of God. He was first deposited in the *Ṣulb* (backbone) of Adam and continued to descend from ancestor to ancestor, till he was eventually deposited in the *Ṣulb* of ʿAbdullāh ibn ʿAbd al-Muṭṭalib. Then he was born as the Messenger of God to all mankind, and seal of all the Prophets of Allah. The *Nūr* theory even asserts that the Prophet cast no shadow. As-Suhaylī took this theory to task, explaining how it is in glaring contradiction with the facts of the life of the Prophet – that he was a human being with a body and a soul, eating food and drinking water and visiting the market places to buy his needs and provisions; that he fought other men in battle and was wounded and his blood flowed as a result of his wounds; that he eventually died and his noble body was buried at the mosque of Madinah in the apartment of ʿĀʾishah.

11.2 Among the late books on *Sīrah* are the books of the *Āthār*. These books are mainly on the lives of the Companions and their fate and whereabouts and places of residence in the *Amsār* (regions of the Muslim state). The two most famous of these collections are the following:

(1) The *Muṣannaf* of ʿAbd al-Razzāq ibn Hammām aṣ-Ṣanʿānī (126–221 A.H.). He lived a long life, and became blind in his last days. He studied under many famous teachers

and travelled far and wide in search of knowledge. He authored many books, but the most famous of these is the *Muṣannaf*.

(2) The *Muṣannaf* of Ibn Abī Shaybah Abū Bakr (d. 235 A.H.).

12. **The Secondary Sources**

Above we have named the most important primary source books of the *Sīrah*. To these, we must now add the secondary sources. These fall into two distinct categories: biographies and commentaries written by modern Muslim authors; and studies by Orientalists from the West and Soviet Russia.

Of the first category, the best works are perhaps those by Muslims of the subcontinent of India, but unfortunately many of them are not available in Arabic or any European language.

Professor Muḥammad Ḥamidullah's books on *Sīrah* are monumental and are now considered as classics in this category.

Haykal's *Ḥayāt Muḥammad* has been recently rendered into English by the late Shahīd Ismā'īl al-Fārūqī, may Allah enter him and his wife Shahīd Lamyā al-Fārūqī in His infinite Mercy. But Haykal's work, though otherwise valuable, suffers from the fact that, being apologetic, it omits the miracles and other metaphysical phenomena of Muḥammad, *ṣallā Allāhu 'alayhi wa sallam.*

Well-written works in European languages exist but have outstanding deficiencies. Some are no more than excellent narratives of the life of Muḥammad that remain oblivious to broader and more fundamental aspects of the meaning of that life.

As to the second category, there are some outstanding studies, very analytical, and of novel imaginative approach. A great many of them suffer from gross prejudice and lack objective understanding of the subject. Some are more sympathetic in the sense that they admit that Muḥammad was indeed sincere, but his sincerity is regarded as merely subjective. Such is the approach of Sir William Muir, in his *Life of Muhammad,* a book of extraordinary elegance and literary beauty. The approach of the Rev. W. Montgomery Watt is similar. Both Muir and Watt assert that Muḥammad sincerely believed that he was a messenger with a divine mission, but for them his claim is not substantiated by solid facts – rather they believe it is falsified by these facts. However, for the specialist, selected readings of the Orientalists' books on the *Sīrah* are essential.

13. What are the Objectives of Studying the *Sīrah*?

Maxime Rodinson, in his book *Muhammad,* said that before he started writing he paused to ask, why another book on Muḥammad when hundreds of books on him already existed in European languages? He said that, being a Marxist, he wanted to give his own dialectical-materialist interpretation of the phenomenon of Muḥammad. A friend of mine who studied under Montgomery Watt told me that Watt used to tell his students at Edinburgh University that an argumentative Pakistani student of his was instrumental in arousing his interest in the life of Muḥammad. But for the Muslims in this age, what could be the motives for attempting a thorough study of the *Sīrah*?

13.1 First of all, Muḥammad, *ṣallā Allāhu 'alayhi wa sallam,* is the good example for Muslims. A Muslim has a religious obligation to know about his life in order to approximate as much as he can to the Muslim ideal in manners and conduct.

13.2 Secondly, insofar as Muḥammad was the embodiment of the Qur'ān, the study of his life is one way of gaining greater insight into the meaning and message of the Qur'ān itself. The *Sīrah,* thus, gives the Qur'ān an added clarity and a unique relevance to human reality.

13.3 Thirdly, the *Sīrah* is, in fact, a social history of the inception and the development of Islam. Its study affords us a unique opportunity to review the history of the first movement of Islam as it gradually took root – first in the minds and hearts of a few individuals, and then as it was tossed in the hustle and bustle of a fearful struggle for its survival, upholding the banner of *Tawḥīd*.

13.4 For the contemporary Muslims who are struggling to recast their lives and their society and its political and economic orders, a dynamic movement-oriented study of the *Sīrah* affords both inspiration and immensely valuable lessons. The Islamic way of reforming and reordering defunct and chaotic human affairs was ordained by Allah, *subḥānahū wa ta'ālā,* and practised by the Prophet. It worked miracles in the context of the pre-Islamic Arabian society with its grave deviations and degenerate ways and institutions. The model of the Prophetic way of affecting human and social reform is legendary in its power to heal, reconcile and achieve.

The reality of Muḥammad is foremost a mercy unto mankind. The study of the *Sīrah* is meant to capture the dimensions of that mercy and to attempt to invoke it, in the hope that our disordered and shattered lives and societies may be touched by the healing hand and the blessing of the Messenger of Allah, who is more merciful to the believers than themselves and their fathers and mothers.

14. Grave Methodological Problems

A systematic analysis of the *Sīrah,* utilizing the tools of contemporary scholarship and the criteria of academic rigour is urgently needed if a healthy tradition in Islamic studies is to be evolved.

Through a well co-ordinated and concerted long-term effort, the Orientalist movement has waged a vicious campaign of slander against the personality of the beloved Prophet. Every facet of his life was studied with the objective of distorting it and creating a thick smoke of doubts and misgivings about it. All kinds of false, mean and unjust accusations were hurled against his noble person, his motives, his relationship with God and with his fellow companions. Especially his private life, his family life, was subjected to the most devious interpretations and the most unnatural and unwholesome explanations. An equally vicious campaign was unleashed against the *Sunnah* and the *Ḥadīth*.

The *Sunnah* was pronounced space-and-time bound, reflecting the conditions of a primitive environment, and an impoverished society of unruly, crude, rebellious nomadic bedouins, who had never experienced civilization or the rule of law. The Islamic law *(Sharī'ah)* was represented as the legal code suitable for a savage, primitive people, who lived in a certain environment at a given time in history. The Islamic state itself (if the concept has any meaning at all) was a primitive government reflecting the societal conditions of a primitive social organization, and suitable only for those conditions.

The *Ḥadīth* was likewise savagely assaulted. It was diminished as representing, in many cases, the personal knowledge of the Prophet – thus without universal validity. Only the Qur'ān has universal validity. Many rulings and judgements of the Prophet were historically circumscribed, and are not therefore to be considered part of the religion of Islam, not binding on the Muslims. For instance:

The treatment of Banū Qurayẓah must be viewed as an extreme case, not paradigmatic of the way the Muslims ought to treat the People of the Book. They are to be treated with kindness, friendliness and charity.

The institution of *Jizyah* may also be historically relative. Can we demand today of our non-Muslim compatriots that they pay *Jizyah*? Should we treat them as second-class citizens, obliged to pay poll-tax? No, is the answer, they say because the Muslims in such places as the Sudan, Egypt, Malaysia, etc. do not hold their position of predominance by virtue of military conquest and so cannot claim any special rights or privileges by the right of conquest.

The ruling over the issue of *ar-Riddah* by Abū Bakr is considered as irrelevant to the issue of the religious freedom of a person. *Riddah* is here re-interpreted as a case of political rebellion against the state, not a case of renegation from Islam. Islam, they say, permits a Muslim to renege, if he wishes, with no penalty involved. The Qur'ān declares 'There is no compulsion in religion' so a renegade from the Islamic faith is not to be executed.

Last, but not least, the stoning of the adulterer is not an

authentic Islamic legal ruling, because the Qur'ānic verse ordering it has been abrogated. It is not sufficient to adduce evidence in favour of it from the *Sunnah,* the *Ḥadīth* or the practice of the Caliphs. All these were incidents within Islamic history suitable for that age alone, but do not constitute part of the universal reality of the *Dīn.*

Such instances could be multiplied considerably. They pose very grave doubts which, if accepted, would lead to the utter discrediting of the *Sunnah* and the *Ḥadīth.* Insofar as a great deal of the religion of Islam, especially the practical, detailed aspects of a Muslim's life, and their explanations, is derived from the *Ḥadīth* and the *Sunnah,* and not found in the Qur'ān, the discrediting of the *Sunnah* is in fact the destruction of Islam itself. Moreover, if the Messenger of the Religion, the founder of the faith, is himself discredited, what can remain of Islam henceforth?

But the most serious question is: Are the *Ḥadīth* and the *Sunnah,* history-bound? Is their truth, consequently, relative, and without universal application? In other words, is the reality of Muḥammad, *ṣallā Allāhu 'alayhi wa sallam,* a relative phenomenon?

The reality of Muḥammad here alluded to is a connotation, a concept. As a concept, Muḥammad is a Prophet and the seal of Allah's messengers to mankind. He is the embodiment of the eternal Qur'ān. Thus to maintain the relativity of the *Sunnah* of Muḥammad, *ṣallā Allāhu 'alayhi wa sallam,* is to maintain the relativity of the Qur'ān as well as the relativity of Islam, and indeed, for that matter, of all revealed religion. How far are we then from the materialist relativist interpretation of Islam, and revealed religion in general? Why do we quarrel with Maxime Rodinson's Marxist interpretation of Muḥammad?

Another way of looking at this issue is to consider the argument, advanced nowadays by some very well-meaning Muslim activists impatient with the decadence and incompetence of the *Ummah.* Their argument can be stated in two versions, one soft or weak, the second a strong or hard-line version:

15.1 **The Weaker Version**

The weaker argument for the relativity of the *Sunnah* runs as follows: at least, some portions of *Ḥadīth,* even authentic *Ḥadīth* (in Bukhārī, Muslim, etc.) must be viewed as the personal expression of the man Muḥammad, *ṣallā Allāhu 'alayhi wa sallam,* of his nature as an Arab of a particular culture and environment – the way he ate, his favoured or abhorred foods, his dress and medicine (eye ointment, for instance), his knowledge of worldly matters, where no specific Qur'ānic ruling (or other divine directive) exists. This part of the *Ḥadīth* and the *Sunnah* must be viewed as historically relative, therefore devoid of any universal import, and not able to generate injunctions of any degree of religious obligatoriness. This argument must be accepted, claim its proponents, or we land ourselves in all kinds of absurdities. If it is not accepted, Muslims must insist on eating what the Prophet ate, that is dates, even if dates are not available, on sitting on the floor and eating with their hands, always, as a matter of religious obligation, even if they are invited by a host who has his feast well arranged on an elaborate table setting. They must insist on wearing flowing Arab clothes, even in cold weather. The obvious absurdity inherent here becomes all too obvious if this kind of reasoning is logically extended – thus we should not use gas or electricity, cars, aeroplanes, telephones, indeed all Muslims should then strive very hard to live and die in Madinah in Saudi Arabia. Some advocates of this weaker version of the relativity of the *Ḥadīth* and the *Sunnah* conclude that it is of the utmost importance that we should accept, indeed we must accept, some elements of *Ḥadīth* and *Sunnah* as history-bound with no universal significance for Muslims or non-Muslims alike.

A second argument is the following:

The practices of the Prophet, *ṣallā Allāhu 'alayhi wa sallam,* were the best way of implementing the universal Qur'ānic principles at that time – the moral value or wisdom in those principles was then best served by the particular practices of the Prophet or of his Companions.

Let us consider the following examples:

Firstly, *Jizyah*. The way that *jizyah* was implemented by the Prophet and his Companions served the following universal Qur'ānic principle:

1. It promoted the supremacy of Allah's Word, where that Word (or Law) was already the Law of the Land (Madinah and indeed the whole of Arabia):

   > Fight them, so that there is no more religious persecution *(fitnah)* and all religion will belong to Allah Alone.[15]

2. When the land had been subdued to the law of Allah, *subḥānahū wa ta'ālā,* and thereafter 'there is no compulsion in religion'. Those who chose to remain non- Muslims could do so freely, and were still citizens of the Muslim state enjoying full religious and autonomous rights (see the constitution of the State of Madinah). They could not be forced to pay *Zakāt,* since *Zakāt* is exclusively a religious obligation on Muslims. They could not be drafted into the army, since *Jihād* is also a religious function of the Muslim state. In consequence, non-Muslims were required to pay an alternative tax, namely the *jizyah.* The sum they had to pay could not be incommensurate with their incomes or over-taxing to their economic resources. If they were poor or for any reason unable to pay it, then it had to be waived, and they might even qualify for some kind of financial aid.

The manner in which *jizyah* was applied was indeed congenial to peaceful and friendly relations between Muslims and the People of the Book in the past. However, the argument goes, it is not now possible to divide the citizens of any country into political or religious classes. Thus, while the application of the *jizyah,* by the Prophet and his *Khulafā' ar-Rāshidūn,* served the wisdom behind the universal Qur'ānic principle of the supremacy of the *Sharī'ah* and the Muslim *Ummah,* at that

> particular point in history, any attempt to do so now by a small, weak Muslim nation-state (Egypt, Pakistan or the Sudan) would have dire internal and international consequences, not only for Muslims in these countries with a large non-Muslim minority, but also for the Muslim *Ummah* at large.

Another example of this argument concerns the attempt to apply the *Ḥadd* of *ar-Riddah* in the context of a modern Islamic state in, say, Malaysia, Egypt, Sudan or Pakistan. Is it desirable, or indeed befitting the lofty image of Islam, with its record of religious tolerance, to apply this punishment? Allah says in the Qur'ān:

> There is no compulsion in religion.[16]
>
> Will you coerce people (O Muḥammad) until they become Muslim?[17]
>
> Remind (them) you surely are but a reminder (O Muḥammad)
> You are not an oppressive authority over them (the unbelievers).[18]

15.2 **The Strong or Hard-Line Approach**

The hard-line version of the relativity of the *Ḥadīth* and the *Sunnah* maintains that, in a sense, the whole *Sīrah* is bound to its history, to the largely primitive and bedouin surroundings of 7th-century Madinah. Proponents of this line of argument claim that, even within the Qur'ān itself, there are verses that are 'relative'. The abrogated verses are used as examples of such 'relativity'. While this argument proposes to use the Qur'ānic notion of verse-abrogation to its advantage (as a proof that some portions of the Qur'ān are 'relative') it also makes a shift to water down to a considerable extent the notion of verse abrogation itself. It would not accept that successive periods and stages of the *Sīrah* necessarily abrogate each other. Thus the Madinan period does not necessarily abrogate the Makkan period; the second stage of the Makkan period does not abrogate the first, nor, similarly, does the late Madinan period necessarily abrogate the early Madinan period.

What does this mean for our contemporary understanding of the *Sīrah*? It means that Muslims are at liberty to evaluate the applicability of the Islamic rulings and commandments as their contemporary situations approximate to the corresponding stage of the *Sīrah*. Thus:

— It is all right if Muslim women (e.g. in the context of Europe or the USA) remain married to non-Muslims, if they have converted to Islam while their husbands have remained adherents of a scripture. That is not to say that Muslim women should marry non-Muslims, but is merely a way of coping with a contemporary problem in a compassionate and humane way – the problem of married women who convert to Islam while their husbands remain non-Muslim. To force a divorce would be very harsh for them, and for their offspring and their spouses.

— The same would be said about the need for Muslim minorities not to demand full application of the *Sharī'ah* in their country as a whole. But of course, it would be all right if they use effective political means to work for their legitimate human rights, including, if situations permit, regional or federal autonomy of those areas where Muslims constitute a predominant majority. That might be a suitable target for Muslim minorities in India, Asia, the United States, Europe and elsewhere.

In general, if this hard-line argument for relativity of the *Ḥadīth* and the *Sunnah* is pursued, it has very sinister implications for the *Sharī'ah* itself.

As to the status of Muslim women, both the soft and the hard approach groups would advocate greater participation for her in public affairs. The covering of the face, the confinement in the house, would not be tolerated by either group. If it turns out that it is ordained in the *Ḥadīth* or the *Fiqh,* then that must be explained away as merely a passing accident of the *Sīrah* and of Islamic history. Never mind the views of Aḥmad ibn Ḥanbal, or even the Companions of the

Prophet. These views are spatio-temporal manifestations of the universal message of Islam, which it is up to us to re-interpret, and re-examine, so as to make it relevant to our contemporary situation.

In particular, *ḥijāb* was enforced in the late Madinan period they argue, and most probably, was only directed to the wives of the Prophet. But if it can be proved otherwise, that it was in fact meant to be universal, then it must not be viewed as overriding the legislation pertaining to Muslim women in the pre-*ḥijāb* early Madinan period. In the early Madinan period there was among Muslims a great deal of intermingling between the sexes. Even the wives of the Prophet used to mix with the Muslims, dine with them, visit Muslims in their homes and were visited, etc. The argument of those who argue the relativity of the *Ḥadīth* and the *Sunnah* is that the status of women of the pre-*ḥijāb* period is more appropriate to our contemporary times. Similar views could be held about other issues such as *Shūrā,* the separation of the three powers of the state (the executive, legislative and judiciary). They may argue that a Muslim ruler may combine all of these powers if the contemporary situation required it.

15.3 **The Rebuttal of Hard-Line Relativism**

Whereas the soft approach may be partly justifiable, even acceptable if suitably modified, the hard-line, rigid approach is very difficult to justify. For one thing, there seem to be rational as well as Islamic reasons not to reject soft 're-lativism' outright, if it is suitably amended. A pedantically literal interpretation of the *Sīrah* leads to nonsensical positions. It is not possible to follow the Prophet or to emulate his deeds literally. This is not sanctioned by Islam itself and is impossible to carry out. Could all Muslims go and live in Madinah as the Prophet did? Could we all insist on having only she-camels for means of transport? etc. In Muslim history also, such a pedantic insistence on following the *Sunnah* was rejected. For example, the rejection of the practices of 'Abdullāh Ibn 'Umar, who, when journeying to Makkah to make *Ḥajj* had insisted on following literally the track of the Prophet on a former trip, sitting where the Prophet sat, resting where he rested, even if the time of the day would not permit that, etc. That was called the *Shadāyid* (i.e. the extremes) of Ibn 'Umar. Ibn 'Abbās (Abdullāh) followed a more rational course. He followed the example of the Prophet, when the context was either that of *'Ibādah* (religious rite) or a legislative matter pertaining to the essence of Islam. But where the Prophet's action was merely habitual, for instance, he rested when tired or took a path when he needed to do so, Ibn 'Abbās would not emulate him. This approach was called the *rukhaṣ* (the discretion) of Ibn 'Abbās. Moreover, we have the famous *Ḥadīth* concerning the pollination of date trees, and the incident of the Prophet's positioning of the Muslim troops at the Battle of Badr. The Prophet admitted that his stationing was far from ideal, and accepted the suggestion of al-Ḥubāb ibn Al-Mundhir, an ordinary soldier, concerning an alternative stationing of the troops. A second incident is that of going out in the Battle of Uḥud. If the practical decisions of the Prophet are part of his *Sunnah,* then of course some of that *Sunnah* is merely the personal opinion of the Prophet, therefore 'relative' and without universal binding force. Of course, a sound criterion by which to distinguish between personal and legislative *Sunnah* is badly needed.

However, that much could not be said for the argument of hard-line 'relativism'. If all the *Ḥadīth* and *Sunnah* are space-time relative, then the whole body of religious ordinances and commandments of Islam must peter out and disappear. If the understanding and religious practice of the Companions of the Prophet is only valid for them, our understanding and practice of Islam will be valid only for us. Why are we justified in thinking our understanding of Islam is superior to theirs? That we are contemporary to our situation is no advantage over them, who were equally contemporary to their situation. If we are superior in our understanding of Islam, simply because we came later in history, then this logic should be reversed, because the Companions were closer to the source of illumination, the Prophet and the fresh coming of the Qur'ān, and its relevance to their living situation. Criticizing the Companions without due reverence and respect is discourteous and un-Islamic. The Prophet definitely advised against it. True, the Qur'ān sometimes criticizes them, but that should not be used as a pretext for fellow Muslims to do so. It is unintelligent and impolite to make casual comments about Abū Hurayrah or other Companions in view of their poverty, etc. Those Companions lived with the Prophet, fought with him, sacrificed everything for the sake of Allah. We get the benefit of Islam through their endeavours, sacrifices and *Jihād.* Far from condemning them, we ought to be grateful to them, and humble ourselves out of respect for them.

16. **Epilogue**

The *Sīrah* and *Sunnah* of the Prophet are the unique heritage of this *Ummah* of Islam. Other nations and *Ummah* lost the authentic records of their sages, Prophets and great moral teachers. Today we know very little about Confucius, Buddha, Brahman, Moses or Jesus. By contrast, we know a great deal about the life of Muḥammad, *ṣallā Allāhu ʻalayhi wa sallam.* That knowledge is a great treasure, a great asset. We should strive to study and appreciate it, make it relevant to our contemporary situation. We should find out the relevant and authentic wisdom of the Prophet for every domain of our lives. The *Sīrah* and *Sunnah* could be immense resources for rebuilding and reconstructing the Islamic social sciences in every field of study. The *Sīrah* can be the springboard in our endeavours to Islamize human knowledge as a whole. In order to do that, the *Sīrah* must be intensively studied, in accordance with the very wide conception we have tried to indicate in our survey of the sources of the *Sīrah.* We have noted that some of the early sources are still missing, either in part or totally. An effort must be made to recover not only the whole work of Ibn Isḥāq, but also those source books on the *Sīrah,* written by the Companions and *at-Tābiʻūn,* mentioned above.

The manuscript collection of as-Sulaymāniyah (Istanbul) and the Scorial Library of Spain must be carefully and expertly sorted out and classified. Moreover, the Qur'ān as a source for the *Sīrah* must be thoroughly researched. This also goes for the *Ḥadīth* books. I have already indicated my opinion that all the *Ḥadīth* books must be researched, including the books of *Sunan, Āthār,* the *Musnads,* and all other newly edited books on *Ḥadīth* (such as the *Ṣaḥiḥ* of Ibn Khuzaymah). This is not to say that weak *Aḥādīth* are to be included in the *Sīrah.* But we may find valuable information in these lesser books of *Ḥadīth,* where that information does not contradict the Qur'ān or the authenticated collections. The voluminous studies of Orientalists are not to be ignored, but an objective methodology of *Sīrah* studies must be developed by Muslim specialists in the field which will satisfy the rigorous criteria of objectivity and factuality. Islam is based on the truth and justice, and is meant to be addressed to 'people of understanding' among all mankind. Thus our methodology must not fail to satisfy the criteria of rationality.

So our methodology in *Sīrah* writing may not be based on sentimentality or mythology. It should be based rather on a defensible quest for the truth which incorporates reason, not necessarily the empirical reason of the sciences of today but rather a consummate, higher and far-reaching rationality. What is needed is a rationality that does full justice to the unseen and the unobservable reality which cannot be detected by the empirical means of human reason. If that is carried out, Islam will be better appreciated by mankind at large.

The complete rewriting of the *Sīrah* here envisaged will require the energetic labours of a whole, dedicated academy of sincere Muslims, learned men and women, who are versed both in Islam in its pristine form, and also in the sciences as they exist today.

Notes and References

1. The *Ḥadīth* are not to be identified with the *Sunnah,* because whereas the former consists merely of the verbal utterances of the Prophet, *ṣallā Allāhu 'alayhi wa sallam,* the *Sunnah* includes his actions, explicit or tacit approval of things happening or done in front of him, his judgements and rulings, the way he conducted affairs of state in times of war and peace, in good health or in sickness, international relations,

religious rites, his appearance, his manner of socializing, talking, etc. Some *aḥādīth* may merely reflect the Prophet's personal views or his private nature and therefore do not constitute part of his religious *Sunnah* to be emulated by the believers. Similarly, some of his conduct and actions are a special perfection, a special distinction of his Prophethood, and not to be emulated by the believers, e.g. marrying more than four wives. See: Zakaria Bashier, *Islamic Movements in the Sudan: Issues and Challenges.* The Islamic Foundation, Leicester, 1987.

2. Among those who praised Ibn Isḥāq highly and asserted that his authority and moral integrity are unquestionable is al-Ḥāfiẓ Ibn Sayyid an-Nās, in the introduction of his book *'Uyūn al-Athar fī Funūn al-Maghāzī wa as-Siyar.* Also al-Ḥāfiẓ Ibn Ḥajar, referred to Ibn Isḥāq as the Imām of *Maghāzī.*

3. See Fārūq Ḥamādah, *Maṣādir as-Sīrah an-Nabawīyah wa Taqwīmuhā,* ad-Dār al-Bayḍā'. Dār ath-Thaqāfah, 1980 (Morocco), pp. 49ff.

4. *Ibid.*, pp. 52ff.

5. Ibn Sa'd's work is a monument of scholarship and a treasure-house of information on both the life of the Prophet and the *Āthār* of his Companions. It is considered very valuable because of the knowledge and information it gives on the Companions, women as well as men, and their ranking in a special hierarchy *(Ṭabaqāt).* It is also very valuable for the information it contains on the social history of Madinah. The literary style, and the manner in which the book is constructed are legendary. The most distinguished contemporary professor of a specialized discipline will not produce anything comparable to it. Its elegance and neatness bear the hallmark of exemplary contemporary scholarship.

6. *al-Sajdah* 32: 26.

7. Some portions of Ibn Isḥāq's *Sīrah Rasūl Allāh* have been recently recovered and published. But the whole work has not as yet been found. From accounts in Ibn Hishām, Ibn Sa'd, aṭ-Ṭabarī and from *Ta'rīkh Makkah* (by al-Azraqī), we gather that the three parts of Ibn Isḥāq are:
(1) *al-Mubtada'* (the early history of man).
(2) *al-Mab'ath* (the inception of the Prophethood).
(3) *al-Maghāzī* (the military expeditions of the Prophet).

Muḥammad Ḥamidullah (of Paris) has edited and recently published in Morocco a revered portion of Ibn Isḥāq. See: Fārūq Ḥamādah, *Maṣādir as-Sīrah an-Nabawīyah wa Taqwīmuhā,* ad-Dār al-Bayḍā' (Morocco 1980).

8. Especially valuable are W.M. Watt's work:
(a) *Muhammad at Mecca,* Oxford University Press.
(b) *Muhammad at Madina,* Oxford University Press.
(c) *Muhammad, Prophet and Statesman,* Oxford University Press.

9. The valley of Bakkah is also mentioned in the Old Testament – the Book of Genesis, and Psalm 84: 5–6; reference is also found in the Old

Testament to *Zamzam* (though not by name) and to Ishmael and his mother Hagar.

10. 'Abbās Maḥmūd al-'Aqqād: 'Ath-Thaqāfat al-'Arabiyyah Asbāq min al-Thaqāfat al-Ighrīqiyyah wa al-'Ibriyyah', an essay published in the Collected Works of al-Āqqād, Cairo, 1979.

11. *al-Naḥl* 16: 120.

12. *at-Takwīr* 81: 8 and 9. Says Allah, *subḥānahū wa ta'ālā:* 'And when the girl-child that was buried alive is asked: For what sin she was slain.'

13. For an elaboration of this point, see Zakaria Bashier, *The Meccan Crucible*, FOSIS, London, 1978.

14. See: Ibn Hishām, Ibn Sa'd, aṭ-Ṭabarī on this point. Also: Zakaria Bashier, *Hijra: Story and Significance.* The Islamic Foundation, Leicester, 1983.

15. *al-Anfāl* 8: 39.

16. *al-Baqarah* 2: 256.

17. *Yūnus* 10: 99.

18. *al-Ghāshiyah* 88: 21.

CHAPTER 1

Pillars of the Prophet Muḥammad's Society

A. THE FIRST PILLAR: THE QUR'ĀNIC DIMENSION

1. **Prologue**

To appreciate the dimensions of the change that came upon Yathrib with the arrival there of the Prophet, we need to recall the quality of life there before that momentous event. Yathrib was a society torn by conflict and war, its life dominated by the unrelenting hostilities between the two major Arabian tribal factions, the Aws and the Khazraj. Of South Arabian, Yemeni origin, the two tribes descended upon the fertile oasis after the dramatic destruction of the Ma'rab Dam. The Jewish tribes who settled in Yathrib, far from easing the situation, allowed themselves to be drawn into it. They split into two groups, each allying with one of the parties to the conflict. During the notorious Bu'āth war that raged for many years before the arrival of the Prophet, the Jews of Banū Qaynuqā' sided with and fought alongside the Khazraj tribe; the Jews of Banū an-Naḍīr and Qurayẓah sided and fought with the Aws. During the prolonged blood-letting, scores of people were wantonly killed, the fields and land ravaged. And not only did Arabs kill Arabs, also Jews killed Jews.

It is against this dismaying background of despair and destruction that the reconciling power of the Prophet's healing touch was most deeply needed and appreciated. It was those years of hatred and death that drove the Yathribites to the Prophet for a way out of their hopeless predicament.

The Prophet's arrival signalled a new and exciting era in the history of the village. Hitherto a small, insignificant agricultural settlement, Yathrib was suddenly wrested from the obscurity in which it had been shrouded. Not only did it become the centre of history in Arabia, but also the hub of a cosmological event of stupendous character. It became the focal point of Divine revelation.

More than anything, it was the sound of the Qur'ān that transformed the whole atmosphere of the place, its every aspect and element, into a new and sublime reality. The Archangel Gabriel was a frequent visitor, descending with portions of the Qur'ān, in response to the situation. For the Qur'ān was not revealed in its entirety on one occasion, but gradually in portions. To this mode of its revelation, the Qur'ān itself refers:

> And (it is) a Qur'ān that We have divided, that you may recite it unto mankind at intervals, and We have revealed it by (successive) revelations.[1]

Exegetes have described this special manner in which the Qur'ān was revealed as *Munajjaman*[2] (in portions). It was not revealed, as former Scriptures were believed to have been, in the form of a complete book. The impact of the Qur'ān was so great for this reason, that it interacted dynamically with people and events, every revelation being concerned with a concrete happening or event.

The Prophet himself had the greatest affection for the Qur'ān. He had a perpetual longing and anticipation for more and more of it. When it did come to him, he would be seized with an immense awe and apprehension, lest he missed any verse of it. In his anxiety to ensure a complete grasp of it, he used to recite it in great haste. Because of this, he was admonished by God in the Qur'ān in the following verse:

> Do not stir your tongue with it to hasten (memorizing) it, it is upon Us (to ensure) its collection and reading, so, when We read it, (just) follow its recitation. Surely, it is upon Us to explain it.[3]

Despite the labour and hardship which used to attend the coming of *Waḥī* (revelation), the Prophet used to await it with eager fondness. He even once pleaded with the Archangel Gabriel not to prolong his absence from him. Such a plea was indeed indicative of the acute sense of deprivation he felt at any prolonged absence of the Archangel. We recall here the Prophet's distress and anxiety when the Archangel Gabriel absented himself for six months after his initial visit at Ḥirā.[4]

The Prophet's spiritual agony was apparently so great at the Archangel Gabriel's prolonged absence that the polytheists of Makkah said that his Lord had forsaken him. To this, the Qur'ān retorted by comforting the Prophet, assuring him of God's love and compassion.[5]

The Prophet became the first thorough *Ḥāfiẓ* (memorizer) of the Qur'ān. So infectious was his love of the Qur'ān that of his wives, 'Ā'ishah, Ḥafṣah and Umm Salamah also became *Ḥāfiẓah.* From amongst his close entourage, Abū Bakr, 'Umar, 'Uthmān, 'Alī and Ibn 'Abbās also became well-known *Qurrā'* (readers).

Bukhārī named seven of the Prophet's Companions as the best-known *Ḥāfiẓ* of the Qur'ān. These were: (1) 'Abdullāh Ibn Mas'ūd *(Muhājir),* (2) Sālim, freedman of Abū Ḥudhayfah (also *Muhājir*), (3) Mu'ādh Ibn Jabal *(Anṣār),* (4) Ubayy Ibn Ka'b *(Anṣār),* (5) Zayd Ibn Thābit *(Anṣār),* (6) Yazīd Ibn aṣ-Sakan *(Anṣār),* (7) Abū ad-Dardā' *(Anṣār).*

A more realistic view is that the reading of the Qur'ān was so widespread that the actual number of *Ḥuffāẓ* was much larger than al-Bukhārī's[6] estimate. In the incident of *Bi'r Ma'ūnah*[7] alone, seventy *Qurrā'* were killed. During the Apostasy Wars (so-called *ar-Riddah* wars)[8] another seventy *Qurrā'* were killed in the one battle of *al-Yamāmah.*

2. Al-Madinah, the Qur'ānic Village

It was the constant habit of the Prophet to read and recite from memory lengthy chapters of the Qur'ān, in the night prayer. Many pious believers followed his example. The Prophet loved to listen to their night recitations. The practice of reciting the Qur'ān, day and night, was so widespread in Madinah that it could be heard from every house, every street and corner. The Prophet's Mosque, located at the very centre of Madinah, buzzed with the Qur'ānic recitations. For the *Ahl aṣ-Ṣuffah* (People of the Platform), almost their sole task was the constant recitation of the Qur'ān, whose sound could be heard pouring out of the Mosque from some distance. The Mosque was not the only place in which the Qur'ān was recited. The whole city was reported to have been characterized by a bee-like buzzing sound of recitation of the Qur'ān, coming from every direction. Men, women and children would not go to bed without first reciting a measure of the Qur'ān. Far into the night, the more pious men would stand in night prayer, reciting long *sūrahs* from memory. The beauty and sweetness of the Qur'ānic language, the nobility of its message, the power and vividness of its imagery, had a masterful sway over their hearts and minds. They felt greatly inclined to a mode of sublime recitation and chanting. The Qur'ān's powerful call to the wide horizons of God and the Hereafter, its disdain for the petty, soul-confining quarters of this world, enchanted them, often moving them to thoughtful sadness, even tears. Though they found the Qur'ān's call to God and the liberation of their souls from worldly chains attractive and compelling, they were also deeply aware of their inability to break loose from their needs and desires. Hence their predicament and sorrow; the tears they shed were but the expression of their unfulfilled though cherished longing.

The Prophet was fond of listening to those night recitations of the Qur'ān, and particularly fond of the Ash'arites' mode and style. The Ash'arites of Yemen were famous for the beauty and perfection of their Qur'ānic rhythm. Abū Mūsā al-Ash'arī, the celebrated arbiter, on behalf of 'Alī at Ṣiffīn[9] was renowned for the excellence and perfection of his Qur'ānic style. One night, the Prophet chanced to pass by his door when he was engaged in recitation. So impressed was the Prophet that he stood at his door for a considerable period. At length, the Prophet went away without disturbing the chanting of Abū Mūsā:

> 'You have one of the clarinets *(mazāmīr)* of David', said the Prophet, when he met Abū Mūsā the next morning.
> 'Were you listening to me, O Messenger of God?' responded Abū Mūsā, very excited and pleased at the rare, priceless Prophetic compliment. 'Had I known that you were there, I could have chanted it even better for you, O Prophet', added Abū Mūsā.

So keen and discriminatory of the Qur'ān was the ear of the Prophet that he was reported to recognize the residences of the Ash'arites, by their recitation at night. The Prophet was also very fond of the Qur'ānic style of 'Abdullāh Ibn Mas'ūd. He used to say:

> 'Who desires to hear the Qur'ān as it has been revealed unto me, let him listen to the recitation of Ibn Umm 'Abd (meaning Ibn Mas'ūd).'

The Prophet's Companions used to vie with each other in learning and memorizing the Qur'ān. They used to take great care to make their wives and children learn it. The Prophet himself attended personally to his Companions' Qur'ānic lessons, assigning a teacher to every newcomer. Qur'ānic teachers were speedily dispatched to tribes that entered Islam.

Insofar as the Qur'ān was the overriding preoccupation and concern of Madinah, the epithet *Qur'ānic Village* is most apt.

3. **The Dominant Qur'ānic Themes**

Before we end our discussion of the Qur'ānic pillar as the very foundation of the Prophet's society and state at Madinah, we must indicate some of the more recurrent among the Qur'ānic *sūrahs* in the first two years of the Prophet's stay therein.

No doubt, some of those *sūrahs* were continuations of the late Makkan period. Of these were such as dealt with the essence of all revealed religion – namely the call to the worship and service of the One True God, Lord of earth and heaven and Creator of all existent things. The calls of earlier Prophets were portrayed as essentially one and the same, namely, to monotheistic worship. The stories of the previous Prophets and Messengers of God from Adam to Moses and Jesus Christ were recounted now and again. Their striving to educate and guide their people was told and retold. The responses of various nations to the Divine Call were recorded as the essence of an eternal drama in human history. Special emphasis was placed on the story of the virgin birth of Christ and also on the story of Moses and the Divine favour in the deliverance of the Israelites.

The Qur'ānic accounts of Moses and the Israelites become more recurrent during the initial period of the coming of Islam to Madinah. The reason for this is obvious – the presence of Jews in Madinah and the Qur'ānic method of addressing itself to concrete realities. But the Madinan scene was also dominated by the phenomenon of hypocrisy and by impending conflict with the Quraysh. Other issues related to the role and status of the Prophet and his authority in the nascent Muslim state. Madinah was also a society in the making, and the fact of the emigrants, homeless and penniless, had to be dealt with. The establishment of prayer, of fasting and of *Zakāt* were also important issues for the emerging community and reflected in the Qur'ānic revelations of this initial Madinan period.

B. THE SECOND PILLAR: BUILDING THE PROPHET'S MOSQUE

1. **The Thatching of Moses**

The building of the Prophet's Mosque was begun almost immediately after his arrival in Madinah. It must be kept in mind that prayer is the pillar of Islam. The mosque was built on the very spot upon which al-Qaṣwā', the Prophet's camel, had stopped. The sizeable plot of land (35 by 30 yards) belonged to two orphaned children. It was immediately bought and paid for, and the work started. The first job was to level the ground, and remove some old graves. Some palm trees and thorny shrubs were also cleared. Then the construction of the mosque and two apartments for the Prophet's wives began. One apartment was meant for Sawdah, the other for 'Ā'ishah whose marriage to the Prophet was then imminent.

The mosque was a very simple edifice indeed. Not that the Muslims were unable to put up a much grander structure; rather it was the Prophet's desire that it should be a most simple building in the tradition of the one built by Moses.

The Prophet personally took part, alongside other Muslims, in the building work. He carried bricks, stones and earth. As the Muslims laboured, they sang ballads and songs in expression of their joy and happiness at the Prophet's stay amongst them. The Prophet also sang along with them. They sang:

> O Lord, there is no (worthy) living excepting one (oriented) for the Hereafter, so help (O Lord) the *Anṣār* and *Muhājirah.*
> O Lord, there is no good, excepting that of the Hereafter.
> So help, O Lord, the *Anṣār* and *Muhājirah.*

The Prophet's personal participation served to bring home to the Muslims the central importance of labour in their lives. It also helped to intensify their efforts and enthusiasm. Delighted with the Prophet's participation in the building work, the Muslims sang:

> If we sat back while the Prophet laboured, that would be our most misguided endeavour.

2. The Killers of 'Ammār

A prominent Companion of the Prophet, the celebrated 'Ammār Ibn Yāsir, distinguished himself by his excessive zeal and industry in carrying building materials to the site. The Prophet saw him carrying twice the normal load. Of him the Prophet said, compassionately:

'O 'Ammār, you will be killed by a tyrannical faction!'

This prophecy was fulfilled when 'Ammār was killed, some thirty years later, by the soldiers of Mu'āwiyah Ibn Abī Sufyān. 'Ammār was then fighting on the side of 'Alī Ibn Abī Ṭālib, in the Battle of Ṣiffīn.

The final structure of the mosque was quite simple, as the Prophet had desired. The foundations were made with stones and the walls with grey mud bricks. The roof was supported on columns made from the trunks of date trees and covered with branches of the same. The roof covered only a small portion of the mosque. The rest was an open, unroofed courtyard, enclosed by a short, grey mud-bricked wall, no higher than a man. There were three doors, in the east, west and south. The roofed portion had a little platform where the *Ahl aṣ-Ṣuffah,* the impoverished, ascetically-inclined students of Islam, lived continuously. Being without homes of their own, without families or occupation, they devoted their entire lives and energies to the study of the Qur'ān and practices of the Prophet. Their main job was to spread the message of Islam. When the call for *Jihād* came, they were among the first to take up the banner and march forward.

The ground of the mosque remained as it always was, not covered by anything. But one day it rained and the ground became muddy so the Muslims brought in some dry rubble and sand. Seeing this, the Prophet exclaimed:

'What a good carpet you have brought in.'

The mosque was a natural and simple structure, absolutely devoid of any pretensions of grandeur. As the Prophet wished, it resembled the 'thatching of Moses'. When the Muslims asked what the thatching of Moses looked like, the Prophet replied: 'The thatching of Moses was such that when he stood up, his head would touch the roof. However, the matter of this life is more transient than would even deserve a building of this magnitude.'

The implication of the Prophet's statement is that Muslims should not waste their time and energy building grand edifices. Rather they should concentrate on good deeds and the worship of God.

The finished building was, by the conscious desire and design of the Prophet, very humble indeed. The private apartments, built for his personal residence were even simpler, consisting of one large room for each of his two wives. This was the Prophet's style, from which he never departed. It was the style of a Prophet and not the grand, pompous style of kings and princes. The simplicity of the Prophet's Mosque and private apartments should not be ascribed to the limited financial resources of the Muslims at that time. Even when those resources became abundant, the Prophet never changed his austere style of living.

The reader may consider, indeed marvel at, the enormous (and continuing) contribution the Prophet made to the world and humanity at large. Yet none of that greatness was prevented by his austere and ascetic life-style, nor by his disdain for the pomp and glitter of this world. The same may be said of the magnitude of the radiance of the Prophet's Mosque.

The Prophet's insistence on working with the Muslims in the actual building is illustrative of his Prophetic style. No king or prince would join in manual labour. One Muslim who was overwhelmed by the sight of the Prophet carrying earth and bricks, rushed to relieve him, and offered to carry the load:

> 'No! No!' replied the Prophet graciously, 'you are not in greater need of God's mercy than I am, but you can take another load, if you like.'

Such humility and natural courtesy were characteristic of the Prophet's leadership. Far from conducting himself as a dictatorial overlord, he conducted himself as a compassionate father or a loving, caring friend.

At least five times every day, the Prophet made himself available at the Mosque, to lead the prayers and recite the Qur'ān. When he delivered sermons he would stand. His voice though most natural, was characterized by a deep, clear and sweet eloquence. When pleased and at ease, his face would assume a curious radiance likened, in many accounts, to that of the moon. Though his sermons were almost always very short, they invariably left the profoundest impression on the minds of his audience.

3. The Significance of the Prophet's Mosque

The Prophet's Mosque, though built in the humble way we have described, had the most glorious place and influence in the history of Islam.

It witnessed the Prophet's congregational prayers, attended by almost all Muslims, five times a day. It witnessed the recitations of the Qur'ān, by the Prophet himself and by his pious Companions, on many an evening and morning. It was the place to which the Archangel Gabriel descended on many occasions with revelations from God. Because of this Mosque, the land was blessed and Madinah became holy, and the Muslims were honoured by God's last divine call to the human race. This Mosque witnessed great assemblies of peace, war and victories. Learned discussions were echoed and re-echoed by its humble walls. Within those walls, God's final message to mankind was completed and perfected. Students of Qur'ānic truth and Prophetic wisdom all but lived there day and night. Muslims assembled there, discussed their plans for peace and war, and shared their experiences. They spoke of past experiences in Makkah, and of what was to come in the years ahead. Tales of distant lands went round, and the possibility of spreading God's final word to humanity held the greatest attraction for them. Often, their eyes filled with tears of love and affection as their hearts mellowed with the Qur'ānic tenderness.

In his simple Mosque, the Prophet received foreign dignitaries and noble deputations. He dispatched Muslim ambassadors to the kings of the world from this Mosque, and there too received delegations offering submission to God and His Word, and paying homage to his person and leadership.

The Prophet's Mosque remained unchanged during his lifetime, except that its courtyard was enlarged to make room for the ever-increasing numbers of Muslims. The only other minor change was the fixing of lamps to the main columns for the night and dawn prayers. The introduction of lamps was a welcome innovation by a Muslim from ash-Shām by the name of Tamīm ad-Dārī. He was more than rewarded by the Prophet's comment:

> 'You have illuminated our mosque. May God illuminate your life.'

Before the lamps were installed, the Mosque used to be lit by bonfires, placed in the middle of the courtyard.

The present-day, green-domed Mosque was built by successive Muslim governments, from the earliest times. The Ottoman and the recent Saudi extensions are the most conspicuous. The size of the Mosque has increased enormously, quite possibly more than a hundred times. Even today, a new extension is being carried out. Yet it is very difficult to find a place inside it, during Ramaḍān or any of the seasonal days.

There is some disagreement as to whether the Prophet's Mosque is the mosque referred to in the Qur'ān as 'the mosque founded on piety and God-fearing from the first day', or whether that refers to the Mosque of Qubā. In our view, it is the latter – the view held by most of our sources, although Ibn Kathīr and others are inclined towards the other view. Be that as it may, the status of the Prophet's Mosque, and its place in Islam, is second only to the sacred sanctuary of Makkah. Madinah thus is the second city of Muslim pilgrimage. The lifelong wish of thousands of Muslims around the globe is to be able to see for themselves its famous, glorious green dome, and pray in it. Prayers in this Mosque have a special religious significance, and rewards for them are very high indeed.

Some of the most melodious of Arabic poetry has been composed, throughout the history of Islam, to express profound sentiment for the Prophet, *ṣallā Allāhu 'alayhi wa sallam,* and for his green-domed Mosque of Madinah. This poetry is widely diffused in the local folklore of Muslim countries of North Africa and lands to the east of Arabia. In Arabia itself it is officially frowned upon. This colourful poetry, sung in praise of the Prophet and his Companions is called *Adab al-Madā'iḥ* (the literature in praise of the Prophet).

C. THE THIRD PILLAR: THE PERSONALITY OF THE PROPHET

1. **The Advent of the Prophet**

The Prophet's society at Madinah was indeed unique, its uniqueness owing to: (a) the presence of the Prophet, his personal example and influence, and (b) the continuous revelations of the Qur'ān, relating to the events of everyday life therein. Thus, it was an extraordinary society, curiously related to the Divine Realm and enormously influenced by it. During the ten years which passed between the Prophet's coming to the city and his death, the Archangel Gabriel, the vehicle of divine revelation, was a constant visitor, overseeing, and generally supervising, Madinah by the leave and commandment of God.

The Prophet's arrival among the Yathribites was indeed the arrival of hope and deliverance. Before it, they were in a desperate state of sickness of both body and soul, exhausted by years of senseless and bloody conflict. Without light or hope, they had longed for a deliverer, a comforter, to reconcile their deep divisions.

Then the Prophet came, the light of divine guidance in his hand, and compassion in his radiant face. He gave them the comfort for which they thirsted. He was for them the mercy and the compassion he was said to be in the Qur'ān: God described the mission of the Prophet as 'a mercy to mankind':

> We have not sent you, but as a mercy for mankind.[10]

To some aspects of this mercy by the Prophet, the Qur'ān refers as follows:

> Those who follow the Messenger, the Prophet who can neither read nor write, whom they will find described in the Torah and the Gospel (which are) with them, he

will enjoin upon them that which is right and forbid them that which is wrong. He will make lawful for them all the good things, and prohibit for them only the foul.

And he will relieve them of their burden and the fetters that were on them. Those who believe in him, and honour and support him, and follow the light that is sent down with him, they are the successful ones.[11]

The Prophet Muḥammad lived in the full light of history. We possess a vast body of material relating to the smallest details of his life and career, compiled by historians and scholars who took great pains not to omit anything. Even the most embarrassing details have been recorded, and instances of the Prophet's conduct reproved, even condemned, by the Qur'ān. This speaks quite favourably for the honesty and objectivity of Muslim historical sources. Far more significant is the fact that a record of the Prophet's life has been preserved in the Immortal Qur'ān itself. Not only is every aspect of his overt life recorded, evaluated and commented upon, but the very musings of his heart, his inner thoughts, are quite often exposed, as in the affair of his marriage to Zaynab bint Jaḥsh.

From this well-preserved, reliable record of the life of the Prophet Muḥammad, some aspects of his vast reservoirs of mercy and compassion can be examined and exemplified. In two extraordinarily beautiful verses of the Qur'ān, the Prophet's mercy is summed up thus:

Surely, there has come unto you a messenger of your own selves, it is grievous unto him that you are overburdened, full of concern for you, and for the believers full of compassion, merciful. But if they turn away, say (O Muḥammad) Allah suffices me. There is no god save Him. On Him, have I relied, and He is the Lord of the Tremendous Throne.[12]

The second verse reports how dear the character and person of the Prophet was to the Muslims, and of his exceptional love and care for his Companions:

> The Prophet is more mindful of the believers' (interest) than themselves, and his wives are their mothers . . .[13]

The Prophet's Companions experienced fully and reciprocated his love for them. They loved him as they had never even loved their own parents, and were prepared to (and some did) sacrifice their lives to protect his. They used to address him often with *fidāka Abī wa Ummī* (may my father and mother be a ransom (sacrifice) for you). Khubayb ibn 'Adī, told his executor that he would prefer to die than contemplate a thorn in the Prophet's foot. During the *Hijrah,* Abū Bakr defended him with his life; 'Alī ibn Abī Ṭālib slept on his bed whilst he escaped his would-be assassins. During the Battle of Uḥud, when he became exposed to the Quraysh fighters, he was defended by a small group of men and women who shielded him with their own bodies against the swords, arrows and blows of the enemy. Those included the celebrated Muslim woman Nusaybah bint Ka'b, and such brave Muslims as Sa'd ibn Abī Waqqāṣ, 'Alī Ibn Abī Ṭālib, 'Umar Ibn al-Khaṭṭāb, Ṭalḥah ibn 'Ubayd Allāh and others, including Abū Bakr.

2. A Pen-Portrait of the Prophet

Although earlier sources, notably Ibn Hishām, do not give a detailed description of the person of the Prophet, later sources describe him in the minutest detail. The following portrait is basically that of Ibn Kathīr, who seems to be drawing on diverse sources, chiefly Bukhārī and Muslim.

According to Ibn Kathīr,[14] there seems to be unanimous agreement that the Prophet was exceptionally handsome. His complexion was white, mixed with a reddish tan. But the rest of his body was 'as white as a rod of silver'. There seemed to be a curious radiance from his face, likened by some to the 'moving sun', by others to the glitter of a sword in the sun. But the most common description of it is that of the full, round moon. The same curious light seemed to beam from his wide, pensive eyes. When he smiled, light seemed to be reflected from his beautiful white teeth. Indeed, such was the beauty and radiance of his countenance that whoever had a private audience with him for the first time would be strongly overawed by it.

Of medium size, neither tall nor short, his figure was, nonetheless, commanding and impressive. His head, unusually large, gave space for a large and noble brow. The eyebrows were large, arched and joined. The hair jet-black, thick and slightly curly and, when he left it uncut, it could reach down below his ears. His eyes were very wide, and very black, pensive and glittering. His eyelashes were long and black, adding to the lustre of his eyes. It was his eyes (slightly marred by redness in the white of them) which more than anything seemed to convey some of his great spiritual and psychological strength and some of his iron resolve and singleness of mind, his total reliance on his Lord.[15] They beamed with his characteristic serenity and firm determination. In general, they reflected that vast reservoir of intelligence and discernment, and contributed most to his awe-inspiring appearance. When he was displeased, anger showed in his face and, no doubt in his eyes, turning more reddish. A vein between his eyes became swollen. But with his exemplary tact and modesty, he used to turn his face aside, so that his audience would not see his displeasure.

His forehead was wide and exposed. It shone with a light and smoothness resembling the surface of a still ocean lit by a full moon, and totally at ease, having achieved the highest peace of total submission to God Almighty. His nose was noble, high, gracious and slightly aquiline. It was, nonetheless, fine and in perfect proportion, somewhat slender at the end. The nose led to a finely-cut but generous mouth. He had the gift of fine, decisive, commanding speech of phenomenal eloquence. His accent was the purest of Arabian speech, in a deep, melodious tone. There was a gap (called *Faljah* by the Arabs) between his upper front teeth, which were finely cut and snow-white in colour, always kept so by the Prophet. He loved to brush his teeth often, at least five times a day, before each prayer. So white and shining were his teeth that they sparkled with little bursts of light as he spoke. The *Faljah* in his teeth added to the moon-like beauty of his face. His beard was full, round, black, reaching to his chest, no doubt adding to his manly magnificence. His physique was fine, even slender, yet sturdy and well-built. His broad shoulders and wide chest gave the impression of conspicuous strength with youthful energy and vitality. When he walked, it was as if descending a hill – none could be faster. His Companions found it difficult to keep pace with him. Though fast, his steps were sharp and firm. His figure tilted slightly forward as he moved around, as if he was on a definite errand.

Although the Prophet's face was reddish-white,[16] possibly as a result of his long and active travels to Syria and around Makkah, the rest of his body was described as silver-white. In particular his back and tall, finely moulded neck were said to be silver-white when exposed from under his mantle. Describing his unusually long and beautiful neck, 'Alī ibn Abī Ṭālib is reported by Ibn Kathīr,[17] to have said 'it was like an *Ibrīq*[18] (tubular necked jug) made of silver'. It was this peculiar quality of radiance that most impressed and mystified his fond Companions. Abū Hurayrah said that he was as white 'as if the sun moved in his face'. A woman Companion by the name of ar-Rubayyi' bint al-Mu'awwidh said:

> 'If you see him, you would say: it is the sun rising in the morning.'

A Persian woman from Hamadhān made pilgrimage with the Prophet. When asked about his appearance, she said:

> 'He was like a full moon, I have not seen anyone so beautiful in my life.'[19]

It was the radiance of his face, no doubt a spiritual gift, that so impressed the beholders. This light beamed from every feature in his face. Especially his long, soft, rather thin cheeks that radiated with pleasantness and happiness added to his magnificence. Summing up his physical appearance, a poet referred to the whiteness of his face as a sign of his generosity and munificence, especially towards the poor and the needy:

> A fair countenance for whose sake rain would fall.
> A guardian for the orphans.
> A comfort for the lonely widows.[20]

3. His Character Traits

For his description of the general manners of the Prophet, Ibn Kathīr draws largely upon a statement by Hind Ibn Abī Hālah at-Tamīmī, narrated on the authority of al-Ḥasan Ibn 'Alī (Ibn Abī Ṭālib). Said al-Ḥasan (grandson of the Prophet): 'If he turned, he would turn with his whole body towards the person addressed. His gaze was more often lowered, more often than not his gaze was cast down to the earth. He looked down to the earth more than he looked up to the sky. He walked behind his Companions, always the first to greet whom he chanced to meet, observing things as he moved along.' Pensive and sorrowful in general appearance, continuously wrapped in his thoughts and meditations, the Prophet was unusually quiet and reserved. Yet, he was industrious, never found just doing nothing. Even at home, he would take part in the *miḥnah* (household work) of his wives. When there was nothing to be done, he would deem it his duty to amuse them, making them laugh with happiness. He quite often attended to his personal chores, washing and sewing his clothes and mending his shoes, etc.

He entertained long intervals of silence, and would generally like to listen rather than lead the conversation. He would not speak without a need or a purpose. When he talked, he did so with his whole mouth. His sentences were short and pregnant. He was given to *jawāmi' al-kalim* (the loaded expressive sentence), not too short or too long but sufficient. His manners were fine, neither coarse and unfriendly nor meek or insignificant. He was never angry for personal motives. He freely forgave and brushed aside personal insults. However, he showed great anger when a matter of principle was mocked or violated. When he was so upset, he would not be pleased until that matter had been redressed or avenged. But personal indignities and little insults would not make him angry, nor would they make him retaliate against his offenders. He would bear them graciously and patiently. Bedouins used to address him harshly and use crude and improper language. They even sometimes pulled his beard as they talked. But the Prophet would bear all of this with a gracious smile.

When engaged in conversation, he would use his whole palm, pointing with it in wonder and amusement. If he was angry, he looked aside; if pleased, he would lower his gaze. Most of his laughter was no more than smiling but occasionally he laughed until his teeth were exposed. When he thus laughed, bursts of light were seen between his teeth.

When at home he divided his time in three portions – one for his wives, one for God, and one for himself. But his personal time he shared with his Companions, receiving them, looking after them, and enquiring about their affairs. When his Companions came to visit him, he received them in kindness, waiting personally upon them, serving and honouring them. He enquired about their needs and tried his best to see to it that those needs were satisfied. Quite often he directed them to do or say things which would benefit them and ease their hearts and hardships. He would even ask them to convey to him the needs of those who could not convey them in person, saying that 'whosoever conveys to the ruler the needs of those who cannot convey them, God would establish and strengthen him on the Resurrection Day'.

When drinks were served in his home, normally with only one bowl going round, he would be the last to drink. Similarly, he often ate only after his Companions had eaten, especially when he sensed that they were suffering from hunger, which was not unusual.

When his Companions assembled around him, his manner was the noblest, light-hearted and elevating. He would show every kindness and compassion towards them, never saying anything or bringing up a topic which would grieve them or lower their spirits. Far from attempting to mock them or demoralize them, he would say things which would help them overcome their vices and weaknesses. In this way, he would raise and foster what was best in them, encourage them and make them want to do good deeds. He honoured them with his gracious hospitality. It was always his habit and concern to please and honour his Companions. He would take great care to especially honour those who had merit or were previously honoured by their own people (even before coming to Islam). Witness the honour he bestowed upon

Abū Sufyān at the conquest of Makkah. In return for his kindness and honouring of them, they remained for ever captivated by his love and favour. They loved him more than they loved their own parents, more even than themselves, ready to do anything to please him, to die if need be in his defence and in defence of the new faith and society.

The Prophet and the assembly of the Companions around him can be likened to a full bright moon and a cluster of luminous stars around it. As he shone ever brighter, so they too became more luminous. His style of leadership was not that of an overbearing lord, obsessed by promoting his own image and strengthening his personal grip. Nor was it the style of an envious professor irritated if one of his students excelled. Far from trying to dim and lessen the merit of his Companions, he for ever sought to exalt and improve them, and lead them towards the realization of what was best and most noble in them (may Allah bless him ever more and more).

It is little wonder, therefore, that no Prophet or Messenger of God, no king or prince was so loved, honoured or obeyed by his Companions and followers as the Prophet Muḥammad.

Although normally reserved and contemplative, Muḥammad was by no means an introvert. On the contrary, he was a social being of unusual charm. His company was of the sweetest, and his visitors would tend to overstay in his house, no doubt drawn and held by the peace and joy they used to experience when in his company.

The habit of overstaying in the Prophet's home, notwithstanding the very limited room in his private apartments, became so widespread, and the Prophet too shy to mention it, that God had to intervene and Qur'ānic verses were revealed to draw the Companions' attention to the inconvenience and hardship which this overstaying inflicted upon their too-gracious host.

The pre-Islamic Arabian society in general, and the Yathribites in particular, were not known for compassion. This is attested by the surprised protestations of a bedouin, when he saw that the Prophet hugged and kissed al-Ḥasan, his grandson. Moreover, Yathrib, at the time the Prophet came there, was just emerging from a prolonged and savage war. The Prophet's mild temperament, his unusual graciousness, the caring love and compassion he showed to his citizens and followers was in marked contrast to anything the Yathribites had so far experienced. The way he used to receive and treat them in private audience, made each one of them feel that no-one else was more loved or honoured by the Prophet than him. Such was the justice and equality with which all of them were treated that they gradually became accustomed to look upon him as their own loving father – the ideal and dearest of fathers. Thus the Muslims became dependent upon the Prophet for their support, material as well as spiritual, and under his protection and guidance they felt happy and tranquil. For the forty or sixty poor *Muhājirūn* of *Ahl aṣ-Ṣuffah,* he was quite literally the sole supporter and guardian, providing food and lodging from whatever little he possessed. This unusual relationship between the Prophet and the Muslims has been recorded by the verse of the Qur'ān, quoted earlier, that the Prophet became closer to the believers than themselves, and his wives became their mothers.[21] Indeed, the Prophet was a father to many a fatherless child in Madinah, orphaned because of the Bu'āth War. He is indeed the father of those who, for whatever reason, have suffered deprivation of parental or fatherly love, to the end of all time.

The Prophet's forbearance in attending to the needs of his Companions was immeasurable. He would sit listening to them for hours, not showing the least sign of impatience or inconvenience. When extending his hand in salutation, he would never be the first to withdraw it, nor would he be the first to break off a conversation or a council, unless something really pressing came up. Often, when he was not busy in some serious matter, a little girl from the neighbourhood would dash into his house, take him by the hand, and demand: 'Let us go out to play.' He would obey her and she would spin him about playing merry-go-round.

His liberality towards his Companions and the citizens of Madinah was without limits. Never was he asked something or some favour and he failed to grant it, unless, of course, it was beyond his means. Even then, he would passionately pray and implore his Lord on their behalf, and quite often his prayers were immediately granted. On some occasions, he would teach them selected prayers and invocations, exalting God and asking His forgiveness. They would comply and their hardships were relieved. One day the Prophet was wearing a new robe, a gift from overseas, from some king or prince. A bedouin's eyes fell on it, praising its beauty and desiring it. The Prophet took it off and tenderly placed it around the bedouin's shoulders. The bedouin was overcome with emotion and gratitude.

Towards those who harmed and opposed him he was usually charitable and forgiving. Yet if they insisted on their enmity and sought to obstruct God's call to mankind, and it became clear beyond a shadow of doubt that they were bent on destroying his mission, then the Prophet would not shy away from having to deal with them, as the situation might demand. One of his favourite strategies was to deal the first blow to them decisively, speedily. He would not suffer humiliation or defeat at the hands of his combatant adversaries, if he could help it. Nor would he let their treacherous designs go unchecked or unpunished. However, if they relented and surrendered, he would forgive them at once, totally and unreservedly. In this way, some of his former enemies became his best friends and protectors.

The Prophet's style of living was, by choice and design, most austere. He would accept gifts and hospitality from his friends and Companions. Yet if he sensed charity in them, he would reject them outright. Although totally modest and unpretentious, he was nonetheless high-minded and noble in his attitude towards people and things. Given the asceticism he chose, his needs were indeed minimal and whatever need he felt was for the compassion and mercy of his Lord, the Almighty God. Because of his utter reliance upon God, the Prophet was called *Al-Mutawakkil* (The God-reliant). In his love for God, he felt self-sufficient. For the glitter of life, its luxuries and comforts, he had no desire. He was reported to find his greatest delight in prayer, especially at night. When he was not in communion with God through prayer, his favourite things were to keep clean, fit and looking well. If he had an indulgence it was for good perfume – offensive smell being most detested by him. Of the innocent pleasures of life, he enjoyed the company of attractive, youthful women, especially when they were distinguished by sharp wits, good humour and upright and virtuous character – qualities which 'Ā'ishah enjoyed to the full.

4. The Qur'ānic Universe that was Muḥammad

Asked about the character of the Prophet, 'Ā'ishah said: 'His character was the Qur'ān.' He was nothing less than the embodiment of every Qur'ānic virtue and noble disposition, unfolded and realized in practical life. So comprehensive was the Prophet's character that it assumed the proportions of a vast Qur'ānic universe in which every perfection, excellence and noble pursuit commended by the Qur'ān for man was exemplified and realized.

It is not therefore possible for any ordinary mortal to encompass his life, nor to describe his greatness adequately. This is an infinite, eternal endeavour. Professor Hart[22] said that of all men who have ever lived, Muḥammad had the greatest influence on human history. As a Muslim, and a humble student of his gracious, noble life, I would add, after agreeing with that opinion, may Allah's peace and blessings be upon him.

D. THE FOURTH PILLAR: INSTITUTION OF BROTHERHOOD AMONG MUSLIMS

1. The Story of 'Abd ar-Raḥmān and Sa'd

As many Muslim emigrants were without means of livelihood, the Prophet laid the obligation of supporting them on the *Anṣār.* He solved the problem by instituting brotherhood between the *Anṣār* and *Muhājirūn.* To each *Muhājir,* the Prophet, *ṣallā Allāhu 'alayhi wa sallam,* assigned an *Anṣārī* Muslim to be as his brother. This brotherhood was a bond more effective and substantial than blood relationship, so much so that, at first, the Muslim brothers used to inherit from each other. Later, this practice was abrogated and inheritance was solely through blood relation. In most cases the brothers consisted of one man from the *Anṣār* and one from the *Muhājirūn*. The exception to this pattern was the Prophet himself and members of his house. The Prophet himself took 'Alī as his brother, and Hamzah and Zayd ibn Ḥārithah were made brothers, all four *Muhājirūn*. This fact must be explained by the Prophet's unwillingness to appear to favour one clan of the *Anṣār* above the others, knowing how sensitive they were due to their history of conflict and rivalry, especially the Aws and the Khazraj sub-clans.

The most remarkable example of solidarity among new Muslims is that between Sa'd ibn ar-Rabī' and his new brother, 'Abd ar-Raḥmān ibn 'Awf. Sa'd was a very rich man and had two wives. On becoming a brother to 'Abd ar-Raḥmān ibn 'Awf he offered, without hesitation, to divide all his wealth equally with him. In an extravagant tribute to this new relationship he even offered to divorce one of his wives so that 'Abd ar-Raḥmān might marry her if he wished. The generosity of Sa'd ibn ar-Rabī' was matched by the nobility of 'Abd ar-Raḥmān, who adamantly refused to take advantage of the goodwill of his new brother. Having duly thanked him and prayed warmly to God to bless him, his wealth and his family, 'Abd ar-Raḥmān asked to be shown the main market-place. This was located in the Jewish quarter of Banū Qaynuqā'. 'Abd ar-Raḥmān went there and began to trade. After a short time, he not only managed to support himself, but to raise enough money to get married. The presence of 'Abd ar-Raḥmān in the market-place must have been an early sign of the socio-economic changes that were taking place as a result of the new Muslim presence there. Before the coming of the Muslims, the Jews of Banū Qaynuqā' had obviously enjoyed a virtual monopoly of trade and crafts in Madinah. Given the traditional Jewish genius in commerce, the Aws and Khazraj had been no match for them. But now, the business-minded Quraysh aristocracy were there, of whom 'Abd ar-Raḥmān was a good example. His presence must have indicated to the Jews of Banū Qaynuqā' that they had, from that time on, to put up with some measure of competition from the equally trade-oriented *Muhājirūn*.

2. **The Pairing Off of Muslim Brothers**

Among the *Anṣār* who were assigned a new brother for whom they were responsible, the following may be noted, together with the names of their *Muhājirūn* brothers:

Mu'ādh ibn Jabal	*(Anṣārī)*
Ja'far ibn Abī Ṭālib	*(Muhājir)*
Khārijah ibn Zayd	*(Anṣārī)*
Abū Bakr aṣ-Ṣiddīq	*(Muhājir)*
'Itbān ibn Mālik	*(Anṣārī)*
'Umar ibn al-Khaṭṭāb	*(Muhājir)*
Sa'd ibn Mu'ādh	*(Anṣārī)*
Abū 'Ubaydah ibn al-Jarrāḥ	*(Muhājir)*
Sa'd ibn ar-Rabī'	*(Anṣārī)*
'Abd ar-Raḥmān ibn 'Awf	*(Muhājir)*
Salamah ibn Salamah	*(Anṣārī)*
Az-Zubayr ibn al-'Awwām	*(Muhājir)*

Another view has it (according to Ibn Kathīr) that Az-Zubayr ibn al-'Awwām (husband of Asmā', daughter of Abū Bakr, thus a relative of the Prophet who was married to Asmā's sister) was paired with 'Abdullāh ibn Mas'ūd – a *Muhājir* and personal attendant of the Prophet. This confirms the Prophet's policy with members or very close associates of his own household.

Aws ibn Thābit	*(Anṣārī)*
'Uthmān ibn 'Affān	*(Muhājir)*
Ka'b ibn Mālik	*(Anṣārī)*
Ṭalḥah ibn 'Ubayd-Allāh	*(Muhājir)*
Ubayy ibn Ka'b	*(Anṣārī)*
Sa'īd ibn Zayd	(Husband of Fāṭimah, daughter of al-Khaṭṭāb)
Abū Ayyūb al-Anṣārī	(*Anṣārī* and host of the Prophet)
Muṣ'ab ibn 'Umair	(first Muslim scholar – Ambassador to Yathrib)
'Abbād ibn Bishr	*(Anṣārī)*
Abū Ḥudhayfah ibn 'Utbah	*(Muhājir)*
Abū Ḥudhayfah ibn al-Yamān	*(Anṣārī)*

ʻAmmār ibn Yāsir	*(Muhājir)*
Abū Rawāḥah ʻAbdullāh ibn ʻAbd ar-Raḥmān	*(Anṣārī)*
Bilāl ibn Rabāḥ	*(Muhājir)*

The Prophet, *ṣallā Allāhu ʻalayhi wa sallam,* was brother and friend of all Muslims, *Anṣār* as well as *Muhājirūn.* We have seen that he carefully avoided taking a formal brother from any clan of the *Anṣār,* lest this should resurrect old rivalries. However, in order to conform to the general pattern of organizing the Muslims into pairs of brothers, he instituted the following brotherhood for himself and members of his house:

Muḥammad ibn ʻAbdullāh and ʻAlī ibn Abī Ṭālib;
Ḥamzah ibn ʻAbd al-Muṭṭalib and Zayd ibn Ḥārithah;
ʻAbdullāh ibn Masʻūd and Zubayr ibn al-ʻAwwām

The institution of brotherhood was not simply a short-term measure designed to deal with an immediate economic crisis, but a major and permanent feature of the new social order that was emerging under the leadership of the Prophet. It represented a conscious, deliberate choice in favour of a collective, co-operative spirit, over individualism and competitiveness. The Muslim society of the Prophet was essentially classless. Hence no struggle between classes could exist and social conflict did not arise. The Prophet himself set the example that demonstrated the orientation and humanity of the new Muslim civilization. He shared his free time, his private apartment and his own food with his Companions.

In particular he shared his meagre meals with the forty or sixty members of the association of *Ahl aṣ-Ṣuffah,* inviting them to his house almost every day.

The brotherhood among Muslims, a permanent basis for social organization in Islam, is confirmed by the injunctions and directives of the eternal Qur'ān itself:

> Surely believers are brothers unto each other, so make peace and reconciliation amongst your brothers.[23]

> Believers, men and women, are guardians *(Awliyā')* unto each other, they enjoin the right and forbid the wrong, and establish prayer and pay *Zakāt,* and they obey Allah and His Messenger. As for these, Allah will have mercy on them. Surely Allah is All-Mighty, Wise.[24]

3. The Concept of *Muwālāt*

The term which the Qur'ān uses to depict this specific, intimate relationship among Muslims is *Awliyā'* (sing. *Walī*). Now, the '*Walī*' is one who accepts total responsibility for looking after somebody else – in Islamic legal terminology, *Walī* could be a father or the next of kin. Also, the Muslim legitimate ruler is deemed a *Walī* over the affairs of Muslims. Thus verse 71 of *Sūrah at-Tawbah* (Repentance) is a unique Qur'ānic reference to the kind of extraordinary, organic relationship that bound the Muslims. In a very real sense, Muslims are a closely-knit family, or a unit still closer:

> You find the Muslims in their mutual love and compassion, like one body. Should any organ of it fall ill, the rest of the body will share in the fever and the sleeplessness that ensues.[25]

Without the organic unity which the concept of *Muwālāt* seeks to establish among them, the Muslims cannot succeed in discharging their enormous responsibility to which the same verse refers, namely, to enjoin righteousness, forbid wrong and establish Allah's socio-political system on earth – the establishment of prayer and *Zakāt.* Nor would it be possible for them to establish Allah's authority on earth through that of His Prophet and His Book. It is, therefore, no wonder, that this same verse of *Sūrah at-Tawbah,* should at the same time refer to the absolute importance of obeying Allah and His Messenger. This obedience is not only necessary to foster and strengthen *Muwālāt* as a system of social organization for a Muslim community in any time or place. It also provides an ultimate goal and objective for that community. In other words, only if the Muslims succeed in setting up *Muwālāt* amongst themselves and strictly observing it, can it be possible for them to establish and guard the supreme authority of Allah and His Messenger on earth.

Thus, the concept of *Muwālāt* seems a broader and more organic concept than that of brotherhood. It has wider social, political, legal and economic implications, as brought out in verse 71 of *Sūrah at-Tawbah,* where the concept is expounded. *Muwālāt* is referred to, here, as the effective principle by means of which the Muslim community is organized. So comprehensive is this organization that every individual Muslim is drawn into it, with no-one left out. Even Muslims held far away in Makkah, against their will, were the responsibility and concern of the Muslims. The Muslims in Madinah were constantly thinking and worrying about their safety and well-being. In this context, an interesting Qur'ānic verse sought to end this worrying in the case of these Muslims, who chose to stay in Makkah, after the *Hijrah* had been ordained:

> Surely those who believed and migrated and strove with their wealth and their lives for the cause of Allah, and those who took them in and helped them, those are the guardians *(Awliyā')* one of another. And those who believed but did not migrate, you have no duty of guardianship *(Muwālāt)* towards them till they migrate.
> But should they seek your help, in a matter of religion, then it is your duty to defend them, except against a faction with whom you have a treaty (of non-aggression).[26]

Thus, the military aspect of *Muwālāt* is weakened, almost dropped, in the case of those Muslims who continued, wilfully, to live in Makkah, after the *Hijrah.* The Muslims' duty to help and defend them, came after their duty to help and defend covenanted non-Muslim partners. However, the general bond of brotherhood and solidarity still existed between the negligent Muslims of Makkah, and the general body of Muslims in Madinah. But no *Muwālāt* between the two groups existed, unless exceptionally.

This *Muwālāt* seemed to have provided a solid basis for a sort of *pax Islamica.* Whoever of the Muslims committed himself to an absolute, full and exclusive *Muwālāt* with Muḥammad and the Muslims was eligible for the protection and support of all Muslims. The *Hijrah* to Madinah was symbolic of such a full commitment. All Muslims had an equal right to extend this protection, and were equally obligated to withhold it from any person or faction engaged in active conflict with the Muslims. There is a reference to this equality in the *Ṣaḥīfah* of Madinah, as we shall see in the sequel. A common way of referring to this *Muwālāt* is by saying that the *Dhimmah* (covenant) of Muslims is one and indivisible. The equality referred to in the following clause –

> *al-Muslimūn 'Udūlun yas'ā bi-dhimmatahim adnāhum wa-hum yadun 'alā mān siwāhum*
> 'Muslims are equals, the least among them can extend their covenant (to a third party) and they are but one hand against their mutual enemy'

– seems to be the legal one of *Muwālāt.*

Zaynab, the Prophet's daughter, gave herself the right to extend this protection to her husband, al-'Āṣ ibn ar-Rabī', without even obtaining the permission of her father who was sitting a stone's throw away in the Mosque. The Prophet endorsed her action, without fuss.

E. THE FIFTH PILLAR: THE ESTABLISHMENT OF CONGREGATIONAL PRAYER

1. The Ordinance of Prayer and *Adhān*

Although the Muslim five daily prayers were prescribed in Makkah, they were not fully implemented in their congregational form until after the *Hijrah.* It is generally accepted that the ordinance of these five daily prayers was received by the Prophet from God during the *Isrā'* and *Mi'rāj.*[27] Yet such was the disarray of life for Muslims in Makkah that they were not able to observe them except once in the morning and once in the evening. Now that Muslims were safe and secure in Madinah, the duty of establishing all the congregational prayers as ordained by God became an absolute priority. To perform this duty was at once the principal concern as well as the greatest pleasure of the Prophet and the Muslims. The Prophet's Mosque was begun and completed to this end – that Muslims should have a suitable place for establishing their daily prayers together.

There was, however, a problem concerning the best way of calling the Muslims to congregational prayers. Tradition has it that the Prophet was thinking about an effective way of calling people to the five daily prayers, then being held in the Mosque. He had considered the Jewish horn or trumpet, but rejected it as unsuitable. He had then thought of using a bell after the manner of the Christians, but again the idea had not appealed to him. Thus, for some time, the Prophet continued the practice of calling Muslims by sending someone into the streets of Madinah, crying at the top of his voice, *'aṣ-Ṣalātu Jāmi'ah'* ('to congregational prayer'). Then, one day, a Companion by the name of 'Abdullāh ibn Zayd came and told of a dream he had had the night before. In that dream, Ibn Zayd saw a man in green robes, carrying a bell, and wanted to buy the bell from him.

> 'But what do you want it for?' asked the man in green.
> 'I want to use it to summon people to prayer', answered Ibn Zayd.
> 'May I show you a better way of doing this? Call out, at the top of your voice:
> *Allāhu Akbar! Allāhu Akbar! Allāhu Akbar!*
> (God is greatest!)
> I bear witness that there is no god but Allah.
> I bear witness that Muḥammad is the Messenger of Allah'.[28]

The Prophet, *ṣallā Allāhu 'alayhi wa sallam,* accepted Ibn Zayd's dream as authentic. Thereafter, the *Adhān* as it is known today, was called out loudly by Bilāl as seen in the dream of Ibn Zayd. Bilāl was chosen because of the suitable qualities of his voice.

2. **The Change of the *Qiblah***

For some time after his arrival at Madinah, the Prophet and the Muslims turned their face in prayers towards Jerusalem, just as the Jews used to do. Relations between the Muslims and Jews then worsened, due to the latter's campaign of slander and hatred against the Muslims. Thus it became more and more untenable for the Muslims to continue this semblance of common cause with the Jews. The Muslims became restless, and the Prophet himself, silently waited and hoped for a new *Qiblah* to be revealed to him by God. The Qur'ān tells of the Prophet's anguish and anticipation whilst he waited, hoped and prayed for a new *Qiblah:*

> We have certainly seen the turning of your face to heaven (seeking and inviting guidance). Now, assuredly We will afford you a *Qiblah* with which you shall be well-pleased. So turn your face towards the *Ḥarām* (the Inviolable) House.[29]

With this announcement of the *Qiblah,* the Prophet and the Muslims rejoiced greatly and felt relieved and honoured. But the Jews were further annoyed with Muḥammad and the Muslims. They questioned the causes and rationale of the sudden change, and expressed their disapproval of it. Thus the change of the *Qiblah* gave fresh impetus to the mounting arguments and disagreement between the Muslims and the Jews, who regarded the new move as unsanctionable.

To the Jews' misgivings about the change and its rationale, the Qur'ān replied that to God belonged the East and West, and indeed all directions. His freedom in choosing a direction *(Qiblah)* for Muslim prayer cannot be restricted by any person or community. Allah says in the Qur'ān:

> The feeble-minded among the people will say: What has turned them from the *Qiblah* which they formerly observed? Say: Unto Allah belong the East and the West. He guides whom He will unto a straight path.[30]

The Muslims found great joy and comfort in observing the five daily prayers, led by the Prophet. They hurried to the

Mosque whenever the *adhān* was called, most often by the melodious voice of Bilāl, and sometimes by the voice of Ibn Umm Maktūm, the blind Muslim Companion, on whom *Sūrah 'Abasa* (He Frowned) was revealed.

The Muslims found pleasure and solace also in the Prophet's speaking to them after these prayers. They listened with alert attention to new revelations of the Qur'ān, and exchanged news of what was happening around them, particularly of the movements of the Quraysh and their designs against Islam. The Prophet used these assemblies to issue commands, make declarations and disclose plans and new measures of coping with the changing situation in and outside Madinah. The Mosque was also the place where Muslims used to meet new emigrants to Madinah, who continued to arrive in small groups throughout the period preceding the Battle of Badr.

During the first six to eight months after the *Hijrah,* the Prophet's Mosque witnessed great debates with the scripturists of Madinah, especially the Jews. Later on, the Prophet received a big delegation of the Christians of Najrān in Southern Arabia. Those debates and dialogues were reflected in some detail in the revelations of the Qur'ān.

The Prophet personally organized the congregational prayers. He demanded that Muslims should, whenever possible, attend them. Their reward is twenty-seven times that of prayers performed by a Muslim alone. An old, blind Muslim living some distance away from the Mosque sought the Prophet's permission to absent himself from the dawn and night prayers there:

> 'Do you hear the *Adhān*?' asked the Prophet.
> 'Yes', replied the old man.
> 'Then respond to the call of the Prayer', demanded the Prophet, who then added:
> 'Even if you had to come to the mosque, crawling, it is better for you.'

One day, when the *Adhān* was called the Prophet looked around, and apparently discovered that some Muslims, perhaps an unusually large number of them, were absent.

His anger was aroused until it showed in his gracious face. He said:

> 'I wish I might appoint one of you to lead the prayer, and then I would venture outside to the homes of those absentees and set their houses ablaze.'

The congregational prayers in the Prophet's Mosque were normally very well attended. It is thus safe to assume that almost every Muslim, who was not sick or a traveller, used to attend every one of them. Attending the daily congregational prayers with the Prophet, at his Mosque, became the principal manifestation of *islām.*

The five daily prayers, performed at one place, at prescribed times of the day and night, served to set the rhythm of life in Madinah. It conferred a unique vitality and dynamism on public life and mobilized and organized the new Muslim *Ummah,* in a unique and most effective way. The consequences and implications of prayer, so organized and performed with regularity and continuity, were so immense that it is impossible to enumerate them.

What we have said thus far about the Muslim prayer should have shed some light on the social, political, even military, aspects of it, and distinguished it from Christian or Jewish prayer or indeed prayer in any other religion. Muslim prayer seems to encompass and influence every sphere of human thought and action.

3. The Uniqueness of Muslim Prayer

Even in its pure spiritual aspect, Muslim prayer is different from other forms of prayer. In other religions, prayer is utterance, or contemplation perhaps in a state of trance. Muslim prayer, by contrast, is performed by the whole person in action. Not only the contemplative mind, but also memory, intellect, imagination, the heart and the whole body are engaged. This total involvement is symbolic of Islam itself, which is the whole life devoted and submitted to the worship and service of God. The body is involved through the performance of a set of measured rhythmic movements. Memory is engaged in the recitation of portions of the Qur'ān. Intellect and imagination are engaged in response to the imagery and the rational arguments of the Qur'ān's style. The heart and the emotions are engaged by the wisdom and compassion of the Qur'ān's message, reminding man of God's favours to him, of his duty to obey and serve God alone, and of the fact that he is accountable for all his deeds on the Day of Reckoning.

But prayer is meant, above all, to rescue man from his routine labours and set him free to turn his face and heart towards his Lord in remembrance, and gratitude, and in order to seek more of His help and guidance. Such remembrance of God, and such seeking of His guidance and help, are the very heart and essence of the Muslim way of life. The centrality of prayer is expressed by the maxim *as-Ṣalātu 'imād ad-Dīn* (prayer is the arch column of religion), which is part of an authentic *Ḥadīth* of the Prophet – whoever establishes it, establishes the religion of Islam, and whoever abandons it, destroys the edifice of Islam.

The heart of Islam is the prescribed Muslim prayer, and the essence of this prayer is the remembrance and worship of the One, True God, who is Allah, *subḥānahū wa ta'ālā.* This essence and ultimate purpose of prayer is enacted and built into its very performance. In each single unit of prayer, called *Rak'ah,* the *Sūrah al-Fātiḥah* (the opening of the Book, also called *Umm al-Kitāb,* the essence of the Book) is recited. No *Rak'ah*[31] is correct or complete without it. The *Fātiḥah* is perhaps the most often repeated Qur'ānic text, and for that matter, any Divine text, that exists today on this earth. A central theme of *al-Fātiḥah* is the verse:

> It is You Alone that we worship and
> It is Your help that we seek.
> So guide us unto the Straight Path.[32]

In addition to the comprehensive functions of the prayer to which we have alluded, there is a most important, inward function. To this, the Qur'ān refers:

> Recite that which has been revealed to you of the Book, and establish prayer *(ṣalāt),* for surely, prayer *(ṣalāt)*

> prevents (and protects) from indecency and wrong-doing, and for the remembrance of God is more worth-while.[33]

Prayer is the most effective vehicle for remembrance of God, and such remembrance the most worthwhile preoccupation for a Muslim. Even so, the five prescribed Muslim prayers do not take more than an hour, and could be correctly performed in a shorter period of time.

In the final analysis, the Muslim community is not a community of people drawn together for any commercial or other material purpose. Fundamentally they are and remain a religious community, a brotherhood of faith, moved by an awareness of God, and of the Hereafter. This other-world consciousness has been emphasized over and over again by the letter and spirit of the Qur'ān, and recounted endless times in the sayings of the Prophet. When he ordered the building of his Mosque, he said:

> 'I want it to be a simple building, like the thatching of my brother Moses. But in reality this world is more transient than would deserve even such a simple building – *wa al-Amr a'jal min dhālik* (the matter is more transient than that)'.

This other-world consciousness in Islam must not be lost sight of. The whole community must be made continually aware of it. The establishing of the prescribed five daily prayers, and the fact that they commence at dawn and finish at night is a most effective instrument for doing so. The very chant that the Prophet chose to sing and repeat while the Mosque was being built is a reminder of just this:

> O Lord! there is no worthwhile living but one oriented towards the Hereafter.
> O Lord, have mercy on the *Anṣār* and *Muhājirah*.

Through the constant, strict observance of the five daily prayers performed at the Mosque under the leadership of the Prophet, the first community of believers in Madinah was transformed into a society of thoroughly spiritualized people. In the process they acquired a definite sublimity, and a lightness and malleability in regard to the commandments and precepts of God. They became so thoroughly permeated by the Qur'ānic and Prophetic light, energy and vitality, that they were themselves transformed into a great reservoir of light, energy and vitality. They became a society of special persons, whose essence was spiritual energy and whose inward constitution was wholly dominated by God-consciousness. The Prophet was a permanent member and the all-present and all-obeyed leader of it. The Archangel Gabriel was a frequent visiting member of this Madinan community.

The Prophet Muḥammad has often been thought of as consisting of light, whose essence is divine light. This conception is widely subscribed to by Muslim mystics, who prefer to refer to the Prophet Muḥammad as *an-Nūr* (the Light).[34] However, the extreme form of this mystical conception of Muḥammad as light has been unanimously rejected by Muslim jurists. One of the first jurists to give it a conclusive rebuttal was as-Suhaylī (in his book *ar-Rawḍ al-Unf*). The Qur'ānic conception of Muḥammad is that of *Basharan rasūlā:* a human messenger of God. If Muḥammad were to be of a special nature he would not be useful as the *good example* he is meant (according to the Qur'ān) to be for the whole of mankind:

> Assuredly, you have in the Messenger of God a good example, for whosoever looks to God and the Last Day . . . and remembers God often.[35]

Although we do not subscribe literally to the mystics' view that Muḥammad's was a special nature, and that he was even an energy being with no material element, we freely allow that he was like an ever-shining light in the life of the Madinans, dispelling their darkness and bringing forth what was best in them. That which is best in every man is a component of the Divine Spirit of God, which was breathed into the material body of Adam. The Arabs of pre-Islamic Arabia were, from the spiritual viewpoint, all but dead. It was the coming of Muḥammad that sparked life and consciousness into their beings. To this the Qur'ān itself refers:

> O you who believe: Obey Allah and the Messenger when he calls you to that which will render you alive, and know that Allah comes (perhaps) between a man and his heart . . .[36]

The Qur'ān also refers to the prophethood of Muḥammad, *ṣallā Allāhu 'alayhi wa sallam,* as a raising from death to life – not only for the Arabs but for all mankind:

> Is he who was dead and We have raised him unto life, and set for him a light, wherein he walks among men, as (the one) whose likeness is that of one in utter darkness, whence he cannot emerge?[37]

It is to this effect of the coming of the Prophet and of his ministry that we refer when we speak of *al-Ba'th al-Islāmī al-Awwal* (the first Islamic Resurrection or Awakening).

We have already quoted the Qur'ān describing the mission of the Prophet as a mercy unto mankind. The Qur'ān also refers to the emancipating aspect of his mission by depicting the Prophet's endeavours as lifting *the 'burdens' and 'the fetters'* under which the pre-Islamic Arabs used to labour.[38] The Prophet is himself more than once rebuked for his great eagerness to see certain persons become Muslims. He is criticized for grieving at the rejection of his call by the Quraysh:

> Ṭā Hā,
> We have not revealed unto you this Qur'ān, that you should become distressed.
> It is but a reminder, unto him who fears (God).[39]

F. THE SIXTH PILLAR: THE MUSLIM STATE

A major difference between Islam on the one hand, and Judaism and Christianity on the other, is that Islam insists that it must have a state. It does not approve of, tacitly or overtly, regarding Caesar as a partner with God. To God Alone belongs what there is in heaven and on earth and what there is in between. This state power must be submitted to His all-inclusive sovereignty. The Christians are free to deny their Lord any authority over their temporal or secular affairs. Muslims, however, are educated in the tradition of their ancestor, Ibrāhīm, who declared:

> 'Say: Surely my prayers and my devotions, and my living and my dying are for Allah *(Rabb)*[40] Lord of the Worlds.'[41]

And to Abraham, Muslims are indebted for their very name *al-Muslimūn. Islām* means total submission to God. A corollary of this total submission is that not only individuals but also the society and state, and all public institutions must also submit totally to God. The Christian maxim: 'Render unto God what is God's and unto Caesar what is Caesar's' is totally rejected by Islam.

1. The Primary Meaning of *Hijrah*

The essential meaning of the Prophet's *Hijrah* to Madinah is that the mission of Islam as a *Dīn* (religion) would not be complete without a state of its own. Thus to establish *Dār al-Islām* (abode or state of Islam) is a religious obligation which every Muslim must attempt to fulfil in his lifetime. If the Muslim state does not exist he has to make a *Hijrah,*[42] strive and struggle, just as the Prophet did, in order to establish it. If it does exist, but he is outside it, he must migrate to it, if that is a possible course of action for him. And if he is living inside a Muslim state, then it is his overriding obligation to defend it and do all he can to see that it prospers and that it reflects the true norms and values of the Qur'ān and *Sunnah.*

It is not possible for Islam, in its totality, to develop and grow in any environment other than that of *Dār al-Islām,* where Muslims enjoy full control. It can grow to some extent in *Dār al-Aman* (a secure haven, e.g. Abyssinia) in the form of a movement or a community depending on the measure of freedom the Muslims are afforded. But its development in *Dār al-Ḥarb* (where it is opposed) will be handicapped, the degree of retardation depending upon the severity of the resistance offered to it. Therefore, Muslims are never advised to live permanently in either *Dār al-Aman* or *Dār al-Ḥarb,* if it is possible for them to live in *Dār al-Islām.* While life in *Dār al-Ḥarb* is dangerous and counter-productive, living permanently in *Dār al-Aman* may do more than rob the Muslim of the opportunity to develop fully as a Muslim, to live as God Almighty has commanded him to live – he must know that he may be exposing himself and his family to considerable risks. However, living in *Dār al-Aman* is, by its very nature, transient. Normally, a Muslim resorts to *Dār al-Aman,* in order to escape the evils and danger, even persecution, of *Dār al-Ḥarb* either because he cannot live in *Dār al-Islām,* or because such an entity does not exist. Thus *Dār al-Aman* is essentially a temporary haven. Yet, in certain circumstances, living in *Dār al-Aman,* may be desirable, or even mandatory. If an opportunity exists for spreading the Qur'ānic Guidance or if the native people of *Dār al-Aman* have requested Muslims to come there, invited them as religious teachers, then it is their privilege and obligation to do so. After all, Islam is a universal call for all mankind to the worship of the One, True God: Allāh, *subḥānahū wa ta'ālā.*

Another factor that necessitates the existence of the Islamic state is that Islam contains a comprehensive system of positive laws, a distinctive social order and unique economic and political theories. It is impossible for Muslims to establish such a social order and implement its various theories, without a state of their own.

Being, as well as a comprehensive system, a programme for action, Islam is neither silent nor passive in its attitude towards rival theories or ideologies. To a very great extent, it was Islam's initial condemnation of Arabian *Jāhiliyyah,* and the refusal of the Muslims to co-exist with it and approve it, that so angered the Quraysh and provoked them to take action against the Muslims.[43] Islam, by its very nature, cannot but find itself in conflict with falsehood, ignorance and any form of pseudo-religion or *Shirk* (polytheism). Thus it is inevitable that Muslims must strive to set up a state of their own, to secure a territory upon which this state is established. The word of God Almighty must rule supreme, an impossible aspiration in either *Dār al-Ḥarb* or *Dār al-Aman*. The setting up of *Dār al-Islām* became an absolute priority and an obligatory duty upon every Muslim.

The Qur'ān itself chides and condemns Muslims who are content to live under a non-Islamic authority, and do nothing about it. The Qur'ān declares:

> He who does not rule by what Allah has revealed – those are the unbelievers.[44]

2. The Prophet's Islamic Movement

With the realization that Islam would not otherwise be allowed to take firm root nor establish its distinctive ideology, the Prophet organized his Companions into a dynamic movement. Their individual characters and personalities, their whole lives, were re-shaped and re-ordered totally, in accordance with the precepts of Islam and the Qur'ānic Guidance. Such was the magnitude of their spiritual, moral, intellectual and even physical regeneration that each one of that Qur'ānic breed proved equal in combat efficiency to ten of the *Mushrikīn* (polytheists) during the Battle of Badr. When they were weakened, later on, by the toll that *Jihād* had taken of them, when advancing age had mellowed their physical powers, each one of that Qur'ānic generation was equal in combat fitness to two unbelievers. The Prophet knew that before the Islamic state could be established, the Muslims would be compelled to strive and struggle, even enter into prolonged wars and conflicts. Accordingly, he carefully trained and prepared them for the Madinan period of Islam when the Islamic state was set up.

Muslims who failed to keep pace with the dynamic development of Islam, whose lives and personalities remained stuck with the environment of the first Makkan period, were criticized by the Qur'ān. Muslims were instructed to withdraw any responsibility towards those who failed to make the *Hijrah,* remaining behind in Makkah for no convincing reason, other than their selfishness and feebleness. The Qur'ān instructed the Muslims not to extend to them any *Muwālāt,* i.e. protection and guardianship. They were abandoned by the Muslims except in very marginal cases, specified by the Qur'ān itself.

3. How the Muslim State was Set Up in Madinah

The Prophet, *ṣallā Allāhu 'alayhi wa sallam,* did not assume political authority in Yathrib by force. Nor did he arrive there as a conqueror or a colonizer. On the contrary, he was warmly invited there by the two dominant factions of the city, and his arrival impatiently awaited. The second 'Aqabah Pledge which the Prophet concluded a year before *Hijrah* with the Aws and Khazraj, paved the way for his entry to the city, and specified his role as a religious as well as a temporal authority. One of its main provisions was the firm commitment which the Yathribites made to defend the Prophet and his Companions, even if that meant waging war against all mankind, the 'red' and the 'black' amongst them.

The Yathribites also firmly committed themselves to accept and uphold the Prophet's authority over the city in all matters, religious as well as political. The uncle of the Prophet, al-'Abbās, who was attending the conclusion of the Pledge, reminded the Yathribites of the grave implications of their commitment. He demanded assurances that the Yathribites would be willing and able to fulfil that pledge, in view of its grave consequences. But the Yathribites were adamant that they wanted the Prophet to come to their city, and that they were prepared and able to defend him against all odds, even if that meant their own total destruction. There is thus no substance whatever to the allegations of a leading Orientalist who claimed that Muḥammad's initial position in Madinah was unclear,[45] and not paramount. In fact, he was the undisputed governor from the first day of his arrival in the city.

4. The Constitution of the New State

The constitution of the new state which the Prophet founded in Madinah is preserved for us, totally intact. The document in which it is set forth is called *Ṣaḥīfat al-Madīnah* or more simply *al-Ṣaḥīfah* (the document). The Prophet himself dictated it, and it was prepared and ratified by the major factions of the city. The first party to the covenant was the Prophet himself, the second party comprised the covenanted factions:

1. The *Muhājirūn* (the emigrants of the Quraysh).
2. The *Anṣār* (the Helpers, citizens of Yathrib).
3. The various clans and tribes of the Jews of Yathrib.

The conclusion of the *Ṣaḥīfah,* in the initial period of the Prophet's coming to Yathrib, must be hailed as a triumph for the Prophet as a diplomat and politician. The *Ṣaḥīfah* established agreement and political harmony and unity among four different groups: (1) The *Muhājirūn,* recent immigrants to the city, dispossessed and displaced, refugees from their original homes in Makkah; (2) the Aws and (3) the Khazraj who had been locked in a bloody and destructive war for many years; and (4) the Jews who were characterized with a notorious haughtiness and a strong feeling of superiority *vis-à-vis* the Arabs, whom they viewed as ignorant gentiles. Yet the Prophet, *Ṣallā Allāhu 'alayhi wa sallam,* managed to bring these widely divergent groups together in one unified political system.

The *Ṣaḥīfah* laid down the foundations of the new society and state upon a solid legal base. Nothing worthwhile was omitted when the provisions of the *Ṣaḥīfah* were being formulated.

The full text of the *Ṣaḥīfah* has been preserved by Ibn Hishām and other authorities. A full study of it with its political implications, has been undertaken by this writer.[46]

The *Ṣaḥīfah* must be looked upon as a great advance for humanity. Perhaps for the first time in human history a state was founded on an ideological basis. The Muslims were declared one *Ummah,* united by bonds of faith and brotherhood. The Prophet's supreme authority was upheld. The *Muhājirūn* and *Anṣār* fused together as one entity.

The Jews were considered full citizens of the Muslim state. They were obligated, under the terms of the agreement to fight alongside the Muslims should Madinah be attacked and to share in the war expenses. In return they were given the privileges of (1) full religious freedom, (2) administration of their own courts unless they referred any case to the Prophet when it would be decided by Islamic laws, and (3) full financial autonomy. However, they were required, under the terms of the agreement, to assist Muslims in payment of ransom money, should that become incumbent upon them.

The *Ṣaḥīfah* increased the solidarity of the Madinans against the Quraysh. No-one under the terms of the agreement was allowed to shelter them or render any assistance to any person with them. No-one was allowed to make a separate peace with them. Waging war or concluding peace was a prerogative of the Prophet, as supreme ruler and commander of Madinah.

Law enforcement was a collective responsibility of the covenanted parties. No-one could shelter or assist a violator of the laws of Madinah even if he was a son of one of them. All disputes which involved inter-group relations were to be referred to the Prophet, and his ruling was to be accepted by all concerned.

Madinah was declared a sacred sanctuary. People of the *Ṣaḥīfah,* i.e. covenanted parties, were devoted to the service of God and to the ideals of peace, justice and brotherhood amongst mankind. It was a truly multi-racial and multi-cultural state, though the Qur'ān and *Sunnah* had overall authority in that the Prophet's religious as well as temporal position was recognized as supreme in the city.

The state of Madinah exemplified Islamic political theory, where the Word of God is Supreme. The *Sharī'ah,* based upon the Qur'ān and *Sunnah* of the Prophet, was supreme above the ruler as well as the ruled. Under this theory, sovereignty belongs to God Alone, man is *Khalīfat-Allāh,* vicegerent of Allah, whose role is to enforce and implement the law of God. All men are considered equal before the law. Absolute ownership is God's Alone. Man can only own wealth and property in a derivative sense. Brotherhood among Muslims and solidarity among all citizens of Madinah seemed a natural consequence of the doctrine of God's absolute ownership of what is in heaven and on earth. *Zakāt* is obligatory for wealthy Muslims, and it was regarded, not as a charity, but as a deserved right for the poor and the underprivileged. Non-Muslim citizens of Madinah paid other taxes, namely war tax, earmarked for the defence of the city; ransom tax, to ransom captives from among Madinans; and blood-wit tax, to compensate for the lives of non-Madinans killed mistakenly by Madinans. The Jews were obligated under the provisions of the *Ṣaḥīfah* to pay these three taxes. On the other hand, Muslims paid *Zakāt*, as well as contributing towards these other taxes. It is significant that the Jews of Madinah were not required to pay *Jizyah*.

At this juncture, it is reasonable to assume that Muslims and Jews retained autonomy over purely religious matters, each community practising its religious rites as it saw fit. Among Muslims there was brotherhood and *Muwālāt* (guardianship). They performed *Ṣalāt* and paid *Zakāt*, enjoined the right and forbade evil and wrongdoing, and worshipped the One, True, God. They had the Qur'ān to recite and learn and follow its teaching. The Jews had their separate community life, their synagogues, rabbis, religious courts and the Torah. But all Madinans, whether Muslims or Jews, were under the general authority of the Prophet and under his supreme political and military command.

G. THE SEVENTH PILLAR: FORMATION OF THE MUSLIM ARMY

1. **The Phase of Peaceful Resistance in Makkah**

Islam is a religious movement whose central aim is the establishment of the service and worship of God Alone. As such, it is bound to provoke the enmity of all kinds of groups whose interests are vested in the service of false gods. This is precisely what happened in the case of the Quraysh. They opposed Islam, persecuted the Muslims and did all in their power to prevent the faith taking root. This phase lasted for the thirteen years of the Prophet's stay in Makkah.

The Makkan period was characterized by passive, peaceful resistance on the part of the Muslims. They bore the abuse and persecution of the Quraysh with patience and forbearance. They never ventured to fight back. No permission to fight was either given by the Qur'ān or by the Prophet, not even in self-defence. Whatever indignation the Muslims showed against the Quraysh was moral and verbal. They never abstained from speaking against idol-worship as senseless and feeble-minded. And they never shied away from asserting the *Tawḥīd* (Absolute Oneness) of God and that Muḥammad was His Messenger to mankind.

The rationale behind the Prophet's peaceful strategy during the Makkan period is not difficult to understand. The Muslims were a small minority of men, women and children. The primary object of this new movement was to share its message with the rest. They stood for peace and greater opportunities for communication. Violence was not their way. They even refused to retaliate against the violence of the Quraysh. Had they resorted to violence, they would have given the Quraysh a pretext to annihilate the movement in the bud. Moreover, Islam was a new movement, a new ideology, and it needed time to be better understood. It needed time to demonstrate its sheer internal force and attractiveness as a new, emerging ideology, without protection and without following. As a persecuted and rejected ideology, only those who subscribed to it out of conviction and sincere belief would be able to come out in favour of it. These would be sincere and strong people, idealists, prepared to endure hardship and suffering for the sake of upholding the truth. They would be disinterested since, in defending the new religion, no benefit was to be expected – if anything, acceptance of the new religion was bound to bring harm and persecution.

For those reasons, permission to fight back in self-defence was not given by the Qur'ān. Those who were most severely persecuted, who enjoyed no clan protection of any kind were given permission to make the minor *Hijrah* to a *Dār al-Aman,* Abyssinia. This whole phase of Islam came to an end with the conclusion of the Second 'Aqabah Pledge.

2. The Permission to Wage War

Shortly afterwards, before the *Hijrah* to Yathrib, the permission to fight back in self-defence was given:

> Permission is given to those who fight (to do so) because they have been wronged; and Allah is indeed able to give them victory. Those who have been driven from their homes unjustly only because they said: 'Our Lord is Allah.' For had it not been for Allah's repelling some men by means of others, cloisters and churches and oratories and mosques, wherein the name of Allah is often mentioned would assuredly have been destroyed. Assuredly Allah helps those who help Him. Allah is Strong, All-Mighty. Those who, if We give them power in the land, establish prayer *(Ṣalāt),* and pay *Zakāt,* and enjoin righteousness and forbid wrong. And to Allah belongs the sequel of events.[47]

3. The Concept of *Daf' Allāh*

It is clear that the permission to wage war against the unbelievers is qualified both explicitly and implicitly. Its historical context clearly relates this permission to self-defence: the Muslims were wronged, maltreated and unjustly persecuted by the Quraysh over thirteen years. At the end of that period they were forced to flee their homes and families, to abandon their wealth, lands, property and their profession and means of livelihood. This is the implicit contextual justification for the permission to fight back. However, there is an explicit statement that fighting is justified against religious oppression as such: the Muslims were persecuted by the Quraysh merely because they said that 'God Alone is our Lord.' The verse quoted above urges believers that if they fail to fight (literally 'push back and repel') against oppressors of religious freedom to worship God Alone, then all monotheistic religion will be destroyed. The effort to fight against religious oppression was called *Daf' Allāh* (the repelling for God), a clear indication of God's approval of it.

The same verse strongly implies that God's help will be extended to Muslims only if they exert themselves vigorously in repelling the oppressors. A further qualification is the correct orientation and purpose of the Muslims. The verse implies that God's victory would only be forthcoming if the

Muslims' objectives and goals were God-inspired. If their efforts were so inspired, then as soon as the Muslims became established they would exert themselves in the service of God. Their first priorities would be directed to the establishment of prescribed prayer, the implementation of *Zakāt* and the establishment of justice and righteousness as commanded by God. Victory would not be forthcoming if the Muslims fought to establish despotism, if they intended only to empower some ambitious individual. Similarly, victory would not be forthcoming if the Muslims fought primarily for the sake of self-aggrandizement or for material, worldly gains. Last, but not least, victory would not be achieved if the Muslims, though sincere, were unjust in their dealings with others or prone to rebellion, dispute, disagreement and disobedience to their legitimate leadership.

In sum, war is sanctioned, by the verse quoted, so long as it constitutes *Daf' Allāh* as explained above, and is directed against those who resist by force the Islamic effort *(Da'wah)* to establish Allah's authority on earth. The second reason for war, namely to eliminate material resistance or impediments to Islamic *Da'wah* is also, as explained above, implicit in the verse of *Sūrah al-Ḥajj* (41). The two reasons given as justification for sanctioning war are clearly defensive in nature, although the second is somewhat subtle. If unbelievers do not attempt by use of force to obstruct the Muslims' effort to establish Allah's authority on earth, then the Muslims would have no justification for waging war against them, according to the verses of *Sūrah al-Ḥajj*. Their mere refusal to accept Islam would not be a valid justification for war against them. Otherwise, the Muslims would themselves become repressors of religious freedom, and an oppressive power fighting people because of their convictions or religious belief. But the Qur'ān forbids religious repression:

> There is no coercion (compulsion) in religion, righteousness has become distinguishable from error.[48]

In many places in the Qur'ān, the Prophet Muḥammad is reminded that it is not part of his mission as Prophet and

Messenger to compel people to become Muslims. He is repeatedly reminded that he has no control or authority over the minds and hearts of men. Only God has such control and authority. The Prophet's mission is that of a caller, a reminder, a warner. If he is to become a ruler or a judge and if he is to assume the role of a governor, then he must do that by the will of the people and after securing their approval. This was precisely what happened in Yathrib, when he was invited to assume legal and political authority by the dominant tribes of Aws and Khazraj. Thus no-one can say that the Prophet usurped political power in Yathrib.

The general command to wage war was given to the Muslims as follows:

> And fight them, until there is no more persecution, and religion becomes Allah's. But should they cease (quit fighting you) then there is no aggression except against transgressors.[49]

The same general command to wage war is given in *Sūrah al-Anfāl:*

> And fight them until persecution is no more and all religion becomes Allah's. But if they cease, then assuredly Allah is Seer of what you do.[50]

In both these Qur'ānic verses of *al-Baqarah* and *al-Anfāl,* the justification for fighting is stated as the need to fight *fitnah,* or persecution, preventing the worship and service of God. In both verses, believers are advised (a) that they should quit fighting if the other side stops its practice of religious repression and (b) not lapse into new levels of unprovoked aggression. The verse of *Sūrah al-Anfāl* even reminds the Muslims that Allah is All-Seeing, with the implication that any unwarranted offensive wars could amount to transgression, and Allah 'loves not the transgressors' be they Muslim or non-Muslim.

4. **The Formation of a People's Army**

As soon as the Prophet had settled in Madinah, it became clear that the emergence of the Islamic state created a new situation in Arabia. Not only was the hitherto unchallenged dominance of the Quraysh threatened and undermined, there were, within the city itself, parties whose authority and dominance were also undermined. These internal factions included the hypocrites, headed by 'Abdullāh Ibn Ubayy ibn Salūl, who had been about to be enthroned as King, and the Jews. Tensions rose inside Madinah, indeed in the whole of Arabia, and most particularly in Makkah. The situation further deteriorated through the actions of the Muslims themselves, who appeared determined to dislodge the Quraysh from their place of dominance and leadership.

Insofar as the Muslims were very few there was no alternative but to make it obligatory upon each one of them to join the war, in defence of the city and in the offensive against the Quraysh. Thus the Muslim people's army was formed. The Prophet himself not only assumed the position of supreme commander, becoming a Messenger-Commander (in the tradition of David and his son Soloman), but he also personally participated in the actual fighting in the Battle of Uḥud. Military experience gained in the war of al-Fijār, in pre-Islamic days, as well as his great physical fitness, were tested and proved to be of the highest quality. So superior was the Prophet's fighting skill that 'Alī Ibn Abī Ṭālib said:

> 'When fighting was intensified, and we were hard pressed by the polytheists of the Quraysh, we took refuge behind the Prophet, none of us was nearer to the advancing column of the enemy than the Prophet.'

When we recall that at Uḥud the Prophet was almost fifty-five years old, his physical fitness and military valour are all the more surprising. That combat fitness was a result of life-long self-discipline, largely sustained by eating little, and strenuous, regular physical efforts and exertions. Even in peace-time, his fitness was proverbial: Abū Hurayrah described his movements: 'His pace was so fast and light as if descending from a hill, and he walked with his head tilted slightly forward.' Abū Hurayrah and other Companions found it very hard to keep up with him. He said it was as if the earth was rolled up for the Prophet, and that the

Companions became breathless, in their efforts to keep pace whilst he walked comfortably.

We learn that the Prophet led in person at least nine military expeditions against rebellious Arabs (desert bedouins). During those expeditions, he endured the hardships of any ordinary soldier, taking his share in walking and riding the few camels or horses available, and looking after his personal effects himself.

He was a military commander and strategist of the highest calibre. He based his strategy on information, collected and gathered by his agents and military informants, which he assessed and evaluated with great skill. He struck at his enemies effectively and, whenever possible, unexpectedly. He often managed to surprise his enemies and so strike the first blow. This was made possible by his superior military intelligence, tactics and strategy; the superior combat capability of his fighters and their swift movement across the desert; his practice of keeping his destination and target secret to the last feasible moment – a practice greatly aided by the high discipline of his fighting men; and the assistance of *ar-Ru'b,* the fear thrown into the hearts of his adversaries by God at the distance of a month's march.

The fighting capability of the Muslim soldiers, their courage and daring, were instrumental in their success. For the Muslim soldiers set out to obtain either of two desirable goals – victory or martyrdom in the way of God. Fighting for the religious freedom of man and in order to fulfil the Commandments of God were a source of pride for them. The Muslims were perhaps the first people to organize their military efforts in the form of a people's army, in which all participated. There was no question of wages or salaries – if anything, each warrior had to bear his own military expenses. Far from being a mercenary army fighting for material rewards (as Orientalists have tried so hard to argue), the Muslims were fighting to gain the pleasure of God and His paradise in the Hereafter. For them, fighting in the way of God was the greatest distinction and honour a person could hope for.

5. The Prophet's Intelligence Service

The Prophet developed a sophisticated and disciplined intelligence service. He had agents bringing him prompt and accurate reports of the movements and plans of the Quraysh and the bedouin Arabs around Madinah. A proof of the efficiency of his intelligence service was his success in frustrating the Quraysh commerce with Syria, and his great success in foiling attempts by the surrounding, unruly bedouins to attack Madinah. It was also a measure of the superiority of his intelligence service that he discovered and was able to forestall many attempts and plots on his life, by Banū an-Naḍīr and other Jewish adversaries.

An important division of his intelligence service, under the charge of Ḥudhayfah ibn al-Yamān, was consigned to the surveillance of the hypocrites, who represented the internal enemy. Ḥudhayfah knew more about the intrigues of the hypocrites than even 'Umar ibn al-Khaṭṭāb, the Prophet's second lieutenant and minister. The Prophet used to pass to Ḥudhayfah any information on the names and movements of the hypocrites as soon as it was disclosed to him by the Archangel Gabriel.

Many minor expeditions dispatched from Madinah in the time before the Battle of Badr, were, partially at least, for reconnaissance, in particular, about the Quraysh and the bedouins around Madinah. One such expedition was that commanded by 'Abdullāh ibn Jaḥsh, whom the Prophet sent to Nakhlah in the vicinity of Makkah. 'Abdullāh did not limit himself to his directives and attacked a caravan belonging to the Quraysh during the sacred months. His action more than anything else precipitated the Battle of Uḥud.

An important part of the Prophet's strategy was not only to assess the enemy, but to assess his own fighting force. The faint-hearted were, on more than one occasion, turned back, and refused the honour of fighting alongside the Muslims. Children were also turned back, but some women were allowed along. The Prophet's maxim – 'War is but a winning trick or a good plan' – indicates the great importance which he placed upon the use of intelligence and preparation in warfare. Such a ploy was indeed made use of during the

Battle of al-Khandaq (the Battle of the Ditch). The Prophet asked a recent Muslim convert by the name of Nu'aym ibn Mas'ūd, whose conversion to Islam was unknown to the Quraysh or the Jews of Madinah, to play the role of a double agent. Nu'aym played that role efficiently and managed to sow suspicion and dissension among the clans of the enemy.

Notes and References

1. *Sūrah al-Isrā'* (The Night Journey), 17: 106. The Arabic text runs:

وَقُرْءَانًا فَرَقْنَٰهُ لِتَقْرَأَهُۥ عَلَى ٱلنَّاسِ عَلَىٰ مُكْثٍ وَنَزَّلْنَٰهُ تَنزِيلًا ﴿١٠٦﴾

2. The Arabic word *Munajjaman* means that the Qur'ān was revealed in portions of a few verses each, in response to the events and changing circumstances of the Muslims. Sometimes a new ruling, directive or guidance was revealed. This mode of revelation made it easy for the Muslims to memorize and learn the new revelations, as they had been revealed. Although the Qur'ān was committed to writing, during the life of the Prophet and at his dictation, by scribes of *Waḥī,* yet committing it to memory was the widespread practice of Muslims, many of whom were unlettered.

3. *Sūrah al-Qiyāmah* (Resurrection) 75: 16–18.

4. See: Zakaria Bashier's *The Meccan Crucible,* FOSIS, London, 1978, chapter four.

5. *Sūrah aḍ-Ḍuḥā* (The Mid-Morning). According to many authorities, *aḍ-Ḍuḥā* was revealed after the initial revelation at Ḥirā of *Sūrah al-'Alaq* (The Clinging Clot).

6. Bukhārī's list may indicate that those seven *Ḥuffāẓ* were perhaps the best and the most famous.

7. The incident of *Bi'r Ma'ūnah* (the Water of Ma'ūnah) happened in Ṣafar in the 4th year of the *Hijrah.*

8. The wars of the Apostates *(ar-Riddah)* happened just after the passing away of the Prophet Muḥammad. The bedouins refused to pay *Zakāt* (Muslim religious fund for social welfare). Abū Bakr, the successor of the Prophet, waged war against them and broke their resistance.

9. Ṣiffīn is the name of a major battle between 'Alī ibn Abī Ṭālib, the fourth successor of the Prophet, and Mu'āwiyah ibn Abī Sufyān, his rival and major contender for the Caliphate.

10. *Sūrah al-Anbiyā'* (The Prophets) 21: 107.

11. *al-A'rāf* (The Heights) 7: 157. The Arabic text of this noble Qur'ānic verse is as follows: (notice that this verse likens the Qur'ān to light):

ٱلَّذِينَ يَتَّبِعُونَ ٱلرَّسُولَ ٱلنَّبِيَّ ٱلْأُمِّيَّ ٱلَّذِى يَجِدُونَهُۥ مَكْتُوبًا

عِندَهُمْ فِى ٱلتَّوْرَىٰةِ وَٱلْإِنجِيلِ يَأْمُرُهُم بِٱلْمَعْرُوفِ وَيَنْهَىٰهُمْ

عَنِ ٱلْمُنكَرِ وَيُحِلُّ لَهُمُ ٱلطَّيِّبَٰتِ وَيُحَرِّمُ عَلَيْهِمُ ٱلْخَبَٰٓئِثَ

وَيَضَعُ عَنْهُمْ إِصْرَهُمْ وَٱلْأَغْلَٰلَ ٱلَّتِى كَانَتْ عَلَيْهِمْ ۚ فَٱلَّذِينَ

ءَامَنُوا۟ بِهِۦ وَعَزَّرُوهُ وَنَصَرُوهُ وَٱتَّبَعُوا۟ ٱلنُّورَ ٱلَّذِىٓ أُنزِلَ مَعَهُۥٓ ۙ

أُو۟لَٰٓئِكَ هُمُ ٱلْمُفْلِحُونَ ﴿١٥٧﴾

12. *al-Tawbah* (Repentance) 9: 128, 129. The Arabic text of this verse is as follows:

لَقَدْ جَآءَكُمْ رَسُولٌ مِّنْ أَنفُسِكُمْ عَزِيزٌ عَلَيْهِ

مَا عَنِتُّمْ حَرِيصٌ عَلَيْكُم بِٱلْمُؤْمِنِينَ رَءُوفٌ

رَّحِيمٌ ﴿١٢٨﴾ فَإِن تَوَلَّوْا۟ فَقُلْ حَسْبِىَ ٱللَّهُ لَآ إِلَٰهَ إِلَّا هُوَ ۖ عَلَيْهِ

تَوَكَّلْتُ ۖ وَهُوَ رَبُّ ٱلْعَرْشِ ٱلْعَظِيمِ ﴿١٢٩﴾

13. *al-Aḥzāb* (The Clans) 33: 6.

ٱلنَّبِىُّ أَوْلَىٰ بِٱلْمُؤْمِنِينَ مِنْ أَنفُسِهِمْ ۖ وَأَزْوَٰجُهُۥٓ أُمَّهَٰتُهُمْ ۗ وَأُو۟لُوا۟ ٱلْأَرْحَامِ

بَعْضُهُمْ أَوْلَىٰ بِبَعْضٍ فِى كِتَٰبِ ٱللَّهِ مِنَ ٱلْمُؤْمِنِينَ وَٱلْمُهَٰجِرِينَ

إِلَّآ أَن تَفْعَلُوٓا۟ إِلَىٰٓ أَوْلِيَآئِكُم مَّعْرُوفًا ۚ كَانَ ذَٰلِكَ فِى ٱلْكِتَٰبِ

مَسْطُورًا ﴿٦﴾

14. Ibn Kathīr: *Al-Bidāyah wa an-Nihāyah,* Vol. 5, p.19, Bayrout.

15. Due to the Prophet's great reliance on Allah, *subḥānahū wa ta'ālā,* he was called *al-Mutawakkil* (the God-reliant). Muslim historical sources say that *al-Mutawakkil* was the name used in the Torah to refer to the Prophet Muḥammad and to predict his dominant characteristic. But in the Gospel (Barnabas) he was referred to as Aḥmad (Paracletus).

16. Some authorities ascribe the redness which seemed to mar the

facial complexion of the Prophet to the effect of long exposure to the sun. I am inclined to believe that the redness in his generally white face is not an acquired trait, but natural. This reddishness was not uncommon among the Quraysh. As a matter of fact, it was a recurrent characteristic among the Hashimites. The Prophet's uncle, the infamous Abū Lahab, was so nicknamed because of the striking flame-redness of his face. In general, the Quraysh were fairer than the rest of the Arab tribes, due to their mixed genealogy. The great ancestor of the Quraysh was Ismā'īl (son of Ibrāhīm). Ismā'īl, according to Muslim historical sources, was left in the valley of Makkah by his father. When he attained manhood, he married an Arab woman of Yemeni origin. The tribe of the Quraysh were the fruit of that mixed marriage.

17. Ibn Kathīr, *al-Bidāyah wa an-Nihāyah*, Vols. 5–6, pp. 16, 17, Maktabah Dār al-Ma'ārif (Bayrout), 1977.

18. *Ibrīq* is an Arabian jug. It has a long, slender, round neck. The most complete description of the person and character of the Prophet is ascribed to Hind Ibn Abī Hālah, son of Umm al-Mu'minīn Khadījah, the Prophet's senior wife, from her former marriage to Abū Hālah. As a stepson of the Prophet he had the closest association with him for many years.

19. *Ibid.*, vols. 5–6.

20. The original Arabic can be found in the books of Islam which deal with the praise of the Prophet.

21. *al-Aḥzāb* (The Clans) 33: 6.

22. In his book *The 100 Most Influential Men in History*, Professor Hart ranked the Prophet Muḥammad first.

23. *al-Ḥujurat* (Apartments) 49: 10.

24. *al-Tawbah* (Repentance) 9: 71.

25. A well-known saying of the Prophet, reported by all reliable sources of *Ḥādīth*, e.g. Muslim and Bukhārī.

26. *al-Anfāl* (War Spoils) 8: 72.

27. The *Isrā'* is the night journey, which took the Prophet from Makkah to Jerusalem, while the *Mi'rāj* was his subsequent ascent to heaven from the Dome of the Rock in the sacred city of Jerusalem. The two episodes took place in one night in Makkah. It was during the *Mi'rāj* that prayers were ordained.

28. The story of the dream of Ibn Zayd, and how the Muslim *Adhān* was instituted is mentioned by both Ibn Hishām and Ibn Sa'd.

29. *al-Baqarah* (The Cow) 2: 144.

30. *Ibid.*, 2: 142.

31. *Rak'ah* is a unit of Muslim prayer. Each *rak'ah* consists of bowing down from the waist, and a full prostration in which the forehead touches the ground.

32. *al-Fātiḥah* (The Opener) 1: 4, 5.

33. *al-'Ankabūt* (The Spider) 29: 45.

34. Some mystics take this theory of the Prophet Muḥammad as pure light very literally. They even claim that his body was transparent, casting no shadow in the sun. This doctrine is obviously false. As well as being in contradiction with the Qur'ān which refers to Muḥammad as a human messenger *(Basharan rasūlā),* it is also in contradiction to the established facts of his human life – eating, marrying, being wounded in battle and bleeding as a result, etc.

35. *al-Aḥzāb* (The Clans) 33: 21.

36. *al-Anfāl* (War Spoils), 8: 24.

37. *al-An'ām* (Cattle) 6: 123.

38. *al-A'rāf* (The Heights) 7: 157.

39. *Ṭā Hā* 20: 1–2.

40. The Arabic word *Rabb* is often translated as 'Lord'. However, the '*Rabb*' has a wider range of meaning than 'Lord' – 'Creator', 'Sustainer', 'Provider', 'Preserver', 'Loving and Caring Guardian'.

41. *al-An'ām* (Cattle) 6: 163.

42. See Zakaria Bashier, *The Hijra: Story and Significance,* The Islamic Foundation, Leicester, 1983.

43. See Zakaria Bashier, *The Meccan Crucible,* on this point.

44. *al-Mā'idah* (The Table) 5: 44.

45. See W.M. Watt, *Muhammad, Prophet and Statesman,* Oxford University Press, 1961, pp. 83–101.

46. Zakaria Bashier, *The Hijra: . . . ,* op. cit.

47. *al-Ḥajj* (Pilgrimage) 22: 40–1.

48. *al-Baqarah* (The Cow) 2: 256.

49. *Ibid.*, 2: 193.

50. *al-Anfāl* (War Spoils) 8: 39.

CHAPTER 2

Two Documents of the Prophet's State

A. THE *ṢAḤĪFAH*

1. Laying Down the Foundations of the First Muslim State

The 'Aqabah pledges, in particular the second, hold the key to a proper understanding of the monumental events that took place in Yathrib following the Prophet Muḥammad's arrival there. In the second 'Aqabah Pledge, the Aws and the Khazraj, the two leading tribes of Yathrib, pledged themselves to install, defend and uphold the authority of the Prophet therein. They pledged to obey and defend the Prophet *fī yusrinā wa 'usrinā wa munshaṭinā wa mukrahanā wa athratun 'alaynā,* i.e. in good times and bad, whether they liked it or not, and even against their self-interest. In another place, Ibn Hishām reports that the Yathribites were so emphatic in their commitment to the Prophet that they declared their readiness to defend him even if they had to go to war with mankind as a whole, the 'black' and the 'red' amongst them.

At no time after that pledge was the Prophet's authority *vis-à-vis* the Yathribites in any doubt. Immediately after the handshaking was over, he issued his first decree as the leader-to-be of Yathrib. He delegated twelve men, to be called 'the twelve Nuqabā', with the authority to lead and organize the new Muslim movement in Yathrib.

When he arrived at Yathrib in his *Hijrah,* he lost no time in addressing himself to the task of giving his authority a broader legal and political base. Having secured the support and allegiance of the Aws and the Khazraj, he was the *de facto* governor of the commonwealth of Yathrib, to be renamed al-Madinah. But Madinah also contained the Jews, as well as the new emigrants of the Quraysh – the *Muhājirūn*. Any effective government had to secure the goodwill and support of all three groups. At the very least, their consent to and acceptance of the new authority were necessary. A framework was needed spelling out the means by which the legitimate interests of these three groupings could best be served.

In order to do this, the *Ṣaḥīfah* was dictated by the Prophet, gathering the emigrants *(Muhājirūn)*, Helpers *(Anṣār)* and Jews into a single, unified *Ummah*, with the Prophet as its leader and governor. These three parties were called the people of the *Ṣaḥīfah*, signifying the fact that they were its principal signatories.[1] It is not certain whether or not a formal ratification actually took place. What is certain, however, is that these three parties clearly endorsed the document and committed themselves to the strict observance of its provisions. The *Ṣaḥīfah* assigned specific roles to these parties, spelling out the obligations as well as the rights of each group. It would have been impossible for the Prophet to assign these rules without a high measure of co-operation and goodwill, and explicit approval, from the parties involved. In particular, the role which the *Ṣaḥīfah* assigned to the Jews indicates a willing and enthusiastic participation by them in the promotion and security of the new state. The *Ṣaḥīfah* committed the three parties to uphold and defend the authority of the Prophet and to co-operate in the enforcement of law and order. It would not have been realistic or reasonable to make such demands or expect such commitments of an unwilling party. It seems logical to suppose that the contents of the *Ṣaḥīfah* were drawn up after consultation with the three parties, especially the Jews, and that its various provisions were both well known to all the parties and clearly endorsed by them. In view of the substantial privileges which the Jews secured for themselves in the *Ṣaḥīfah*, it would have been unreasonable for them not to endorse it.

For the two Muslim parties, endorsing the *Ṣaḥīfah* presented no problems whatever. They were committed Muslims, and their endorsement of the *Ṣaḥīfah* is unsurprising. An investigation of the circumstances that persuaded the Jews to endorse the document would be interesting. There were altogether eleven Jewish settlements in North Arabia at that time. They were initially concentrated in the Madinah region. There were three main groups and eight lesser ones. The main Jewish tribes were Banū Qaynuqā', Banū an-Naḍīr, clients of the Khazraj, and Banū Qurayẓah, clients of the Aws. The lesser groups were further divided into two main groups. The first group (opposed to the Prophet, according to Ibn Hishām) included confederates of Banū Zurayq, Banū Ḥārithah, Banū 'Amr, Banū an-Najjār and Tha'labah. The *Ṣaḥīfah* does not contain any reference to the Jewish confederation of Banū Zurayq. The other four of these lesser Jewish opponents of the Prophet were among the initial parties to the *Ṣaḥifāh*. The second group of the lesser Jewish tribes included confederates of Banū Sā'idah, Banū Jusham and Banū al-Aws.

It would seem that this second group never opposed the Prophet. They were not included by Ibn Hishām among Jewish opponents of the Prophet. The *Ṣaḥīfah* includes them among parties that committed themselves to the alliance of the Prophet Muḥammad. It would appear, then, that at least these three Jewish tribes, confederates of Banū Sā'idah, Banū Jusham and Banū al-Aws, kept their covenant with the Prophet to the end. No conflict with the Muslims is reported with these three groups of peaceful Jews. It would seem that they made full use of the rights and privileges accorded them in the *Ṣaḥīfah*.

The dominant feature about the Jewish settlements, in and around Madinah, was that they fitted into an elaborate system of tribal alliances and confederations. That was the norm in pre-Islamic Arabia. To obtain peace and security, a newcomer or otherwise weak individual would avail himself of the *jiwār* (protection) of a strong or prominent tribe or personality. As is well known, when the Prophet Muḥammad lost the *jiwār* of his uncle, Abū Ṭalīb he was forced to seek that of al-Muṭ'im ibn 'Adī. It is perhaps for this reason, and in a security-oriented *Ṣaḥīfah,* that the Jewish tribes of Madinah were not mentioned by name. Instead they were referred to by naming their Arab allies. Thus the Jewish tribe of Qaynuqā' were referred to as the Jews of Banū al-Khazraj. The Jews of the Qurayẓah were perhaps referred to as the Jews of al-Aws, and so on. That the Qurayẓah were allied to the Aws is confirmed by at least two incidents:

(1) First of all, Abū Lubābah (one of the twelve *Nuqabā'* of the second 'Aqabah Pledge), a prominent Aws, was on very friendly terms with them. When the Qurayẓah were besieged by the Muslims after the Battle of the Ditch, they sent for him. He was touched by their ordeal and tried to warn them of the danger of fighting the Prophet. In a moment of tenderness, he disclosed the thinking of the Muslims concerning them.

Later on, Abū Lubābah chastized himself for showing tenderness to the enemies of the Muslims. The Qurayẓah had conspired with the Quraysh and had prepared to launch an attack on the Muslims, from inside Madinah, an inexcusable betrayal of the provisions of the *Ṣaḥīfah* which had been endorsed by the Qurayẓah earlier.

Abū Lubābah did what he did out of compassion for their plight, although it was self-incurred. His objective was both to warn and persuade them that it was vain folly to continue resisting the Muslims.

That they were confederated with the Aws is also attested by their demand that Sa'd ibn Mu'ādh, chief of the Aws, be appointed a judge to decide their case after the siege ended.

The Jews' association with Arab tribes was necessitated by the manner in which they came to settle in Arabia. Historical sources state that they fled Jerusalem when it was invaded and destroyed by the Persians. It would have been impossible for them to settle in Yathrib without protection from the war-like tribes of the Aws and the Khazraj. In time, the Jews developed centres of power, commercial as well as cultural. Not only were they scripturists in possession of the teachings and knowledge of the Torah, they were also talented tradesmen and craftsmen. Coming from Palestine, they were a civilizing influence. None of this seems to have changed their status as confederates of the Arab tribes, whose *jiwār* they depended on for their security. This is not to suggest that they were without any means of defence of their own. On the contrary, with capable blacksmiths among them, they were the main producers of weapons. The Banū Qurayẓah even boasted of being *Ahl al-Ḥalaqah,* i.e. men of weaponry.

Reference in the *Ṣaḥīfah* to the Jews through their Arab confederates, seems therefore quite unremarkable.

2. The Origin, Date and Authenticity of the *Ṣaḥīfah*

Neither Ibn Isḥāq, the original author of the biography of the Prophet, nor Ibn Hishām, the celebrated editor of Ibn Isḥāq, give precise details of the date or circumstances in which the *Ṣaḥīfah* was dictated by the Prophet. However, since, in general, they consistently follow the order of events, mention of the *Ṣaḥīfah* at the very initial period of the Prophet's stay in Madinah indicates its very early date. Moreover, its very themes and the nature of its provisions confirm the supposition that it was concluded at the very start of the Prophet's career as the leading figure in Madinah. Although his status as a Prophet accorded him both spiritual and political authority *vis-à-vis* the Muslims, Islam recognizing no distinction between the religious and the secular, he had as yet to secure the Jews' recognition of his political authority. That recognition he was able to secure both *de facto* by the consent of the majority of the inhabitants of Madinah, and *de jure* by the conclusion of the *Ṣaḥīfah* as a binding legal document between Muslims and Jews. Such an act must have presented itself as an urgent priority for the Prophet. The supposition that it was concluded at the very start of his political career is both logically sound and fits in nicely with the natural order of events.

Whether the conclusion of the covenant was also attended by the customary hand-shaking that signalled formal ratification of a binding document among the Arabs, our sources furnish no information. But the legal formulation of the *Ṣaḥīfah* itself and the repeated references therein to the people of the *Ṣaḥīfah* leaves little doubt that it was formally approved by the various parties mentioned in it.

As relations with the Jews of Madinah were initially cordial, the Prophet apparently met no difficulty in securing their formal acceptance of his offer of an autonomous Jewish political entity with the Muslim *Ummah* or State. It could very well be that the Prophet himself initiated the matter by contacting them and proposing it. Having got a sympathetic hearing from the Jews, he proceeded to put it in a precise legal form and commit it to writing. The document was presumably then presented to the various parties, *Muhājirūn, Anṣār* and Jews, who readily declared their acceptance of it and their commitment to it.

Apart from a few repetitions, the text of the *Ṣaḥīfah* is very impressive both in its formal and material aspects. No less impressive is the fact that it is expressed in very precise and elegant language. The comprehensiveness, the vigour and the legal texture of the document are all the more striking when we remember that its author, the Prophet, did not know how to read or write. He was the unlettered Arabian Prophet, *an-Nabī al-'Arabī al-Ummī*.

> It is He who has sent to the unlettered people a Messenger from amongst themselves, to recite to them His Signs, to purify them and to teach them the Scripture and Wisdom, although they had been before in manifest error . . . [2]

3. **English Translation of the *Ṣaḥīfah***

We give below an English version of the *Ṣaḥīfah* of Madinah, as recorded by Ibn Hishām. No attempt is made to follow literally the lay-out of the original. On the contrary, we have, in places, deliberately departed from the original paragraphing, and added numeral prefixes to the main paragraphs of the translation, for the purposes of easy reference in the subsequent discussion of the document:

> Said Ibn Isḥāq:[3]
> 'The Messenger of Allah wrote a document (stipulating the relationship) between *Muhājirūn* and *Anṣār,* in which he made peace with the Jews and pledged himself to them that they will be established in security regarding

their religion, wealth and property. He pledged to honour certain rights for them and demanded that they fulfil certain obligations. The *Ṣaḥīfah* reads:

1. 'In the name of Allah, the Compassionate the Most Merciful. This is a document written by Muḥammad the Prophet, *Ṣallā Allāhu 'alayhi wa sallam,* (governing the relations) between the believers and Muslims from Quraysh and Yathrib, and those who followed and joined them and strove with them. They are one *Ummah,* distinct from all men. The *Muhājirūn* from Quraysh, according to their established customs, are bound together and shall ransom their prisoners in the kindness and justice common among believers.

2. The Banū 'Awf, according to their established customs, are bound together as before, each group shall ransom their prisoners in the kindness and justice common among believers. The Banū Sā'idah, the Banū al-Ḥārith, the Banū Jusham and the Banū an-Najjār are likewise.

3. The Banū 'Amr ibn 'Awf, the Banū an-Nabīt, and the Banū al-Aws likewise.

4. Believers shall not leave anyone among them in destitution by failing to give for him redemption money or blood-wit in kindness.

5. A believer shall not take as an ally a freedman of another believer against him.

6. The God-fearing believers shall be against whoever rebels or him who seeks to spread injustice, or sin or aggression or spread enmity between believers; the hands of everyone of them shall be against him, even if he be a son of one of them.

7. A believer shall not stay a believer for the sake of an unbeliever nor shall he aid an unbeliever against a believer.

8. The bond of God is one, the least of them (believers) may give protection (to a stranger) on behalf of them. Believers are protectors one of the other, to the exclusion of outsiders.

9. The Jew who follows us is surely entitled to our support and the same equal rights as any one of us. He

shall not be wronged nor his enemy be assisted *"Ghairu mazlūmīn walā mutanaṣṣirīna 'alayhim"*.

10. The peace of believers is one and indivisible; no believer shall make a separate peace without other believers, when they are engaged in war in the way of God, except when conditions are deemed fair and equitable to all.

11. In every foray *(Sarīyah)*, a rider must take another behind him. The believers must avenge the blood of one another, if anyone of them fails fighting in the cause of God. The God-fearing believers follow the best and most upright guidance.

12. No polytheist shall take the property or person of Quraysh under his protection nor shall he intervene on their behalf against a believer.

13. Whoever is convicted of deliberately killing a believer without righteous cause, shall be liable to retaliation, unless the next of kin is satisfied (with blood money). The believers shall all be against him, and they are bound to keep him under their custody (until either the next of kin is satisfied or retaliation takes place).

14. It shall not be lawful to a believer who has accepted this document as binding, and who believes in God and the last day, to help an evil-doer or to shelter him. The curse of God and His anger on the day of resurrection will be upon him if he does, and neither repentance nor ransom will be received from him.

15. Whenever you have a disagreement amongst you, it must be referred to Allah, *subḥānahū wa ta'ālā*, and to Muḥammad, *ṣallā Allāhu 'alayhi wa sallam.*

16. The Jews shall contribute to the cost of war, so long as they are fighting alongside the believers.

17. The Jews of Banū 'Awf are one *Ummah* with the Muslims; the Jews have their religion and the Muslims have theirs, their freedmen and their persons shall be protected except those who behave unjustly or sinfully. For they hurt but themselves and their families. The same applies to the Jews of Banū an-Najjār, Banū al-Ḥārith, Banū Sā'idah, Banū Jusham, Banū al-Aws, Banū Tha'labah, and the Jafnah, a clan of the Tha'labah

and Banū al-Shuṭaybah. Doing good deeds is a protection against sinfulness. The freedmen of Tha'labah are as themselves. The close friends of the Jews are as themselves.

18. None of them shall go out to war, save with the permission of Muḥammad, *ṣallā Allāhu 'alayhi wa sallam.* But none shall be prevented from taking revenge for a wound inflicted upon him. Whoever kills a man, kills himself and his household, unless it be one who has wronged him, for God would accept that.

19. The Jews must bear their expenses and the Muslims bear theirs. Each must help the other against anyone who attacks the people of this document. Their condition must be one of mutual advice, consultation and charity rather than harm and aggression.

20. No man is liable for a crime committed by his ally. Support must be given to him who is wronged. The Jews must spend of their wealth, along with the believers, so long as fighting continues.

21. Yathrib shall be a sanctuary for the people of this document. A stranger under protection shall be as his protecting host, unharmed and committing no crime. A woman shall not be given protection without the consent of her family.

22. If any dispute likely to cause trouble should arise among the people of this document, it must be referred to Allah, *subḥānahū wa ta'ālā,* and to Muḥammad, *ṣallā Allāhu 'alayhi wa sallam.*

23. God approves and is pleased with the piety and goodness in this document.

24. Quraysh and their helpers shall not be given protection.

25. The people of this document are bound to help one another against any attack on Yathrib. If they are called to make peace and maintain it, they must do so; and if they make a similar demand on the Muslims, it must be carried out except with one who insists on fighting against their religion.

26. To every small group belongs the share which is their due as members of the larger group which is

party to this covenant. The Jews of the Aws and their clients, are entitled to the same rights as any other party to this document, together with the goodness and charity from all parties to it. Charity and good deeds exclude sinfulness and wrongdoing.

27. There is no responsibility except for one's own deeds.

28. God approves of such truth and goodness as is included in this document.

29. This document shall not constitute any protection for the unjust or the wrongdoers.

30. Whoever goes out to fight or stays at home is safe in the city, unless he has committed an injustice or a crime.

God is the protector of whoever honours (his commitment to the *Ṣaḥīfah*) and is God-fearing and so is Muḥammad, the Messenger of God, *ṣallā Allāhu 'alayhi wa sallam . . .'*

The foregoing is a translation of the Arabic text of the *Ṣaḥīfah* as given by Ibn Hishām. The text comes immediately after the report of the arrival of the Prophet in Madinah, and takes precedence over even the establishment by the Prophet of brotherhood between the *Anṣār* and the *Muhājirūn.* The only major event that preceded it was the building of the Prophet's Mosque in Madinah.

4. The Political Import of the *Ṣaḥīfah*

The *Ṣaḥīfah* must be acknowledged as a great achievement for the Prophet at the beginning of his career as a statesman. It was way ahead of its time, perhaps the first written constitution in history governing political as well as legal relations of a state. Recalling that the Prophet Muḥammad had had no previous experience as a ruler, the acumen of this extraordinary document is truly impressive. It provides a political and legal framework for the state of Madinah, well in advance of its actual realization. The government of Madinah, under the leadership of the Prophet, before it came into being, enjoyed the advantage of having put the political rights and obligations of the citizens in very clear written form.

The document heralded the birth of a unified community and a single government in Madinah. The authority and prerogatives of the Prophet were well defined and his position as undisputed ruler clearly established on a firm, contractual, legal foundation. His authority was also, and more significantly, lodged securely in the love and obedience of the two majority tribes of the city, the Aws and the Khazraj. The *Muhājirūn* were, of course, dedicated followers and supporters.

It is very significant that the Madinan state, though founded by a Prophet, and came into existence in the wake of a religious conflict and revolution, should have as its constitution a document stipulating a pluralist, multi-racial and multi-cultural, society, comprising two distinct religious communities, Muslim and Jewish. Thus the *Ṣaḥīfah* provided for the Madinan government a basis that was civic and political rather than religious and sectarian. The Prophet was recognized as the ruler by non-Muslim as well as Muslim citizens of Madinah. The Madinan society and state was declared as one, unified *Ummah,* on the basis of the ratification and enforcement of this document.

The three main groups or communities, *Anṣār, Muhājirūn* and Jews were accorded local and communal autonomy with regard to certain matters:

1. Freedom to practise their religious rites as they saw fit.
2. To enforce law and order, prevent crime and punish criminals and wrong-doers.
3. Carry out commercial and economic activities and earn a living as they chose. (This seems to be the natural assumption of the call upon them to provide money for the defence of the city, should fighting break out.)
4. Management of communal affairs and solidarity and mutual support for all members. Prisoners to be ransomed and blood-wit collected and paid. No

member of the community was to be left in destitution.

5. To a certain extent, the *Ṣaḥīfah* allowed the various parties, at least by implication, the right to make legal decisions. A dispute was to be referred to the Prophet only if it proved too difficult and prolonged, otherwise it could be resolved locally, at the level of the community. However, two matters must be dealt with at the central level by the Prophet himself: these were (i) matters pertaining to war and peace in general, and (ii) matters pertaining to the relationship of Madinans with the Quraysh. No party to the *Ṣaḥīfah* had the right to go to war without securing the Prophet's permission in advance, even if they were suffering an injustice and had sustained wounds. Also, no party to the *Ṣaḥīfah* had the right to make a separate peace with their common enemy. The Prophet's permission must first be sought and secured and they must make sure that the conditions of the proposed separate peace would be fair and equitable to all parties to the *Ṣaḥīfah*.

Relations with the Quraysh were also put under the jurisdiction of the central authority of the Prophet. In particular, it was not permitted that any party to the *Ṣaḥīfah* should extend friendship, protection or assistance to the wealth or persons of the Quraysh. It was failure to honour this restriction that brought so much doom and destruction to the Jewish party to this *Ṣaḥīfah,* as we shall see in the sequel.

The *Ṣaḥīfah* is remarkable, also, for the very high place it gives to the issue of law and order, and the firmness which it shows *vis-à-vis* crime and disorder. Rebellious actions against the authority of the Prophet would not be tolerated, according to the tone of the document, even if the rebels were sons of the covenanted parties. It was not lawful to give protection of any sort to rebels or criminals, nor was it lawful to shelter them or render any other assistance to them.

All parties to the covenant were to actively and unitedly join in the fight against rebellion and crime.

A vital provision of the *Ṣaḥīfah* was that all covenanted parties must join in the fighting, should the city of Madinah be exposed to external aggression, as well as contribute to the cost of any such defensive action. The Jews were not excluded from this vital provision of the *Ṣaḥīfah*. The city of Madinah was declared a sanctuary whose sanctity must not be violated. It was the duty of the covenanted parties to safeguard and effectively guarantee it.

The covenanted Jews were given full citizenship in the state – no sign of any distinction between first or second-class citizens. The *Ṣaḥīfah* declared that the covenanted Jews shall have rights and obligations equal with Muslims, and be entitled to the assistance and support of the Muslims should they stand in need of that. The covenanted Jew shall not be wronged, nor his enemy be aided, *'ghaira maẓlūmīn walā mutanaṣṣarīn 'alayhim'*.

Major disputes, disagreements or major conflicts must be referred to the Prophet, though petty quarrels could be resolved locally, as we have seen.

The peace of Madinah was declared one and indivisible, every individual of the city must make peace and war in harmony with the state. However, should an individual Muslim give his *jiwār* (protection) to anyone, not guilty of any crime or an injustice, all Muslims must honour this *jiwār*.

The *Ṣaḥīfah* declared that the basis for legal responsibility is individual. Each person is responsible for his own deeds. No-one shall be punished for the deeds of his allies or even his next of kin. The emphasis on personal responsibility is an important break from the tribal conception of collective responsibility, which was widespread in pre-Islamic Arabia. If a member of a tribe killed a man from another tribe, the killer's tribe as a whole were held responsible. Anyone of the killer's tribe could be taken and killed in retaliation. The shift away from the tribal bonding of collective responsibility was an important objective of the *Ṣaḥīfah* as a whole. Perhaps for the first time in history, we have the example of a state founded on the basis of ideology, and contractual agreement as to the rights and obligations of its citizens.

Citizens of the state of Madinah were either Muslims who were committed to its defence and well-being out of religious conviction and religious brotherhood, or non-Muslims who had secured their peace and safety therein by a written contract.

To the bonding on the basis of faith and law afforded by the conclusion of the covenant of the *Ṣaḥīfah,* we must add a third unifying factor in the foundation pillars of the new Muslim state. This third factor was the territorial base of the new Muslim *Ummah* emerging as a multi-racial and multi-cultural society. Muslims could not have formed a state at Makkah because (apart from other reasons), they lacked a secure, defensible territory upon which to set it up. But Madinah provided an ideal territorial base for that purpose. Well to the north of Makkah, it could not easily be reached by the warriors of the Quraysh. Madinah sits at the gate of *ash-Shām* to the north, where the bulk of the Quraysh commerce was directed. Thus whoever commanded Madinah enjoyed a great agricultural centre with crops and palm trees and plenty of water, thus self-sufficient as far as basic provisions were concerned. Furthermore, being surrounded by hills and mountains, it was easily defensible against outside attackers. Muslims and Jews found themselves, despite their religious differences, sharing the same territory and having to defend it against external aggression. This was one of the considerations which persuaded the Jews to endorse the *Ṣaḥīfah* of Madinah.

The state of Madinah extended to areas on its immediate outskirts where clients and confederates of the Aws, the Khazraj and the Jews lived. The Prophet also made treaties with some tribes living near Madinah, and these too could be included within the jurisdiction of the city. However, it would have been difficult to include tribes which though allied with the Muslims, were living far out of Madinah. Thus the *Ṣaḥīfah* does not refer to any of those allied tribes of either the Muslims or the Jews. It only refers to them vaguely as 'followers' and 'clients'. Nor were these 'followers' and 'clients' considered a major party to the covenant of the *Ṣaḥīfah.* Thus, and despite its reference to 'followers' and 'clients', the covenant of the *Ṣaḥīfah* remains a tripartite alliance, between the *Anṣār,* the *Muhājirūn* and the Jews of Madinah.

It is interesting to note two things in connection with the status of the third party to the covenant, namely the Jews. Firstly, their status, as we have observed before, is that of full and equal citizens. They were obligated under the covenant not only to fight with the Muslims against attackers, but also to contribute towards the overall cost of any such fighting. Secondly, we find no mention in the *Ṣaḥīfah* of *jizyah.* The Jews were not required to pay *jizyah* to the Muslims. Payment of *jizyah* was indeed required of non-Muslim citizens in Muslim lands precisely because they were not willing (nor expected) to fight alongside the Muslims. It was more or less a defence tax. But insofar as the Jews of Madinah were contractually committed to fight alongside the Muslims and also to contribute to the cost of such fighting, there was indeed no need of any resort to *jizyah.*

The *Ṣaḥīfah* is also noteworthy for the protection it accords to strangers travelling in Muslim lands. Hitherto, such strangers had been considered fair game for highway robbers and the violent, aggressive bedouins of the desert. Only within Makkah, did the Quraysh and the Hashimites in particular, manage to secure some rights of security for strangers. They had to conclude a special alliance before they could extend such rights to strangers. The *Ṣaḥīfah* must be praised for this important provision, and for the related but significant provision that any Muslim had the right to grant his *jiwār* (protection) to any such stranger, provided that the protected strangers were innocent of crimes and wrong-doing. Moreover, all Muslims were called upon to honour this *jiwār,* irrespective of the social status of the Muslim granting it. The protection of Allah and His Messenger is one and indivisible, and so is the protection of all Muslims. Muslims are equal in this respect, and their protection can be extended by any one of them. In a well-known saying of the Prophet:

> Muslims are equal *('Udūl),* their protection can be extended by the least of them. They are also one hand against their enemy.

Al-Muslimūna 'Udūlun, yas'ā bi-Dhimmatihim adnāhum, wa hum yadun 'alā man siwāhum.

Muslims are one hand for their friend and ally, and one hand against their enemy.

In the *Ṣaḥīfah,* the expression *'Dhimmatu Allāhi wa-Rasūlihī wāḥidah'* is repeated more than once. It means that the protection and peace of God, His Messenger and that of all Muslims is one and indivisible. The Islamic peace is one and indivisible, and so is the peace of the people of the *Ṣaḥīfah.* Thus no separate waging of war or separate making of peace was lawful for any covenanted party to the *Ṣaḥīfah.*

However, the parties to the *Ṣaḥīfah* were warned against extending *jiwār* (protection) to two categories of persons. No freedman fleeing from his master, could be given *jiwār* against the interests of his master. Secondly, no protection could be granted to a woman without the permission of her family. This last provision may have been designed to restrain women slaves or even women in general from running away. If so, it was most probably meant to restrict any tendency of the Muslims to take women polytheists as wives or vice versa. However, that last restriction was introduced later, a fact which makes us more inclined to believe that the restriction was perhaps directed against such malpractices as abduction or even rape which used to exist in pre-Islamic Arab society. It may also have signalled a new, tougher attitude towards licentiousness and promiscuity in Arab society. One way for women to become prostitutes was to run away from their families and get protection from a wrong-doer or a conspirator.

The interpretation of the provision that no woman be given protection against the wish of her family as a way of restricting intermarriage between Muslims and polytheists, is most unlikely because such intermarriages were not known to trigger any opposition from the Arabian society. Thus parents and families used to readily permit and bless such marriages. It was the Qur'ān, and the practice of the Prophet Muḥammad after the *Hijrah,* that made such intermarriages unlawful. Thus, at the time of the *Ṣaḥīfah,* to arrange such marriages, girls or women did not need to run away from their families.

The provision needs to be interpreted in the framework of the *Ṣaḥīfah* as a whole. Given that matters of security and the general peace of the society were the overriding consideration, the provision must be seen as relating above all to the maintenance, and reinforcement, of law and order. Given the Arabs' well-known sensitivity towards questions of honour, sexual integrity and privacy of their women, the issue was important enough to warrant its inclusion in a separate provision.

5. **The Contractual Strength of the *Ṣaḥīfah***

We turn now to the question of how and to what extent the *Ṣaḥīfah* was seen as binding by the various parties to it. No doubt, both the Prophet and the Muslims viewed the *Ṣaḥīfah* absolutely earnestly. The most solemn emphasis possible was placed upon it by the Prophet, as is evident from his repeated reminders and warning to the Jews of Madinah against any possible breach of any of its provisions.

The conflict with the Jews of Banū Qaynuqā' was the first ever between Muslims and Jews. A Jewish jewellery-seller dealt indecently with a Muslim woman customer. She had refused to unveil, but he managed to expose her nudity by means of a nasty trick. The Muslim woman cried for help and the Jewish dealer was instantly killed by a Muslim. That Muslim was in turn killed by Jews. The Prophet hurried to the scene and addressed the Jewish gathering in the market place of the city, which was situated in the Jewish quarter. He reminded Banū Qaynuqā' of the covenant of the *Ṣaḥīfah* and demanded that they abide by its provisions and not break it again. He warned them sternly against any future violation of that covenant. In reply they arrogantly boasted of their military strength, and imprudently warned the Prophet that he would be defeated, should he try to engage them on the battlefield. The Prophet considered their reply a repudiation of the covenant, and proceeded immediately to take action against them.

Such behaviour on the part of the Prophet could make no sense nor would it seem natural or logical, had it not been for the fact that a covenant existed between the two parties.

The Jews, for their part, never denied the existence of that covenant. It is also significant, in this connection, to mention that he too had to repudiate the covenant before taking military action against them. These events are given in great detail in Muslim historical sources, especially Ibn Hishām.

Again the conflict with Banū an-Naḍīr was precipitated by their attempt to assassinate the Prophet, when he was visiting them in connection with the payment of the blood-wit of two men from the allied tribe of Banū 'Āmir, killed accidentally by a Muslim. According to the provisions of the *Ṣaḥīfah* they were expected to contribute some money towards such payment. The *Ṣaḥīfah* called upon the various parties to it to help each other in such matters. Instead of rendering such help, they conspired to assassinate the Prophet, by throwing down a stone on his head, as he sat in their council. But he was informed by the Archangel Gabriel, and left suddenly. After he reached his Mosque, the Prophet immediately issued a commandment that Banū an-Naḍīr must leave the city.

In similar fashion, Banū Qurayẓah sided with the Quraysh and the Ghaṭfān when they besieged Madinah in the Battle of the Ditch (al-Khandaq). Banū Qurayẓah were persuaded by Ḥuyay Ibn al-Akhṭab to repudiate their covenant with the Prophet, pointing to the greatness of the besieging army and promising a certain defeat of the Muslims in a few days. Banū Qurayẓah were impressed by his logic and by the great size of the attacking army and decided to break their covenant with the Prophet. In vain did he try to talk them out of that position. When the Quraysh and their allies were defeated, Banū Qurayẓah were caught in combat gear making ready to attack the Muslims from within the gates and trenches of Madinah.

6. The Prophet's Insights and the Jewish Anticipation

It would appear, in view of the circumstances in which the *Ṣaḥīfah* was ratified, that the Prophet was moved to conclude it by penetrating insights and intuition beyond anything that could be discerned at the time of the event itself. He realized the importance and usefulness of having the Jews committed to the peace and security of Madinah by a legally-binding document. Initially the Prophet seems to have entertained great hopes of befriending the Jews as Scripturists and monotheists. He hoped and longed for meaningful and effective co-operation with them in the inevitable battle with the polytheists of the Quraysh. He was a regular visitor to their notables and had long religious discussions with their rabbis and learned authorities. He informed them of his great affection for Moses, whom he used to call 'my brother Moses'. Moreover, he told them of the essential continuity of his call and religion with that of Moses, and the oneness of the divine source of both the original Torah and the Qur'ān. The Prophet Muḥammad assumed, naturally and logically enough, that, as monotheists, the Jews were his natural allies against the Quraysh, the latter being adamant polytheists and idol-worshippers. However, much to his astonishment and dismay, the Jews preferred to ally themselves with the Quraysh, in particular, and anti-Muslim forces in general.

The collaboration between the Quraysh and the Jews of Banū an-Naḍīr became known immediately after the Muslim victory of Badr. At this point, the Prophet began to investigate their motives and psychological dispositions *vis-à-vis* himself and the Muslims. He began to find out more about their history and their past, present and future attitudes to both themselves and others.

The mind of those Jewish inhabitants of Madinah was very much shaped by four principal considerations:

1. They regarded themselves as being the chosen people of God. God had decidedly favoured them over and against the Gentiles of every race and religion. All Prophets with Divine Revelations were Jewish and so the anticipated Prophet, to come after Moses, would be Jewish as well.

2. In the northern Arabian peninsula of the time, they were the only community with a living, continuous Divine Scripture. True, there were Christians in Madinah and Makkah, but these were a few, isolated individuals having no or very little impact on the development of events. The Christians of Najrān were in the remote south, and although they represented a community, their views had no immediate

bearing on events in Madinah. The Ḥanīfīs, followers of the religion of Abraham were even fewer in number, with little and fragmented portions of Divine scrolls, said to have been handed down from the time of the Patriarch. Certainly, the great Jewish influence in Madinah must be attributed to this fact. It was because of the divine origin of their learning and wisdom that the Prophet himself was so deeply attracted to them. He prayed, with them, towards Jerusalem, fasted the Day of Atonement *(Yaum 'Āshūrā')* and held feasts in celebration therein. He concluded a friendly, equitable agreement with them with most generous provisions, as are found in the *Ṣaḥīfah* of Madinah. He was fond of attending religious discussions with them and, at one time, entertained high hopes of totally winning them over to his side in his impending dispute with the Quraysh. The fact that they were Scripturists was a source of great pride and honour for the Jews. Over the years, that pride and honour turned into vanity, haughtiness and arrogance. The Jews became so conscious of their status, so proud of their culture and so fond of themselves and their heritage that they had become virtual prisoners of their own image of the world. Unable to participate in other worlds, they were unable to perceive these worlds in objective terms, let alone honour or appreciate them.

3. The third consideration pertains to the way they had to flee Palestine and come to Arabia. The agonizing circumstances that attended their exodus from Palestine had had the most profound impact upon their minds and consciousness. These circumstances bred hatred, mistrust and exclusiveness *vis-à-vis* other societies and cultures. Also, harsh and difficult experiences quite often tend to make those who experience them hard and militant in character, and prone to an aggressive, even belligerent disposition. Those Jews could not forget what they had been through, and as they watched the Prophet's power and prestige grow, especially after the Battle of Badr, they became angry and spiteful towards the Muslim presence in Madinah.

4. Last but by no means least, the Jews had huge and wide-ranging vested interests. Enjoying a virtual monopoly of the commerce, finance and indeed the general wealth of

Madinah, they were fretful of the implications the growing power of the Muslims would have on their position.

At the beginning their hopes were naive and misplaced. They expected to emerge as the chief beneficiaries of the covenant with the Prophet. They expected him to follow them in religion and to side with them in any future conflict with the native tribes of the Aws and the Khazraj. They had in the past even threatened these tribes with the approaching advent of a Prophet, who would help the Jews against them.

Had the Jews been more insightful about their own psychological and cultural tendencies, they would surely not have endorsed the *Ṣaḥīfah*. They would have known that they could not long endure the supremacy of the Arabian Prophet, and a steady diminution of their former eminence. Had they been more far-sighted, they would have known that they would feel inwardly compelled to rebel against the authority of the Prophet, and therefore refrained from voluntarily committing themselves to a peaceful co-existence with him. Nor can they have imagined that rebellion and violation of the covenant would spell for them their doom.

7. The Lasting Significance of the *Ṣaḥīfah*

The *Ṣaḥīfah* was perhaps the first-ever document governing the political conduct of a state, with a clear declaration of its main constituting principles and objectives. In modern terminology, it represents the first written constitution known in history.

But the *Ṣaḥīfah* is also very significant for the lofty principles, the humane and just relations it ordains with regard to the different religious and ethnic groups living in the city of Madinah. As a matter of fact, it is the first known attempt to create a multi-cultural and multi-racial society with different religious dominions living alongside one another. Basic human rights were granted in a fashion unprecedented in history. Every individual, Muslim or Jewish, was granted freedom of worship and freedom to live and work in peace and dignity. His livelihood and property were granted, and his rights to be treated with equity and justice firmly established. To reinforce the concept of equal citizenship to all persons living in Madinah, irrespective of their religious affiliations, the Jews of Madinah were formally committed by the provisions of the *Ṣaḥīfah* to participate in the defence of the city, should it be exposed to outside aggression. They were obligated both to take part in the actual fighting, should it break out, and to contribute towards the cost of such fighting.

The *Ṣaḥīfah*'s strong commitment against crime and lawlessness is very commendable. All citizens were bound, under the provisions of the *Ṣaḥīfah,* to fight criminals and law-breakers, even if those were the sons of any one of the covenanted parties.

Thus the *Ṣaḥīfah* affords the unique possibility of a pluralist state, founded on a sound legal document. The degree of liberty and tolerance implied by the various provisions of the *Ṣaḥīfah* is truly amazing. The ideals of peaceful and fruitful co-existence between different ethnic and religious groups remain difficult to achieve in most contemporary societies.

B. THE PROPHET'S FAREWELL ADDRESS

1. **Prologue**

In his last pilgrimage, the Prophet, at the age of sixty-three, mounted on his she-camel, addressed a gathering of almost a hundred thousand Muslims. That address became a landmark in Muslim history, and a vital document of Islam. It has become famous as *Khuṭbah Ḥajjat al-Wadā',* that is, the 'Farewell Address'. The speech itself is a masterpiece of the Prophet's renowned eloquence, a most noble proclamation and a document of unusual significance. For this reason, it is sometimes referred to as *Khuṭbah at-Tablīgh* (i.e. the Proclamation Address) and, in recognition of the perennial and fundamental themes incorporated into it, as the *Khuṭbah al-Islām*. The first two epithets are used of it by Ibn Hishām himself.

Its text, as given by Ibn Hishām, is terse and short, consisting of the Prophet's address on Mount Raḥmah at 'Arafāt on the 9th of Dhu al-Ḥijjah of the year 10 A.H.

Ibn Kathīr gives a much longer text, consisting not only of the address at 'Arafāt, but also the Prophet's second address delivered on the second day of his stay at Minā, i.e. on the 11th of Dhu al-Ḥijjah. Ibn Kathīr's account is therefore much more comprehensive than that of Ibn Hishām. Some of the further proclamations included in it could not properly be included in Ibn Hishām's version, since these were made separately in the three days following the 'Arafāt address of the 9th of Dhu al-Ḥijjah. However, some later authorities have edited the Farewell Address, so that it includes these further statements and proclamations.

We shall first give Ibn Hishām's text, which is also given by Ibn Kathīr. Then we shall give the additions made by Ibn Kathīr and others.

Said Ibn Hishām[4]:

The Prophet started by praising God and thanking Him, then turning to his audience, he added:

'O people! Listen well to my words, for I do not know if I am ever going to meet you again on such an occasion after this year.

O people! Your lives and your property shall be inviolable until you meet your Lord, just as this day and this month are inviolate.

You are surely going to meet your Lord, and He will question you about your deeds. Thus I have conveyed to you:

Whoever of you is keeping a trust of someone else, shall return it to him.

All usury *(Ribā)* shall henceforth be abolished. But you may keep your capital. You shall not inflict nor suffer injustice. God has ordained that any usury *(Ribā)* due to al-'Abbās ibn 'Abd al-Muṭṭalib shall be henceforth abolished. Every right to avenge homicide in pre-Islamic days is henceforth abolished. And the first such right which I abolish is that arising from the slaying of Rabī'ah ibn al-Ḥārith ibn 'Abd al-Muṭṭalib.

O people! Satan has given up every hope of ever being worshipped in this land of yours. But he will be pleased if obeyed in the lesser of your deeds. So, beware of him, concerning your religion.

O people, intercalation is indeed evidence of great unbelief and confirms unbelievers in their misguidance. They render it lawful one year, and they forbid it the next, so that they appear in conformity with the number of months which God declared inviolate. (But in reality) they resort to this in order to make legitimate that which God forbade and to forbid that which God has made permissible.

But surely time has revolved in its own fashion since the day God created the heavens and the earth. The number of months with God is twelve, of which four are inviolate. Three of these are consecutive and Rajab of *Muḍar* which is between Jumādā and Sha'bān.

O people! surely you have certain rights over your wives and they have certain rights over you. It is of your rights on them that they do not invite anyone to your house whom you do not approve of and also never commit any acts of lewdness or manifest impropriety. Should they commit any of those acts, God has permitted you to abstain from having sexual intimacy with them and to chastise them, yet not severely. But if they refrain (from these malpractices), then they are entitled to their rights of being fed and clothed in a kind and fitting way. Do treat your wives well, be kind to them, for they are confined to your homes and are dependent upon you, not being able to do anything for themselves. You have taken them as wives by the trust of God, and enjoyed their bodies by the permission of God. Think well, O people, and understand what I am saying to you. For I have now assuredly conveyed to you (what I am supposed to convey).

I am leaving with you what if you hold fast to, you will never go astray. The Book of God and the *Sunnah* of His Prophet.

O people, think well about my words, and understand them well. You no doubt know that every Muslim is a brother unto every other Muslim, and that Muslims are indeed one brotherhood. Nothing is lawful for him, of his brother save that he himself gives willingly. Do not, therefore, do injustice to yourselves. O Lord, have I conveyed Your message?'

It is reported that people responded: 'O yes' to the Prophet's last question. He concluded by saying: 'O Lord, bear witness.'

The foregoing is the standard version of Ibn Hishām's account of the Farewell Address. However, he gives a second version which is substantially the same except that it adds that the Prophet elicited responses and affirmations from his audience concerning the sanctity of the inviolate months of the *Ḥajj*.

Ibn Kathīr's[5] version is much more comprehensive, adding to Ibn Hishām's text a number of very important points, apparently made by the Prophet on different occasions during his last pilgrimage.

2. **Ibn Kathīr's Account of the Farewell Address**

Whereas Ibn Hishām bases his version of the Farewell Address upon the address which the Prophet gave on Mount 'Arafāt, Ibn Kathīr includes in his rather lengthy statement of that address a number of other speeches as well. He draws mainly on the books of the Sayings of the Prophet, in particular Bukhārī and Muslim. According to al-Bukhārī, the Prophet made a second speech on the day of slaughter *(Yawm an-Naḥr)*. In that second speech, he repeated his declaration of the inviolateness of human life and the sanctity of private property, which he had made the day before. But in this second speech, he referred also to the inviolateness of human sexual integrity and honour:

1. Said al-Bukhārī, on the authority of 'Alī ibn 'Abd Allāh, on that of Yaḥyā ibn Sa'īd, on that of Fuḍail ibn Ghazwān, on that of 'Ikrimah (Ibn Abī Jahl) on the authority of 'Abd Allāh ibn 'Abbās, that the Prophet addressed the Muslims on the slaughter day. He said:

> 'O people! What day is this?'
> They said: 'A sacred day.'
> He said: 'Which place is this?'
> They said: 'It is a sacred place.'
> He said: 'What month is this?'
> They said: 'It is a sacred month.'
> Said the Prophet: 'Surely your lives, your property and your honour are as inviolate unto you as the inviolability of this day, this month and this place.'

Bukhārī said that the Prophet repeated the foregoing statement a number of times. Then he raised his head and added:

> 'O Lord, have I conveyed Your message?'

Then the Prophet added, according to a second version of the above *ḥadīth*, also narrated by al-Bukhārī: 'Those present shall convey this to those who are absent. Perchance, those to whom this is reported be more diligent and more thoughtful. Do not revert after me, becoming as unbelievers, engaged in smiting each other's necks.'

2. Another significant addition in Ibn Kathīr is based on a saying of the Prophet's, narrated by Imām Aḥmad ibn Ḥanbal and Imām an-Nasā'ī. Both Aḥmad and an-Nasā'ī rest this new addition on the authority of Hilāl Ibn Yasāf:

The Prophet said, in his Farewell Address: 'There are four commandments:

— You shall not associate partners with God.
— You shall not kill the souls which God has rendered inviolate, except in dispensation of justice.
— You shall not fornicate.
— You shall not steal.'

3. A third addition in Ibn Kathīr is based on the authority of Usāmah ibn Sharīk. Usāmah said that he witnessed the Prophet giving a speech on his Farewell Pilgrimage. Said the Prophet:

> 'Take care to be kind to your mothers and fathers, your sisters and brothers, then those of your nearest of kin.'

4. A fourth addition in Ibn Kathīr consists of four points of advice: The Prophet said to his audience:

> 'Worship your Lord alone.
> Pray your five ordained prayers.
> Fast your month of Ramaḍān.

Obey if you were commanded to do so by those in authority amongst you.
If you do these things, then you shall enter the Paradise of your Lord.'

This fourth addition is narrated by Imām Aḥmad ibn Ḥanbal, on the authority of Abū 'Umāmah.

5. A substantial addition in Ibn Kathīr refers to the important topic of inherited rights. This is also narrated by Imām Aḥmad, on the authority of the same Abū 'Umāmah. Said the Prophet: 'God has ordained that everyone should receive what is due to him by way of inheritance. No bequest shall be made to a prospective inheritor. A child belongs to the marriage bed and the violator of wedlock shall be stoned. Their ultimate reckoning shall be with God. Whosoever attributes his ancestry to other than his father, or claims his clientship to other than his actual protector, shall incur the curse of God until Doomsday. No woman shall spend from what is in her house, except by the permission of her husband.'

The Companions said: 'O Messenger of God! Not even food?'

He said: 'Food is the best of our wealth.'

The Prophet then added: 'Whatever is borrowed must be returned, grants and gifts should be mutual, and debts should be repaid and leaders are more likely to incur debts and losses.'

The foregoing statement is attributed to the Prophet by the four authorities on the *Sunnah,* namely Imām Aḥmad, Abū Dāwūd, an-Nasā'ī and at-Tirmidhī.

6. Muslim narrated on the authority of Umm al-Ḥusain, who said: 'I accompanied the Prophet on his Farewell Pilgrimage. I heard him saying: "O people, listen and obey, even if an Abyssinian slave is in command over you, so long as he leads you according to the Book of God".'

7. The last of the significant additions by Ibn Kathīr is one that pertains to the pre-Islamic *Jāhiliyyah* period: The Prophet meant to impress upon his audience that Islam represents a final break with the habits and customs of that *Jāhiliyyah:* 'All customs and practices of *Jāhiliyyah* are under my feet, and so are all blood revenges and money rights arising therefrom until Doomsday . . .'

Some authorities include in the Farewell Address the following theme relating to personal responsibility and the equality of all people in the sight of God:

'O people! Surely, your Lord is One, and your father is one. You all belong to Adam, and Adam was created of clay. No Arab is superior to a non-Arab, or vice versa. No white man is superior to a black man and vice versa. Surely, the noblest amongst you are the most God-fearing amongst you'.[6]

3. The *Lā-ḥaraj* Maxim

Ibn Kathīr's account is notable for the *Lā-ḥaraj* (no hindrance) pronouncement which the Prophet made on a number of issues. These pronouncements were given as responses to those of his Companions asking whether it was permissible to do things which appeared doubtful to them. On his Farewell Pilgrimage the Prophet almost always gave positive answers to those questions. He would typically answer: 'O yes, you could do such and such, with no hindrance *(lā-ḥaraj)* to you.' Or he would simply say: '*Lā-ḥaraj* (all right)'.

Ibn Kathīr relies here on the authority of the two shaikhs, Bukhārī and Muslim. Both Bukhārī and Muslim reported, on the authority of Ibn Jurayḥ on the authority of az-Zuhrī, on the authority of 'Īsā ibn Ṭalḥah, on the authority of 'Abd Allāh ibn 'Amr ibn al-'Ās, that whilst the Prophet, *ṣallā Allāhu 'alayhi wa sallam,* was addressing the pilgrims on the day of slaughter, a man stood up and asked: 'I thought that doing so-and-so comes before doing so-and-so.' Another man, then, also stood up and asked a similar question. To both men the Prophet replied: 'Do it – no embarrassment – *lā-ḥaraj.*' Imām Muslim added: 'The Prophet was not asked about any matter, being done before or after its ordained time, to which he did not give the answer: "All right, no embarrassment. You can do it in that way, nothing is incumbent upon you".'

This *lā-ḥaraj* pronouncement encourages a measured degree of flexibility in matters of religious rites and ordinances, and a major shift away from dogmatism in religious worship. This is not surprising in a religion like Islam, which so emphasizes inner modes and attitudes of the mind and spirit. Ostentatious acts or gestures are not the hallmarks of piety or sincerity in religion. The worth of acts and deeds depends very much upon the goodness of the intentions and motives behind them. The *lā-ḥaraj* maxim also represents a shift towards easiness and naturalness in religious devotions. For one to be a strict religious devotee, one does not need, and certainly is not required, to always take the hard way. It is well-known that this was in fact the Prophet's own way. Whenever he had to choose between two alternatives, he would always opt for the easier one, so long as that did not lead to disobeying any of God's commandments. The Prophet repeatedly said: 'This religion of Islam is a lenient one. So go into it with ease and patience. No-one who attempts to storm his way into it, will come out victorious.'[7]

However, the *lā-ḥaraj* maxim should not be interpreted as an unconditional licence to dodge all religious obligations. There can be no doubt that it does not relate to well-defined, established and central religious observances. Thus lesser rites, not affecting the stated wisdom behind them, are the natural and proper sphere for the application of the *lā-ḥaraj* maxim.

It is indeed interesting that the maxim was declared in connection with performance of the *Ḥajj* which is perhaps the Islamic observance with the most complicated set of rites and rituals. Symbolism in those rites and rituals is most conspicuous. It is perhaps in view of the complexity and multiplicity of those rites, and to the difficulty and the length of the *Ḥajj* itself, that the *lā-ḥaraj* maxim is primarily directed and to which it is especially suited. Its import is nonetheless general, whenever situations are parallel to those prevalent in the *Ḥajj*. The maxim epitomizes a whole set of attitudes and dispositions towards religion in general. If the reservations we have made are borne in mind, the maxim is an excellent prescription against narrow-mindedness and bigotry in religion, so characteristic of some religious communities in the past as well as in the present.

4. Mixed Feelings of Joy and Sadness

The Farewell Address was heard with intent and solemnity. The Prophet's manner of delivering it, the gravity and profundity of his voice, his repetition of the main propositions, all helped to impress upon his audience that it was indeed no ordinary speech. The outstanding eloquence of the address, the noble and sublime message it contained, raised the minds and feelings of his audience to an extraordinary mood of thoughtfulness and expectation.

It was during this Farewell Pilgrimage that God revealed to the Muslims that their religion had been completed and perfected. The Prophet declaimed loudly the momentous revelation:

> 'Today I have perfected for you your religion, and I have completed My favour upon you, and I have approved of Islam as your religion'.[8]

The Muslim multitude rejoiced. Yet this joy was checked by an underlying feeling of unease and anxiety. What next? What was to become of the Prophet, who had already hinted that he might never be at that occasion again?

Ibn Kathīr, on the authority of Bukhārī and Muslim claims that the above verse (5: 3) signifying the perfection of Islam, was revealed on the day of 'Arafah, just before the Prophet delivered his farewell address. On hearing it, 'Umar sobbed passionately and then burst into tears. He understood the sad news implicit in it. People crowded around him, asking in surprise: 'What is the matter? O 'Umar.' He replied: 'After perfection, there is nothing but bereavement.'

He knew and feared the terrible loss impending after the

revelation of this verse – that the Prophet's role in this earthly life was nearing its end.

'Umar's cryptic response was not grasped by all those present. Two other persons, however, got the sad message as quickly as he did: Abū Bakr aṣ-Ṣiddīq and the young 'Abdullāh ibn 'Abbās, the Prophet's cousin, known for his ready wits and genius.

Another verse which also conveyed this message about the impending departure of the Prophet from this life is *Sūrah an-Naṣr:* 'When God's victory and succour comes, and you (O Muḥammad) witness people entering the religion of God in great numbers, then recite the praises of your Lord, and ask His forgiveness, He is oft-forgiving' (Qur'ān, 110).

Ibn Kathīr asserts that this verse was revealed on the second day of the Prophet's stay in Makkah. When *Sūrah an-Naṣr* was revealed, the Prophet knew that the end of his days in this life was approaching. 'Umar also grasped the sad import of the verse, as did 'Abdullāh ibn 'Abbās. Apparently the generality of Muslims did not. When some elder Muslims who participated in Badr, resented the prominence which the young 'Abdullāh enjoyed with 'Umar ibn al-Khaṭṭāb, he called upon him to interpret *Sūrah an-Naṣr* to them. 'Umar asked the older Muslims what this *sūrah* meant and they did not know. Then the youthful Ibn 'Abbās explained it to them, revealing its hidden meaning. 'Umar concurred with Ibn 'Abbās' explanation.

5. The Augmented Text of Ibn Kathīr's Additions

If we regard Ibn Hishām's text of the Farewell Address as the first part of a larger text of it, Ibn Kathīr's additions will then be the second part. Since those additions were given in the form of scattered places throughout Ibn Kathīr's discussion of the topic, they need to be rearranged together as the second part of an enlarged, edited text of the Farewell Address. The Prophet said:

'Surely, your lives, your property and your honour are inviolate unto you, just as this day, this month, and this place. O Lord! have I conveyed Your message? Those present shall convey this to those absent. Perchance those to whom this is reported will be more diligent and mindful than those hearing it.

Do not revert, after I am gone, into unbelief, smiting each other's necks.

You shall not associate partners with God. You shall not kill the souls which God has rendered inviolate except in dispensation of justice.

You shall not fornicate.

You shall not steal.

Take special care to be kind to your mothers and fathers, sisters and brothers, then those nearest of kin.

Worship your Lord alone.

Pray your five ordained prayers.

Fast during the month of Ramaḍān.

Obey, if you are commanded to do so by those in authority amongst you.

If you do these things, then you shall enter the Paradise of your Lord. God has ordained that everyone should receive what is due to him by way of inheritance. No bequest shall be made to a prospective inheritor. A child belongs to the marriage-bed and the violator of wedlock shall be stoned. Their ultimate reckoning shall be with God. Whosoever attributes his ancestry to other than his father, or claims his clientship to other than his actual protectors, shall incur the curse of God until Doomsday.

No woman shall spend from what is in her house except by the permission of her husband.'

The Companions said: 'O Messenger of God, not even food?' 'Food is the best of our wealth', the Prophet replied. The Prophet then added: 'Whatever is borrowed must be returned, grants and gifts must be mutual, debts must be repaid and leaders of people are sure to incur debts and losses. O people! listen and obey, even if an Abyssinian slave is in command over you, so long as he leads you according to the book of God.

All customs and practices of *Jāhiliyyah* are under my feet, and so are blood revenges, and money rights arising therefrom, until Doomsday.

O people, surely your Lord is One, and your father is one.

You all belong to Adam, and Adam was created of clay. No Arab is superior to a non-Arab or vice versa. No white man is superior to a black man and vice versa.'

God said: 'Surely the noblest amongst you are those who are most God-fearing amongst you'.[9]

There ends the second part of the Farewell Address.

6. **Central Themes of the Farewell Address**

Seen in proper historical perspective, the Farewell Address will be understood as an absolute breaking away from the pre-Islamic age of *Jāhiliyyah* – or moral ignorance – and as an inauguration of a new and great civilization. It categorically rejects the thinking and attitudes of *Jāhiliyyah* on the one hand and on the other looks forward to universal future civilization.

In his earnest desire to do away with *Jāhiliyyah* once and for all, the Prophet declared the following principles:

1. All evil customs, traditions, conventions and practices pertaining to *Jāhiliyyah* are to be condemned and henceforth totally rejected. In the Prophet's words, these evil customs are 'under his feet'. The customs referred to by the Prophet in particular were those that relate essentially to paganism, idol-worship or immoral and inhuman masculine attitudes and practices.
2. Against the *Jāhiliyyah* practices of manslaughter, armed robbery, and violation of sexual decency, the Prophet declared the sanctity of human life, of private property and of sexual integrity.
3. Usury or *Ribā* was widespread in Makkah and other Arabian towns, and the basis of socio-economic exploitation. The Prophet declared it unlawful, affirming the war which the Qur'ān has waged against it.
4. The practice of avenging the murder of fellow-tribesmen by indiscriminate killing of members of the tribe to which the murderer belonged, is likewise abolished. The Prophet declared that he

had waived his right to avenge the blood of a cousin of his, killed in the *Jāhiliyyah* period.

5. It was the bad habit of the people of the *Jāhiliyyah* to tamper with the natural order and duration of the four sacred months, so as to dodge their sanctity – if it suited them to launch war during any of these sacred months, they would declare that they had decided to defer the coming of these holy months. In this way, they falsely absolved themselves of the charge of having violated their sanctity. This malpractice of tampering with the calendar was condemned and abolished by the Prophet.
6. Many of the privileges enjoyed by the Quraysh were undeserved. The Prophet abolished them, except for custodianship of the sacred sanctuary – *al-Ḥaram* – and the provision of water for pilgrims.
7. All kinds of injustice, aggression and exploitation are denounced unreservedly. Men are declared equal to one another; discrimination on the basis of social status, wealth, race or colour is declared void.
8. The sanctity of wedlock is affirmed, promiscuity wholly condemned and rejected. Fornicators are to be severely punished. Married fornicators are to be stoned.
9. The purity of descent and genealogy is declared sacrosanct – whoever claims a descent he knows not to be his or hers, shall be cursed by God. The need to preserve this purity seems to have been a major factor in adopting a tough line against fornication and permissiveness. Another major aspect of the war declared against sexual permissiveness is foundation of family life upon the sanctity of the marriage bond.
10. The rights and possessions of future generations must be guarded. The only way to do this is through a strict observance of inheritance rights. So bequests to prospective inheritors exceeding one third of total inheritance are banned. Objective

and correct apportionment of inherited rights, presupposes pure and authentic lines of family descent, a further reason for forbidding extra-marital sexual relations.

The Farewell Address is equally notable for the universal message it has for mankind as a whole:

1. There is the basic and primordial call to mankind to worship Allah alone, not associating any partner with Him. Implicit in the Qur'ānic verse, 'Today I have perfected your religion for you . . .', revealed during the Farewell Pilgrimage, is the claim that pure monotheism is only preserved in Islam. The other supposedly monotheistic religions of Judaism and Christianity have lost that doctrine of pure monotheism, being falsified and tampered with through the ages. This view has been expressed in another Qur'ānic verse which affirms: 'Surely the (true) religion with God is Islam.'
2. There is the warning concerning Satan, as the symbol of all evil. True, this warning is primarily directed to Muslims, but its relevance to all monotheistic worshippers is obvious.
3. There is the emphasis on the priceless worth of human life. Wilful taking of human life cannot be tolerated and must be punishable by death. Even if the life is taken by mistake, the *Diyah* (blood ransom or compensation) must be paid to the relatives of the killed person. The *diyah* is a token of the very high worth of human life, not a price for the life taken. Such a high value does Islam accord to human life that it declared that whoever kills one man deliberately, it is as if he has killed all of mankind.
4. The Farewell Address emphasizes the need and concern that women be treated kindly and compassionately. It reminds husbands that the enjoyment in marriage of a wife's body is a great blessing of God – they should appreciate and be grateful for

this blessing, and partake of it equitably and justly. Husbands are warned not to take advantage of the fact that women depend on them for their livelihood. At the same time, both marriage partners are informed of their mutual rights and obligations. Divorce, while permissible as a last resort in Islam, must be avoided if at all possible. Of all the permitted acts, it is the most detested by God. In desperate circumstances, the husband of an aggressive wife *(Nāshizah)* may even resort to bodily chastisement, but on condition that the chastisement be neither severe nor excessive.

5. Married women are advised not to socialize or fraternize freely with other men, if they wish to preserve the integrity of their marriage, and to obey God's commandments.
6. The eternal value of the Qur'ān and the Prophet's *Sunnah* as the source of Divine guidance are strongly emphasized. The Qur'ān remains the only divinely-revealed text that is totally intact. It has been preserved by God Himself against any attempt to alter or tamper with it. All other revealed texts were falsified and tampered with. The commandment to heed the Qur'ān is addressed to all mankind – to anyone desiring to avail himself of the wisdom and guidance of a divinely-revealed text. The teaching and the wisdom of the Prophet are also a valuable source of divine guidance, available to all mankind. 'Ā'ishah described the character of the Prophet as 'Qur'ānic'. The Qur'ān itself has praised the Prophet thus: 'Surely you are of great character (O Muḥammad).'
7. The Farewell Address strongly draws the attention of mankind to the unity of their origin, their common descent from one father, Adam, and one mother. No valid rational basis for any type of racial prejudice exists, according to Islam. Moreover, the Address reminds us that Adam was created of a very humble stuff, namely clay. The natural link between racial prejudice and arrogance

> is obvious. In the Farewell Address, the Prophet sought to strike at the very root of those evils, the probable cause of a large share of man's suffering, misguidedness and misery. In view of the wide renown of erroneous modern speculations about the origin of man, speculations that claim the prestige of being 'scientific', the worth of the Prophet's declaration on the subject cannot be overestimated. While modern 'scientific' speculations like Darwin's natural selection hypothesis can be used or abused to support the claims to superiority of certain races and so justify and promote racial conflict, the Prophet of Islam, over fourteen centuries ago, sought to eradicate the very ground of such false claims. Truly, Muḥammad was and remains, as the Qur'ān describes him, a mercy for mankind: 'Truly, We have not sent you except as a mercy for mankind.'

It is on account of his eagerness to fulfil the Qur'ān's vision of the unity of mankind, the promise of his ministry, that the Prophet Muḥammad spoke on these themes, for humanity as a whole: that is why he uses the phrase 'O People' though his audience was exclusively Muslim. He was in fact addressing human conscience everywhere and in all times to come. Given the profound divisions and suffering of humanity today, one cannot help but wonder what a mercy would descend upon this miserable world, if the teachings of the Prophet Muḥammad were heeded.

Islam has been described as the greatest leveller of all ideologies, because, as far as the human worth of man is concerned, it will not countenance any kind of discrimination. The Qur'ān declares, in this respect:

> O People, We have created you male and female, and have made you 'different' peoples and tribes, so that you will be acquainted with each other. Surely the noblest among you in the sight of God are those of you who are God-fearing.[10]

The phenomenon of the diversity of colour, language and race has been explained in the Qur'ān as a sign of God's omnipotence and omniscience:

> Of His Signs is the creation of Heavens and earth, and the diversity of your tongues and colours, surely therein are signs for mankind.[11]

It is little wonder that the concept of human brotherhood should enjoy such prominence in the founding principles and formative years of the first Muslim state and society set up by the Prophet in Madinah. Brotherhood among believers was the solid base of that state and society. The Prophet paired the *Anṣār* and *Muhājirūn* as brothers, to look after one another. This principle of brotherhood, so prominent in the *Ṣaḥīfah* is reaffirmed in this last of the Prophetic public proclamations, the Farewell Address.

7. 'I am Merely a Conveyer'

Perhaps no mortal man has been as much loved and adored as the Prophet Muḥammad has been by Muslims. Yet, at no time in Muslim history was Muḥammad thought of as divine or supernatural in any way. The question of worshipping him thus never arises. Certainly he himself never let any opportunity pass to stress that he was merely a messenger, a mere conveyer of God's message to mankind. In the Farewell Address, he reaffirmed his essential role as a humble servant and conveyer of God's message to mankind.

For this reason, the Prophet never forgot to say, after every major theme of the Farewell Address:

> 'Have I conveyed Your message, O Lord? Bear witness, O Lord!'

8. The Common Ground Between the *Ṣaḥīfah* and the Farewell Address

If the *Ṣaḥīfah* represents that universalist, multi-racial, multi-cultural dimension of the first Muslim society and state, the Farewell proclamation affirms the universal message of Islam to all mankind. And if the *Ṣaḥīfah* represents the ideological, legal foundation of the Muslim *Ummah*, a foundation wide in scope and so far-reaching in its ultimate purposes and objectives, the Farewell Address represents the broad lines of Islamic *Da'wah* (mission) to humanity at large.

The two documents share a common concern for, and emphasize, basic human dignity and basic human rights. Both documents affirm the absolute unity of God and His sole prerogative as the Creator of man and of the heavens and the earth. It is because of the creaturehood of man before God, that man is obliged to worship and to thank Him. God's absolute dominion of the heavens and the earth and all that is in them includes man who is well-advised to pray to Him for help and guidance. Such is the theme of the opening chapter of the Qur'ān – *Al-Fātiḥah*. The *Fātiḥah* has been likened to the Lord's Prayer of the Gospel.

It was also a common theme of both *Ṣaḥīfah* and Farewell Address to stress the sanctity of human life, private property and sexual integrity. The concern for freedom, security and peace in the life of man is an overriding consideration in both documents.

In both documents injustice and aggression are condemned, while equality and fraternity of the human race are emphasized. In the *Ṣaḥīfah*, the Prophet's authority in Madinah was founded on his exemplary role as a just and compassionate statesman. In the Farewell Address, the eternal message of the Qur'ān and the wisdom of the Prophet's *Sunnah* were stressed as the only hope for the deliverance of man from error and falsehood. The war against injustices suffered by humanity, implicit in the themes of the Farewell Address, also serves as a demonstration of the Prophet's role as a dispenser of mercy and compassion to all mankind.

If one of the central objectives of the *Ṣaḥīfah* was to prepare the ground for a final onslaught on the Quraysh, the symbol and fortress of idol-worship, the Farewell Address directed much of Muslim energy and attention to ensure the complete destruction of paganism in Arabia. The warnings against Satan were meant to urge the Muslims not to lay down their ideological weapons in the war against evil and idolatry.

The general direction of the *Ṣaḥīfah* was inward towards Makkah and the Quraysh, the direction of the Farewell Address was outward in the direction of the north, where the power centres of the world at that time were located. But the orientation in both documents is the same – to push the frontiers of Islam forward, to peoples and territories that have so far not heeded the call of Islam to pure, unmixed, uncompromised monotheism.

Notes and References

1. Ibn Hishām called the three parties to the concluding of the *Ṣaḥīfah*, *'Ahl aṣ-Ṣaḥīfah'* – the People of *Ṣaḥīfah*, indicating no doubt that they were the originators of it.
2. *al-Jumu'ah* 62: 2.
3. Ibn Hishām: Part I, p.501 (Arabic, Al-Ḥalabī's version).
4. *Ibid.*, Part II, p.604.
5. Ibn Kathīr, *Al-Bidāyah wa al-Nihāyah*.
6. *al-Ḥujurāt* 49: 13.
7. Bukhārī, 'Kitāb al-Īmān', Vol. I, p.16.
8. *al-Mā'idah* 5: 3.
9. *al-Ḥujurāt* 49: 13.
10. *Ibid.*
11. *ar-Rūm* 30: 22.

CHAPTER 3

The House of the Prophet Muḥammad
(Some Aspects of His Private Life)

A. PROLOGUE

This attempt to look into the private life of the Prophet Muḥammad, *ṣallā Allāhu 'alayhi wa sallam,* has been prompted in part by the desire to examine it as the major source of inspiration and influence that it has been for countless generations of Muslims including the present. But it is also motivated by one of the most explosive crises of modern life, the threat to the institution of the family. The collapse of family life is most certainly the one permanent factor behind every malaise or malfunction of modern life. With thousands of young men and women who, having grown up experiencing no love, care, tenderness or protection, are aimlessly roaming the streets of big cosmopolitan cities, creating disorder, destruction and violence, what can anyone foresee if the trend is not soon reversed, but the collapse of human civilization.

There were many Prophets who had very full family lives – the Prophets David and Soloman are reported to have had hundreds of wives – and there were Prophets who never had any intimate relations with women – Prophets like Jesus, and John who preceded him. From the latter, nothing can be learned, in regard to family life. The Prophet Muḥammad belonged to the former category, but with a difference. First, the number of women with whom he had intimate relations were far fewer than his Jewish counterparts. Second, and more significant, is the wealth of detailed information we possess of every aspect of his private life. It is rightly said that he is the one Prophet born in the full light of history – precisely because of the comprehensive and authentic record of his life that has been preserved for us.

With the manifest breakdown of traditional Western patterns of the family, in particular that marriage is an eternal, irrevocable bond between two individuals, a man and a woman, there is reason to explore alternative patterns. If the West has failed so far to tap the resources afforded by the example of the private life of the Prophet Muḥammad, it is because no serious and open-minded effort has ever been made to read correctly the events and details of that life. A leading Islamist[1] failed to learn anything from the private life of the Prophet: 'The world has paid scant attention to Muḥammad as a moral exemplar. Yet . . . it will sooner or later have to consider seriously whether from the life of Muḥammad any principles are to be learned which will contribute to the moral development of mankind. To this question, no final answer has yet been given . . . What has been said so far by Muslims in support of their claims for Muḥammad is but a preliminary statement and has convinced few non-Muslims . . . will they at least be able to show that Muḥammad's life is one possible exemplification of the ideal for all humanity? . . .

'My personal view is that Muslims are unlikely to be successful in their attempt to influence world opinion, at least in the sphere of morals.'[2]

This essay does not attempt a comprehensive treatment of the subject. What is attempted here is a more restricted study of some specific aspects of central importance and interest in the Prophet's private life, in particular the salient facts of his several marriages with special reference to the role played by 'Ā'ishah, the most beloved of his wives, as well as the misgivings which non-Muslim writers have expressed in regard to his marriage to Zaynab bint Jaḥsh. However some attention will be given to wider issues of his private life such as the assemblies at his private residence of women and men seeking knowledge, moral guidance and social as well as spiritual comfort. Also an attempt will be made to work out a synoptic view of the Prophet's daily life at home and the kind of activities he indulged in, once he returned to his house. From all of that it is hoped that a more authentic and factual picture of his private life will emerge and prove substantially different from that still persisting image in the West of the Arabian Prophet, indulging in a life of lust and sensuality. Some unwitting writers even use the term *harem*[3] from the late 'Abbāsid and Ottoman ages to refer to the Prophet's wives, unaware (perhaps wilfully) of the strict discipline and austerity of the life of the family of Muḥammad.

B. THE THREE MAJOR DIVISIONS OF HIS DAY

Ordinary men generally retire to their private residence for rest and pleasure but the Prophet never knew leisure of that sort. His work did not end with his coming home – only a new order of engagements and activities commenced which filled most of his private time. The jurists generally refer to three phases of his private life as follows:

(1) The family phase, where he received his wives and fulfilled his duties as husband, father and father-in-law. Every day, he received all his wives in private audience, in the late afternoon, though of course he spent the night and some part of the day with one of them, by rotation.

(2) A personal phase, which he took for himself. But it was during this time that he received an endless flow of guests and visitors – some attracted no doubt, by the grace of his noble company, others seeking religious and moral guidance, still others with needs, demands, problems and disputes. Thus the Prophet had to fulfil a variety of highly diversified roles, ranging from that of gracious host, munificent giver, teacher, arbiter, governor and judge, as well as friend and companion.

(3) The spiritual phase, normally placed towards the last third of the night, was perhaps the most important of his private life. Ever since he received his initial revelation at Ḥirā, Allah commanded him to observe and perform *qiyām al-layl* (night vigil in prayer). *Qiyām al-layl* was prescribed as the method of self-preparation for the projected role of

the Messenger of God, which the Prophet was destined to fulfil in the remaining portion of his life:

> O you wrapped in your mantle! Observe vigil (in prayer), the whole night excepting a little thereof, perhaps its half or decrease a little of it, or increase a little thereof and recite the Qur'ān a good recitation. We are going to reveal to you a weighty message . . .[4]

No description of the private life of the Prophet can be adequate without taking into consideration all three of these phases of his day. A gross distortion results if an account disregards the first and the last phases. This is precisely what we find in numerous accounts of that life made by non-Muslim Islamists. Yet even in their discussion of the first phase, the Islamists more often than not fail miserably to tackle all the issues involved, the true facts never emerge through their singular approach. What is disquieting, indeed disgraceful, about their practice in this respect is that they use whatever scant and incomplete account they find to make unjust and unwarranted generalizations and judgements about the character of the Prophet.

To redress such a situation, a more factual and balanced account of his private life is called for. The present study attempts, briefly, to provide that need.[5] Certain practical considerations make it impossible to give a fuller, more detailed study of the vast and varied aspects of the private life of the Prophet Muḥammad.

C. THE FIRST PART: THE FAMILY OF THE PROPHET

Islamists among Orientalists have been critical of the Prophet's private life on three accounts:

(i) that his marriages were quite numerous.
(ii) that he married 'Ā'ishah when she was only ten or eleven years old.
(iii) that he married Zaynab bint Jaḥsh, a divorcee of his adopted son, Zayd Ibn Ḥārithah.

It is alleged by some critics that his marriage to Zaynab was incestuous, and that he became infatuated with her beauty whilst she was still married to Zayd.

1. The Several Marriages of the Prophet

As to the several marriages of the Prophet, polygamy was customary among the Arabs, and the Semitic peoples in general in those times. Among many Prophets and Apostles of ancient tribes of Israelites and Hebrews, polygamous marriages were widespread. Some of those Prophets of the Old Testaments were reported to have married tens of wives. However, an examination of the circumstances and manner in which the Prophet practised polygamy shows that sexual appetite was never the dominant factor.

(a) With the exception of 'Ā'ishah, all the women whom he married were widows or divorcees.

(b) A number of those women were quite advanced in age, e.g.:

 (i) Sawdah bint Zam'ah whom he married after the death of his celebrated first wife, Khadījah.

 (ii) Umm Salamah, Hind bint Abī Umayyah al-Makhzūmiyah.

 (iii) Zaynab bint Khuzaymah, twice married and war widowed before the Prophet married her. She was known for her piety and love of charity, a quality which won her the honorary title *Umm al-Masākīn* (the Mother of the Poor).

 (iv) The rest of his wives, with few exceptions, were typically middle aged women, such as Ramlah bint Abī Sufyān, Ḥafṣah bint 'Umar ibn al-Khaṭṭāb, Maymūnah bint al-Ḥārith (twice married before).

(c) A number of the Prophet's marriages were obviously prompted by motives of compassion, notably:

 (i) Sawdah bint Zam'ah, who migrated twice to Abyssinia, and whose husband was one of the pioneering Muslims who, after his return from Abyssinia, died in Makkah. Marrying her was a way of honouring her sacrifice, and early *Hijrah* to Abyssinia. It was also a way of consoling and providing for her.

(ii) Similar considerations led to his marriage to Ramlah, the daughter of Abū Sufyān, the arch enemy of the Prophet and the leader of the Quraysh opposition. Ramlah became a Muslim, despite the attitude of her father and her family, and suffered a great deal in consequence. Then whilst still in Abyssinia, her husband who was a Christian before he converted to Islam, reverted to Christianity, divorced her and deserted her with his little baby in her arms. Thus she was indeed in a very difficult situation living out these moments in a strange land, thousands of miles from Makkah.

(iii) Maymūnah gave herself to the Prophet and wished to be his wife. He honoured her wish, accepting her as a wife, and she was devoted to him.

(iv) The Prophet married Ṣafiyah bint Ḥuyay ibn al-Akhṭab, out of sympathy for her plight, her Jewish father having been killed in the Khaybar battle. She had no one to care for her.

(v) The Prophet married Ḥafṣah b. 'Umar out of regard for her father, who was his aide and minister and enjoyed his love and appreciation for services rendered to the cause of Islam. Umm al-Mu'minīn Ḥafṣah was not particularly young or attractive. But she was deeply religious, steadfast in prayer and fasting. When she became a widow, her father, 'Umar ibn al-Khaṭṭāb, tried unsuccessfully to persuade some of his close friends and brothers in Islam to marry her. The noble-hearted Prophet was moved by the anguish of his close aide and friend 'Umar and offered to marry her himself. Later on, unable to bear her and her proneness to intrigue and excessive jealousy, the Prophet divorced her. But the Archangel Gabriel came with a divine command ordering the Prophet to reinstate her on account of her piety and devotion to God.[6] The Prophet was further informed that Ḥafṣah was indeed one of his wives in paradise. Ḥafṣah lived to play a vital role in the history of Islam. She kept and painstakingly looked after the stock of holy scrolls and relics on which the Qur'ān was inscribed during the Prophet's lifetime.

(vi) Other marriages of the Prophet, also prompted by compassionate considerations include his marriage to Umm Salamah (Hind bint Abī Umayyah al-Makhzūmiyah). Her husband, Abū Salamah of Banū Makhzūm, not only undertook the two *Hijrah* to Abyssinia, but was seriously wounded in the Battle of Uḥud, and died a martyr a month afterwards. The Prophet in his fatherly compassion wanted, as well as to honour her, to provide for her and her numerous children. At first, she politely declined his marriage offer, apologizing that she would be too senior to him, being so advanced in age, and with so many children.[7] As, however, the Prophet insisted, the marriage did take place.

2. Strengthening Bonds of Affection and Solidarity

At the time of the Prophet, tribal loyalties counted a great deal in Arabian society. The whole system of defence, security and safety depended upon those tribal alliances and relations of *Jiwār* (protection). A person's safety and security depended crucially on whether or not he was in the protection *(jiwār)* of some powerful chief or prominent personality. Marriage was one of the most effective ways in which this allegiance was secured. The manner in which the Prophet made use of this fact is strongly indicative not only of his unusual ability as a leader, but also of his consummate knowledge of his people and their social traditions. His marriage to 'Ā'ishah bint Abū Bakr (his first lieutenant or aide) and to Ḥafṣah bint 'Umar ibn al-Khaṭṭāb (his second lieutenant) might be regarded as having political overtones, in the sense that they were meant to further consolidate his already very close relations with these two most important of his Companions and helpers. Yet more overtly political was his marriage to Juwayrīyah bint al-Ḥārith of Banū al-Muṣṭaliq. Having inflicted a crushing defeat upon them, the Prophet quickly moved to alleviate some of their acute sense of humiliation. Juwayrīyah was the daughter of their most respected chief and, by taking her as a wife, their status was transformed overnight. They became the in-laws of the Prophet and it was not becoming to class them as war captives, as would have been the case but for the Prophet's marriage to Juwayrīyah.[8] Although Juwayrīyah is reported to have been good-looking, this was not the main factor in the Prophet's decision to marry her. More important to him and to his cause of spreading Islam and of consolidating its political base, was to maintain the support of the powerful tribe of Khuzā'ah, who were important allies of the Muslims, and of whom the Banū al-Muṣṭaliq were a clan. Also the Banū al-Muṣṭaliq were living within easy reach of Madinah, and their friendship was of strategic military importance. If the conflict with them had been allowed to develop into a blood feud, it might have endangered the strategically important alliance with Khuzā'ah as a whole.

That the Prophet, *ṣallā Allāhu 'alayhi wa sallam,* sought, knowing the circumstances and traditions of his people, to strengthen the cause of Islam through bonds of marriage, is further demonstrated by the fact that he gave two of his daughters in marriage to 'Uthmān ibn 'Affān, his third successor, and to 'Alī ibn Abī Ṭālib.

In summing up, it may be said that the only 'ordinary' marriage the Prophet ever enjoyed was that with Khadījah. All his other marriages were urged by some or other necessities. Even his marriage to 'Ā'ishah was motivated by dreams which were shown to him in two or three nights. In those dreams, he saw the Archangel Gabriel descending with her picture and saying: 'This is your wife, in this life and in the world to come. Marry her, because she has some qualities of Khadījah.'[9] Since 'Ā'ishah was but a little girl, the Prophet said to himself: 'If those dreams were from God, this marriage would take place.' Because of her tender age, 'Ā'ishah could not have been an object of sexual desire for the Prophet. But destiny was planning a very great role for her in the history of Islam, as we shall see later.

The charge that the Prophet entered into his several marriages to indulge his sexual appetite has no justification at all. If the Prophet was possessed of such an appetite, he would not have confined himself to just one wife for the best part of his youth. While Khadījah lived, though she was fifteen years his senior, the Prophet would not have married again. He remained with her for more than twenty years and cherished her memory all his life.

Nothing in the life of the Prophet before the *Hijrah* suggests that he led a life of sexual indulgence. If anything, the opposite is true. Had it been the case that he was sexually overactive, this would have become more apparent in his early manhood, not after he had passed the age of fifty. Any honest, objective commentator must then seek other reasons than sexual appetite for the Prophet's several marriages. The reasons are not hard to find. Marriage bonds were used by the Prophet to improve and strengthen his relationships with his people; by using this means which was familiar to them, it was possible for that message to be heard by every clan and tribe in the vast Arabian peninsula. The bonds of marriage helped also to consolidate his social and political position in Madinah. And again, some of his marriages were the means the Prophet used to accommodate and provide for families which had lost their providers because of either *Hijrah*(s) or of *Jihād* wars. The argument that self-indulgence was the motive behind these marriages is plainly (aside from being false and disgraceful) absurd and preposterous.

3. The Prophet's Marriage to 'Ā'ishah

Certain non-Muslim critics of the Prophet have also made too much of the Prophet's marriage to 'Ā'ishah at the tender age of ten or eleven years. In the Arabian context of that time, such early marriages were, for both sexes, normal. It was a simple society and the normal functions of marrying and producing children were given a much higher priority than public or vocational careers, if any form of these can be said to have existed at that time. Moreover, in hot climates, both sexes mature very early. Even today, in rural areas of that region, girls often marry at between ten and fifteen years old, young men at between fifteen and twenty years old.

When the Muslims migrated to Madinah, many of the *Muhājirūn,* many of them in middle age, got married to young virgin girls. Abū Bakr, 'Abd ar-Raḥmān ibn 'Awf, 'Umar ibn al-Khaṭṭāb and many others married into their hosts' families in Madinah, although they were all previously married with one or more wives. At an advanced age, and during his reign, 'Umar ibn al-Khaṭṭāb got married to Umm Kulthūm bint 'Alī ibn Abī Ṭālib, who was quite young.[10] It is worth remembering that neither the marriage of the Prophet to youthful 'Ā'ishah, or his other subsequent marriages, drew any condemnation or criticism from his many vigilant enemies within the city or beyond it, among the Quraysh. The absence of any such criticism strongly suggests that polygamy and marriage to girls in their early teens were not out of the ordinary. However, 'Ā'ishah herself was quite a unique personality destined to play a unique and vital role in the history of Islam. She was exceptionally attractive and graceful, affectionate and of radiant countenance, but her greatest endowments were her quick wits and a phenomenal memory. From her father aṣ-Ṣiddīq, she inherited a quiet strength and confident attitude. From his learning, she acquired a good knowledge of the history, the language, the poetry and the lineage of Arabia. Of relatively well-to-do background, she was brought up dignified and charity-loving. All these character traits combined to make her a most engaging and intriguing personality. Perhaps no young girl of the Quraysh was more qualified than her to occupy the role of the wife and partner of a Prophet and a statesman. We would even venture to say that she had no equal in either of the two major cities of Arabia, Makkah and Yathrib.

According to the most reliable sources, the Prophet married her when she was nine or ten, and died when she was nineteen or twenty years old. Had the marriage been later, she would have had only three or four years in his company – hardly enough time to equip her for the role of scholar and learned jurist she played so capably in the history of Islam. The Prophet used to direct Muslims to make use of her learned erudition, saying:

> 'Take half your religion from this *Ḥumayrā'* (red-faced lady).'

The tasks of learning the Qur'ān, its interpretation, the *Sunnah* of the Prophet, and the intricate, complex issues of Islamic jurisprudence and law, are so exacting that only a person with her extraordinary intellectual abilities could have been equal to them.

Another fact may also be recalled: before the Prophet showed interest in her, she was engaged to Jubayr, son of al-Muṭ'im ibn 'Adī. A delay on the part of the Prophet might have meant her marrying Jubayr.

The years she spent in the house of the Prophet were just sufficient for her to master the sciences and disciplines that she did master. She is reported to have narrated more than two thousand of the Prophet's sayings *(aḥādīth),* and is therefore one of the most widely quoted persons on the sayings of the Prophet.

Imām az-Zuhrī of *at-Tābi'ūn* said that 'Ā'ishah was the most learned among the Muslims – senior and learned Companions of the Prophet consulted her. 'Urwah ibn az-Zubayr[11] said that 'Ā'ishah was the most scholarly person in the sciences of the Qur'ān, poetry, *fiqh,* medicine, history of the Arabs, their genealogy, and was most competent in distinguishing between *ḥalāl* and *ḥarām.* She ranked, with 'Abdullāh ibn 'Abbās, 'Alī ibn Abī Ṭālib, 'Umar ibn al-Khaṭṭāb and ʻAbdullāh ibn Masʻūd, among the five most learned Muslim Companions of the Prophet.

Later on, ʻĀ'ishah played a major role in politics and war. But her most important role was always that of a jurist and teacher of Islam. In particular, Muslim women learned a great deal from her.

Difficult circumstances tested and proved her strength of mind and character. Not only did she participate in many military expeditions, accompanying the Prophet, but she came through unshaken from the affair of the *Ifk*[12] when her chastity was questioned. ʻĀ'ishah's innocence was revealed in a Qur'ānic revelation, whence her title *al-Mubarra'ah* (the acquitted one) and *aṣ-Ṣiddīqah.* After God revealed her innocence, her mother told her to thank the Prophet. But she said:

> 'Oh no, by God, I am not thanking anyone, except God the Almighty Alone!'

Before her innocence was revealed, she had refused to be questioned by the Prophet, saying:

> 'What am I to say? If I told you that I committed what I did not commit, you would believe me, but if I denied it, you would not believe me. I shall only say to you, what Yaʻqūb, the father of Yūsuf said: lovely patience, and God is the One whose help is to be sought in relation to your allegations.'

These and many similar episodes help to demonstrate her exceptional courage and strength.

Thus in countless ways, she was the most perfect partner of the Prophet. No wonder that, after Khadījah, the Prophet loved her so dearly and favoured her over all his wives. Muslim sources, especially Ibn Hishām and Ibn Saʻd[13] asserted that she was chosen by God to be the wife of the Prophet. Imām Bukhārī[14] reported that twice the Archangel Gabriel showed him the image of ʻĀ'ishah and told him that she was his wife in this world as well as in the next world.

4. The Prophet's Marriage to Zaynab bint Jaḥsh

Among the most appalling of distortions is the charge of incest made by certain critics because of the Prophet's marriage to Zaynab bint Jaḥsh, who had been married to Zayd ibn Ḥārithah, his adopted son. Formerly, Zayd used to be called Zayd ibn Muḥammad. The Qur'ān outlawed this practice, commanding the believers to call their adopted sons by the names of their natural fathers. Zaynab, a cousin of the Prophet, was closely known to him and it was on the insistence and the initiative of the Prophet that she reluctantly agreed to marry Zayd. When life became untenable between them, apparently on account of Zaynab's feeling of superiority over Zayd, a former slave, they were divorced. The Prophet was then commanded by the Qur'ān to marry her, so as to abrogate an outmoded custom that fathers of adopted sons may not marry the divorcees of their adopted sons.

Critics have dramatized the Prophet's marriage to Zaynab in the most obnoxious way. As if he had never seen her before, totally oblivious of the fact that she was his near cousin, the Prophet is said to have fallen in love with Zaynab when he chanced to see her, scantily dressed, during a visit to Zayd's home. That he subsequently married her, is taken by them as a substantiation of their romance hypothesis. Thus those critics would have us believe that the Prophet who had been used to seeing Zaynab all her life and since she was a child, was suddenly so smitten with love, as a result of a passing glimpse, that he had to marry her.

From the Muslim point of view,[15] the whole affair was divinely ordained. The Qur'ān itself supports this view. In a noble revelation, directly referring to the episode of Zaynab, God Almighty said:

> 'When you say to him, upon whom Allah has bestowed His favours, and you have also favoured, keep your wife to yourself; and fear Allah. And you conceal in your heart what Allah is to make public, and you fear the people but Allah is more worthy to be feared by you. And after Zayd had ceased (relations) with her (by divorcing her) we gave her to you in marriage, so that there may be no sin for the believers, in respect of

> (marrying the former) wives of their adopted sons, after the latter have ceased (relations) with them.'[16]

The issue of Zaynab, having been decisively ruled by the Qur'ān, never raised any further interest or controversy in Muslim circles, ancient as well as modern. The marriage was ordered by God, to abrogate an old custom. The Prophet hesitated and failed to act, fearing the gossip of the city. Then the Qur'ānic revelation intervened disclosing his hesitation unapprovingly, and the marriage had to go through.

D. THE SECOND PART: THE PROPHET'S FREE TIME

The Prophet's private time was mainly in the early evening and the first hours of the night. But he also used to retire to his home between the prayers and in the afternoon, between the noon *(Ẓuhr)* and mid-afternoon prayers *(al-'Aṣr)*. Those were the times when he received his visitors and Companions, as well as visiting others. The Prophet's private apartments were focal points of social activity, informal lessons and gatherings. Muslims came to his home to see him, talk to him and enjoy the congenial company of the most pleasant of all men. They might chance to have a question, or a problem, or might desire to share a meal with him. Sharing meals together was a widespread practice among Muslims of the Prophet's time. The Prophet himself encouraged it, both by his own example as well as by his explicit exhortations. The Prophet said:

> 'Do not turn your homes into graves. But make them *Qiblahs* (places to which people look and turn).'

Homes were meant to be for vibrant, happy living. The Muslims were directed to pray in their homes and receive guests and visitors there. Many a night, the Prophet insisted on sharing his meagre meal with poor Muslims, in particular he often insisted on inviting to his home the people of *aṣ-Ṣuffah*, who were poor and living in the mosque, devoted to the study and teaching of the Qur'ān. They were also part of a permanent *jihād* contingent, always the first to answer the call to *Jihād.* The Prophet took it upon himself to support them as much as he could. He used to visit his Companions and accept their invitations to share a meal. He never discriminated between them, accepting invitations from women as well as from slaves.

When receiving Muslims in his home, the Prophet would take it upon himself to wait upon, serve and entertain them, though there was nothing they would have loved to do more than serve the Messenger of Allah. He would be the last to drink and he would eat with them. He sat amongst them and hated to be distinguished or privileged. His manners were not those of kings or princes, but those of a Prophet and a Messenger of God. The Prophet would take great care not to offend his Companions, nor bring up topics uncongenial to them or that might cause embarrassment to them. Even his sermons and lessons were carefully planned – concise, and delivered at such times as would make them most easily understood by his Companions. The Companions reported that the Prophet was very selective in the topics of his sermons and the times and durations of those sermons, lest they should become tiring. Also, far from being dictatorial he would consult them and abide by their collective opinions, even if these were against his own.

1. The Prophet's Conduct at Home

'Ā'ishah was once asked what the Prophet's conduct was like when he was at home. She said his conduct was the embodiment of the manners prescribed by the Qur'ān *(Kāna Khuluquhū al-Qur'ān).* 'Ā'ishah described his manners as the best – he was neither loud nor foul in speech. He would never retaliate for personal insults, but would forgive and forget. She said:

> 'He was like one of you at home, yet he was the most lenient and the most generous. His spirits were high at all times, smiling and even joining in laughter at times. He was ready to give a helping hand to his wives in the

ordinary work of the house, sew his own clothes, mend his shoes. In general, he helped in whatever work his wives chanced to be doing. However, when the call to prayer was made, he dropped everything and hurried to the mosque.'[17]

'Ā'ishah said that the Prophet never hit anyone with his hand or in any other way. He was the most gentle of all men to women, children and servants.

The Prophet was so generous even by the standard of his people known to have cultivated this value to the highest degree that, according to Jābir ibn 'Abdullāh he was never asked for anything that he would not grant.

2. 'Umar Cries

One day 'Umar ibn al-Khaṭṭāb came into the house of the Prophet to find him lying on a simple mattress which left its marks on his body. 'Umar started to sob.

> 'Why are you crying, O 'Umar', said the Prophet.
> 'I thought of Caesar and Chosroes sitting on thrones of gold, wearing silk. And you are the messenger of God, yet here you are sitting on this simple mattress.'
> 'O 'Umar', said the Prophet, 'are you not satisfied that they have this world and we have the next?'

So simple and austere were his living habits that he went half-hungry most of the time. 'Ā'ishah reported that for three consecutive nights, a fire was not kindled in the homes of the Prophet because there was nothing to be cooked. When asked how they managed, she said they depended on water and dates (the two blacks).

Where is the basis for the image of a self-indulgent, luxury-loving ruler with his 'harem' which some critics of the Prophet have contrived to draw for him?

3. Dispute in the House of the Prophet

So austere was the life-style of the Prophet that his wives on one occasion could not contain their disquiet. Seeing that funds were not lacking in the Muslim treasury, they demanded some amenities and some relatively luxurious items. The Prophet refused, saying that he had consciously chosen an austere way of life. Whether there was money in the treasury or not was irrelevant to this choice. When his wives insisted on their demands for an easier life, the Prophet was angered. He vowed to keep away from them for a whole month. At the end of that month, he gave them a choice: they might accept his simple life-style and stay as his wives, otherwise they would be granted a divorce. All chose to stay as his wives.

Despite the austere simplicity of his life, the Prophet's homes were by no means unhappy or devoid of pleasure and delight. It is a great tribute to the personality of the Prophet that those homes, lacking any comfort or even abundance of food, were yet full of love and happiness. The Muslims converged on them in large numbers and stayed for so long that the Qur'ān had to remind them, more than once, that it was not befitting or polite to deny their Prophet a little rest and quiet at home. In particular, a group of the Companions overstayed their visit on the day of his marriage to Zaynab bint Jaḥsh. The Prophet was too polite to make them feel that he and his bride were inconvenienced by their long stay in the one-room[18] apartment of Zaynab. However, Qur'ānic verses were revealed and those Muslims were duly educated about the etiquette of visiting the Prophet:

> O you who believe! Enter not the residences of the Prophet for a meal without waiting for the appropriate time, unless permission be granted to you. But if you are invited enter, and when your meal is ended then disperse. Linger not for conversation. Lo! That would cause inconvenience for the Prophet and he would be too shy from you. But Allah is not shy of the truth.[19]

It is indeed a great credit to the Prophet's person that despite the poverty of available means in his environment, he managed to lead a noble, rich and happy life, devoted to the service of God Almighty and at the same time seeking to express the highest ideals of morality and refined conduct in his relations with others. That the life-style of the Prophet at home was not that of a king was attested by 'Adī ibn Ḥātim aṭ-Ṭā'ī (a legend for generosity) according to Ibn Hishām. After returning from his exile in Syria, he met the Prophet in Madinah. Whilst walking with him in Madinah, an old Muslim woman intercepted the Prophet in the middle of the road. The Prophet stood there talking with her for a long time. 'Adī said: 'I said to myself this is not a king but a noble Prophet.' Again, when they were inside the Prophet's house, the Prophet offered him the only cushion in the room and insisted on sitting beside him on the floor. Again 'Adī was impressed and knew that the man was not a king.

E. THE THIRD PART: DEVOTION TO GOD ALMIGHTY

The Prophet's private day was very long indeed. It did not end until the small hours of the next morning. After he had finished with the first two parts of his day, and got a few hours sleep, he used to get up for night prayer. That would last many hours, occupying fully the last third of the night. The Prophet was commanded by the Qur'ān, in a very early revelation to observe *Qiyām al-Layl* (night vigil in prayer):

> O you! wrapped in your mantle. Keep vigil the night long, save a little, a half thereof, abate a little the rest or add (a little) thereto. And recite the Qur'ān a good recitation. We are assuredly going to reveal to you a weighty message.
>
> Assuredly, night vigil is the most effective way (of self-preparation) and the most suited for fine speech (the recitation of the Qur'ān). During the day you have long business, so remember the name of your Lord, and devote yourself to Him a complete devotion.[20]

Night vigil was thus ordained and made obligatory, at first, so that the Prophet might learn, recite and ponder the message of the Qur'ān. It was the daily spiritual exercise in which he prepared himself for the weighty and most difficult task of confronting the world, of calling humanity to the service of the One, True God, Allah, *subḥānahū wa taʻālā*.

Ever since the Prophet was thus ordered to observe night vigil, he did so, constantly and regularly, every night, irrespective of the circumstances. It was his habit to recite long chapters of the Qur'ān, from memory, in beautiful recitation, whilst standing. It is reported that his night prayer *(Tahajjud)* consisted normally of ten *rak'ahs* (a unit of prayer consisting of standing, reciting a portion of the Qur'ān together with *al-Fātiḥah* (the Opening Chapter), one bowing and two consecutive prostrations). It is also reported that at times, he read the whole of the first two longest chapters of *al-Baqarah* (The Cow) and *Āl 'Imrān* (The House of 'Imrān) in one such *rak'ah*. If he continued at that pace, he could have recited the whole of the Qur'ān in one night. This might very well have been the case, since some later Muslims are alleged to have done the same. The Grand Mahdī of the Sudan was reported to have been in the habit of reciting the whole of the Qur'ān, from memory, in one night. The report, significantly, comes from Nūr ad-Dagm, one of al-Mahdī's teachers, and one of his most outspoken critics.

So long were the Prophet's night prayers, so protracted his night recitations of the Qur'ān, that his feet became swollen from standing so long. 'Ā'ishah lying at his feet pleaded with him passionately:

> 'O Messenger of God. Why do you exert yourself so much, when your Lord has forgiven all your sins?'
>
> 'O 'Ā'ishah, should I not become for that reason His most grateful servant?' replied the Prophet.

F. ROLE OF MUSLIM WOMEN IN THE PROPHET'S SOCIETY

1. **'Ā'ishah**

We have already alluded to the powerful role played by 'Ā'ishah in the life of the Prophet, and her permanent influence in Muslim history. Her major contribution was in the areas of religion and knowledge. She preserved for the *Ummah* a good proportion of the *Ḥikmah* (wisdom) of the Prophet, and in so doing she became one of Islam's leading jurists. Many prominent and learned Companions of the Prophet sought knowledge from her. She not only narrated many *aḥādīth* from the Prophet, but had an excellent grasp of the Qur'ān and its meanings, and, more than perhaps anyone else, kept a record of a great deal of the private life of the Prophet. Her role in society was by no means limited to her intellectual contributions, she witnessed and participated in a number of military expeditions, alongside the Prophet, *ṣallā Allāhu 'alayhi wa sallam.* Prominent among these were the Battle of Uḥud and that of Banū al-Muṣṭaliq. Her steadfastness, endurance and courage during the affair of *Ifk* are an inspiring example for all time. That she should have referred to the example of the Prophet Jacob in his difficult trial, is indicative of her intimate and absorbing encounter with the Qur'ānic wisdom and guidance. 'Ā'ishah's love of charity and her preference for an ascetic life-style cannot but be inspiring and a source of pride to Muslim women of all generations. She shunned the pomp and show of this world – no slight achievement, given the natural instinct, at least among most women, to be adorned.

'Ā'ishah's greatest merit lay in her unfailing, unselfish devotion to the Prophet as a Muslim and as a wife. She was intelligent enough to appreciate the honour and privilege Allah accorded to her in the role of the wife of the Prophet and Mother of the Faithful. When she was confronted with the choice between continuing the life of austere simplicity as the Prophet's wife or a life of luxury and comfort in separation from him, she chose the former unhestitatingly. After the Prophet's death, 'Ā'ishah continued to play a leading role in the society both in the domains of knowledge and politics. In addition to her role as a leading jurist and religious authority, she became a leader of a political faction, following the assassination of the third Caliph, 'Uthmān ibn 'Affān. She called for *Qiṣāṣ* or retribution from the murderers of 'Uthmān, even prior to the settlement of the issue of political succession. Her role in urging the Muslims to demand *Qiṣāṣ* is one of the major controversies in the early history of Islam. More controversial still is the fact that she commanded an army against 'Alī, the venerated cousin of the Prophet and his son-in-law. Some Muslim sources have it that, in her later years, she deeply regretted her role in the matter of demanding retribution from the murderers of 'Uthmān.[21]

However that may be, 'Ā'ishah's presence in the public life of the Muslims throughout the first era of Islam, must be understood for its profound significance for the status of women in Muslim society. In the very nature of things, that presence would have been impossible if an absolute, hard and fast, separation of the two sexes was the dominant norm in that formative age of Islam. That 'Ā'ishah, as wife of the Prophet, was observing the most stringent forms of *Ḥijāb,* made specifically and particularly obligatory for the wives of the Prophet, cannot be doubted. Yet, her major and continual involvement in public affairs was such that it is impossible to suppose that she was rigidly segregated from public life or that it was impermissible or impossible for her to meet and converse with leading figures as well as ordinary Muslim citizens. Nor is it possible to interpret *Ḥijāb* as an absolute wall and barrier between men and women in Islam. The true, original function of *Ḥijāb* is to conceal those features of the woman's body and personality that may provoke infatuation or temptation. *Ḥijāb* cannot be interpreted to mean the total banishment of women from the social sphere in the Muslim society. In practice, the *Ḥijāb* of 'Ā'ishah, the favoured and most cherished wife of the Prophet, and one of the most loved and respected Mothers of the Faithful, did not prevent her from playing the roles of professor, jurist, lawyer-cum-judge, leader of a political party and even a military commander.

How is it possible to reconcile this picture of the role of Muslim women, as embodied and practised by 'Ā'ishah, with later views which totally negate and reject any public or social role for women in the Muslim society? In the opinion of some later jurists, even the voice of women is considered *'awrah* (an obscenity) not to be heard in public. How was it possible for 'Ā'ishah to discharge her role as professor of religion, law, history, and as biographer of the Prophet's life, without having her voice heard in public, even from behind a barrier? This paradox is indicative of the low ebb, to which scholarship of the pre-*Ṣaḥwah* (i.e. pre-Renaissance) period had deteriorated, in Muslim circles.

'Ā'ishah was not an isolated case in that first Muslim society. A careful reading of the lives of Muslim women of the first generation will show that a sizeable number of them distinguished themselves and were very well known in the society at large. Without such knowledge, it would have been inconceivable for early historians such as Ibn Sa'd and Ibn Ḥajjāj to devote whole volumes to the names and careers of hundreds of Muslim women in the first period of Islam. Most intriguing is the abundance of detail and personal information regarding these women. Thus we know not only their names, but also who married whom and the names of their children. In case a woman Companion of the Prophet married more than once, we are given all the names of the husbands and their children. In what follows, we shall give some examples, not meant to be exhaustive by any means, of Muslim women who played significant roles in the social and public life of the early Muslim society of the Prophet and his Rightly-Guided Caliphs.

2. **Other Wives of the Prophet**

In their roles as Mothers of the Believers, the wives of the Prophet continued to be and act, after him, as sources of guidance and inspiration for Muslims. Prominent among them was Ḥafṣah bint 'Umar ibn al-Khaṭṭāb, a model of piety, devotion and high-mindedness. She played a vital part in preserving the scrolls and relics on which the Qur'ān was initially inscribed. Her care and safe-keeping of the Qur'ān verses committed to writing were an integral part of the divine promise to preserve the Qur'ān as the perfect Scripture.

We consider, next, the example of Zaynab bint Khuzaymah. Her active work in looking after the poor and dispossessed earned her the title of *Umm al-Masākīn,* the Mother of the Poor.

Umm Salamah played a significant role in supporting the Prophet and comforting him on the Day of Reconciliation of Ḥudaybīyah (*Ṣulḥ al-Ḥudaybīyah*). These are but a few examples among many others, e.g. the attitude of Ramlah bint Abī Sufyān, when her father then an unbeliever and an enemy of the Prophet, visited her in the house of the Prophet. She did not permit him to sit on the bed of the Prophet. We must also recall the fundamental role played by Khadījah in the Makkan period of Islam.

3. **Nusaybah bint Ka'b (Umm 'Umārah)**

Nusaybah bint Ka'b, an *Anṣārī* woman of the Khazraj of Madinah, defended the Prophet gallantly, during the Battle of Uḥud, at a most critical moment in that battle. She was among the very few who held their ground around the Prophet when the Muslim army was dispersed by the Quraysh charge.

Umm 'Umārah (Nusaybah bint Ka'b) is an excellent example of a Muslim woman who was a pioneer both in accepting Islam and in defending it with all the resources at her command. We must recall, here, that Nusaybah represented the women of Yathrib at the second 'Aqabah Pledge. She must have been a woman of middle age at Uḥud since she was the widow of the celebrated Muslim martyr, 'Āṣim ibn Zayd, and both her sons and her second husband participated with her. Her gallantry and courage were phenomenal; she continued to fight, among less than ten Companions, who managed to hold their ground around the Prophet. She suffered more than twelve wounds, one of which was nearly fatal, being a sword-cut deep in the side of her neck which took more than a year to heal completely. Despite such a wound, her spirit was neither conquered nor even daunted. When, on the following day, the Prophet called upon the Muslims to go out in pursuit of the Quraysh to Ḥamrā' al-Asad, Umm 'Umārah rose to answer that call, but fainted due to the heavy loss of blood from her wound. Later, Umm 'Umārah fought the apostates at Yamāmah and lost her hand in the fighting and sustained major wounds. Moreover, with the Prophet, *ṣallā Allāhu 'alayhi wa sallam,* she witnessed al-Ḥudaybīyah, Khaybar and Ḥunayn.

The Prophet often visited her in her home and took meals there. Sometimes Abū Bakr would accompany him. He promised her and her family his company in Paradise. Ibn Sa'd gives a great deal of information about the character and the family of Umm 'Umārah, a fact that confirms the view that she was a public figure of considerable social eminence.[22]

4. **The Personality and Role of Asmā' bint Abī Bakr**

Asmā' was vital in the success of the *Hijrah,* of the Prophet and her father, helping them to escape the pursuit of the Quraysh. She looked after some part of the business of her husband, az-Zubayr ibn al-'Awwām, who had been rather poor, and was instrumental in increasing his wealth. In much later years, she played an important role in the career of 'Abdullāh ibn az-Zubayr, who challenged the Umayyads and resisted their oppression. 'Abdullāh ibn az-Zubayr managed to liberate al-Ḥijāz but was later defeated and killed by al-Ḥajjāj ath-Thaqafī.

5. **Khawlah bint Tha'labah (The Disputant)**

Khawlah came to see the Prophet about her difficulty with her husband who vowed not to touch her, i.e. not to have sexual relations with her. Twice the Prophet said that she ought to be separated from him. But she was not convinced, and continued to dispute with the Prophet, until Allah revealed *Sūrah al-Mujādalah,* on her case, ruling that no divorce or separation was incumbent upon her. The story is significant for its social and political implications. It says a great deal about the relations that obtained between the Prophet and ordinary Muslims. It says a great deal too about the position of Muslim women in early Islam, the kind of social, intellectual and religious freedom, and the civil rights they used to enjoy. No ordinary woman could even have dreamed of getting access to the rulers of the Roman or Persian empires. Nor could their personal, private problems ever have become a public concern of the highest order, reaching not only the Prophet as Messenger of Allah and as statesman, but also the Qur'ān itself, which obviously considered her case an important social and legal case, meriting the revelation of a special *sūrah* to deal with it.

6. Umm Sulaim bint Milḥān ibn Ḥarām

Umm Sulaim bint Milḥān ibn Ḥarām, a prominent member of Banū an-Najjār, was closely associated with the Prophet's house and family. The Prophet, *ṣallā Allāhu 'alayhi wa sallam,* used to visit her in her house, have meals there and sometimes spent his mid-noon resting period *(waqt al-Qaylūlah)* in her house. She cannot have been very advanced in age as she was pregnant at the time of the Battle of Ḥunayn. She was a staunch Muslim fighter. She witnessed Uḥud, where she was seen carrying a knife, and also Ḥunayn, when she also participated in the battle, and was seen with a knife tied to her waist. When questioned about the knife, in the presence of the Prophet, *ṣallā Allāhu 'alayhi wa sallam,* she replied that she might have to defend herself, if one of the *Mushrikīn* (polytheists) tried to harm her. The Prophet only smiled on hearing her reply and commented that Allah, *subḥānahū wa ta'ālā,* had taken care of that.

Umm Sulaim had indeed an exceptionally strong personality, a clear-cut and orderly mind, and the determination and will of a man. This comes out clearly in the consummate portrayal which Ibn Sa'd[23] gives of her character. Firstly, she accepted the call of Islam independently of her husband who was, it would seem, unaware of the upheaval taking place around him in Yathrib as a result of the arrival of the Prophet there. She succeeded in converting him to Islam. When he was killed soon afterwards, she cherished his memory, refusing remarriage until their son, Anas ibn Mālik, had passed the age of breast-feeding. When she was approached with a marriage proposal from Abū Ṭalḥah (a *Mushrik*) she demanded that he convert to Islam, if he desired to marry her. Abū Ṭalḥah did so and they got married.

A much circulated story about Umm Sulaim is quite indicative of her high-mindedness and strongly independent personality. One of her children from Abū Ṭalḥah died whilst he was away from the house. When he came back, she did not break the news to him, until she had provided him his dinner and had sexual intercourse with him. The sources do not explain why she acted in this unusual way. We can only speculate. Perhaps he had been away for a long time and she knew best what he needed at that time. Or perhaps she was just being patient and behaving as a true Muslim believer should behave in such circumstances, namely to show *iḥtisāb* – that whatever a person has is Allah's trust and He may take it back whenever He desires. This is the meaning of *Innā lillāhi wa innā ilayhi rāji'ūn* – 'We are Allah's creatures and unto Him we return.' The Prophet, *ṣallā Allāhu 'alayhi wa sallam,* has advised Muslims that these are the words, in such circumstances, if they desire Allah's compensation for the disasters and mishaps that befall them. They must reconcile themselves to total acceptance and submission to the will of Allah and His decree.

Umm Sulaim seems to have been related to the Prophet in a very special way, much as an aide or a special functionary or ambassador would relate. He once visited her and prayed in her house two voluntary *rak'ahs.* He said:

'O Umm Sulaim, if you perform the obligatory *ṣalāt,* say: *Subḥān Allāh* (ten times), *Alḥamduli-llāh* (ten times), *Allāhu Akbar* (ten times). Then ask Allah whatever you desire. It will be said to you: Yes, yes, yes.'

Anas ibn Mālik, the personal attendant of the Prophet, narrated that the Prophet used not to enter the house of any woman other than his wives except that of Umm Sulaim. The Companions asked him about this. He said:

> 'I feel pity and compassion for her, because her own brother was killed fighting with me.'

Umm Sulaim narrated that the Prophet used to sleep in the afternoon in her house. She used to lay out a rug for him to lie on. As the Prophet used to perspire heavily, she would scoop the perspiration from his body and mix it with her perfume. One day as he was sleeping, and she was scooping the perspiration from his side, he woke up, and said:

> 'What are you doing, O Umm Sulaim?'
> 'I am scooping up this *barakah* which is oozing from you.'

Anas ibn Mālik narrated that one time the Prophet, *Ṣallā Allāhu 'alayhi wa sallam,* came to visit Umm Sulaim. She brought him dates and cooked butter. He said:

'Take it back to the pot, because I am fasting.'

Then he stood to pray. After he finished praying, he made good invocations for the house of Umm Sulaim. Umm Sulaim then said:

'O Messenger of Allah, I have a special request.'
'What is it?' said the Messenger of Allah.
'It is your servant Anas', Umm Sulaim said.

The Prophet did not leave anything of the good of this world or that of the next, which he did not include in his *du'ā'* (prayer) for us. Then he prayed for Anas, saying:

'O Lord, give him wealth, and offspring and bless that which You give him.'

Anas became the wealthiest of the *Anṣār,* and in al-Basrah, more than a hundred and twenty-nine of his descendants were buried, when al-Ḥajjāj went there, narrated Ibn Sa'd.

The Messenger of Allah, said that he heard the sound of the feet of Umm Sulaim in Paradise, moving in front of him.

When Umm Sulaim had a baby by Abū Ṭalḥah, she sent him to the Prophet who fed him some fresh dates which he softened by chewing before he placed them in the baby's mouth.

7. **Umm Ḥarām bint Milḥān (Sister of Umm Sulaim)**

Umm Ḥarām was the sister of Umm Sulaim, an *Anṣārī* from Banū an-Najjār, the relatives of the Prophet's mother.

Said Umm Ḥarām:

The Prophet came to visit us. He fell asleep whilst in our house (noon resting time).
Then he woke up, laughing. I said: 'Why are you laughing O Messenger of Allah?'
The Prophet said: 'It is some people of my *Ummah* riding the open sea as kings on their thrones.'
I said: 'O Messenger of Allah, pray to Allah so that I will be one of them.'
'You are one of them', said the Messenger of Allah.

Umm Ḥarām sailed with the Muslim army which invaded Cyprus, during the reign of Mu'āwiyah ibn Sufyān. She is buried in Cyprus.

8. The Prophet Visits a Bride

According to Ibn Sa'd, the Prophet, *ṣallā Allāhu 'alayhi wa sallam*, visited ar-Rubayyi' bint al-Mu'awwidh ibn 'Afrā' on the day of her wedding to Iyās ibn al-Bukayr. He sat in her room while two of her maidens were singing and beating their drums and mentioning the names of her ancestors. They were saying in reference to the visiting Prophet:

> 'We have a Prophet amongst us who knows what is going to happen tomorrow.'

Ar-Rubayyi' said that the Prophet, *ṣallā Allāhu 'alayhi wa sallam*, interrupted them at that point and said: 'As to this, do not say it.'

That was a social visit of a very special nature. If the version of Ibn Sa'd at issue here is substantiated, it has an important bearing on the topic of the kinds and degree of mixing between the two sexes permissible in Islam.

9. Other Muslim Women Whom the Prophet Visited

Among the Muslim women whom the Prophet visited was Umm 'Aṭīyah al-Anṣāriyah. She witnessed seven military expeditions with the Prophet. The Prophet, *ṣallā Allāhu 'alayhi wa sallam*, used to visit her and spend his mid-day rest period in her house.

The Prophet, *ṣallā Allāhu 'alayhi wa sallam*, also used to visit Umm Waraqah whom he used to call ash-Shahīdah. She was called ash-Shahīdah because she asked the Prophet, *ṣallā Allāhu 'alayhi wa sallam*, to allow her to attend Badr, saying: 'May Allah grant me martyrdom (or *Shahādah*).' The Prophet replied: 'Surely Allah is going to grant you a *Shahādah* (martyrdom).'

From that day, the Prophet, *ṣallā Allāhu 'alayhi wa sallam*, used to call her *ash-Shahīdah* (the martyr). He gave her a special status, permitting her to pray as Imām for her house and for women generally, and permitted her to have a *mu'adhdhin* (one who calls loudly for prayer). She was murdered by her two servants during the reign of 'Umar ibn al-Khaṭṭāb. They were caught and crucified – the first persons to suffer that death in al-Madinah al-Munawwarah. Before she died, 'Umar used to visit her and also called her *ash-Shahīdah,* following the example of the Prophet, *ṣallā Allāhu 'alayhi wa sallam.*

10. The Phenomenon of Women Combatants

Umm Waraqah (al-Anṣāriyah) was not an isolated case amongst Muslim women in general, nor among the *Anṣārī* women in particular. Al-Bādhān narrated on the authority of 'Abdullāh ibn 'Abbās that a woman came to the Prophet, *ṣallā Allāhu 'alayhi wa sallam,* and said: 'I am the delegate of women to you. This *Jihād* was made obligatory upon men. If they win, they are given worldly rewards, and if they are killed then they are alive with their Lord, well-provided for. But we Muslim women, we serve them, what do we get for that?'

Said Ibn 'Abbās, the Prophet, *ṣallā Allāhu 'alayhi wa sallam,* replied: 'Convey to women you meet that obedience to their husband, and the acknowledgement of their favours is equivalent to that *(Jihād)* – only a few of you are doing this.'

Aṭ-Ṭabarānī narrated this same *Ḥadīth,* with minor alterations, in almost the same words in *at-Targhīb* (3/336).

Despite the fact that Islam did not make military *Jihād* obligatory upon Muslim women, yet the practical *Sunnah* of the Prophet who took one of his wives with him on almost every expedition he undertook is indeed very significant. In addition to this, the phenomenon of the *Anṣārī* women fighters, and the fighters of the Ghifārī women, says something about the desirability of some Muslim women participating in military *Jihād* – though this is never obligatory upon them and never a general rule. The story of the participation of the women from Ghifār is reported in the following vivid way by Ibn Isḥāq:

A woman from Banū Ghifār came to the Prophet, *ṣallā*

Allāhu 'alayhi wa sallam, and said: 'We would like to go out to war with you, so that we may treat wounded men and help the Muslims.'

He said: 'With the blessing of Allah (*'alā barakat Allāh*).'

She said: 'We went out with him to Khaybar.'

The woman said: 'I was a young girl. The Prophet made me ride behind him on his she-camel. When the Prophet got down to pray *fajr*, he noticed some blood on his saddle, where I had been riding. It was my first menstruation and I was very shy, so I stuck to my place. But the Prophet said (comfortingly): 'Perhaps you have menstruated. Go and wash up yourself with water with some salt added to it.' The Ghifārī woman said that when they resumed their march, the Prophet, *ṣallā Allāhu 'alayhi wa sallam*, again invited her to ride behind him on his she-camel.

Prominent Names of Women Who Participated in Jihād

These included, among many others:

1. Umm 'Umārah, Nusaybah bint Ka'b.
2. Umm Sulaim bint Milḥān.
3. 'Ā'ishah bint aṣ-Ṣiddīq.
4. Umm Ḥarām bint Milḥān.
5. ar-Rubayyi' bint al-Mu'awwidh.
6. The Ghifārī women.
7. Ṣafiyyah bint 'Abd al-Muṭṭalib.
8. Umm 'Aṭīyah al-Anṣārīyah.
9. Laylā al-Ghifārīyah.
10. Umm Salīṭ.
11. Umm Sharīk.

Asmā' bint Yazīd ibn as-Sakan, the cousin of Sa'd ibn Mu'ādh, is said to have killed nine men of the *mushrikīn* in the Battle of Yarmouk. Ṣafīyah bint 'Abd al-Muṭṭalib, the aunt of the Prophet, was the first Muslim woman to kill a *mushrik*.

The Society which the Prophet, *ṣallā Allāhu 'alayhi wa sallam*, established was well trained to defend itself – men, women and even children, were prepared for its defence.

11. *Ḥijāb* and the Role of Muslim Women

Until the *Ḥijāb* was ordained, during the marriage of the Prophet, *ṣallā Allāhu 'alayhi wa sallam,* to Zaynab bint Jaḥsh, there was a fair measure of mixing between the sexes. After that, the degree of such mixing was drastically curbed, especially with regard to the wives of the Prophet. But even then some degree of mixing between the sexes continued. Muslim women, after *ḥijāb* was enforced, did not withdraw into total segregation from men, nor into total seclusion from public life. They continued to have a public role, although that role was discharged with the *Ḥijāb* fully observed. Thus *Ḥijāb* is not to be understood as forbidding Muslim women to appear in public. *Ḥijāb* is to be understood as constituting the framework of that appearance and as a regulative principle governing it. It is in this sense that *ḥijāb* was apparently understood in the first Muslim society.

Ḥijāb is primarily intended to curb or prevent free and direct mixing of men and women unrelated by a bond sanctioned by *Sharī'ah.* It is meant to prevent or considerably lessen the chances of infatuation between the sexes. It requires the Muslim woman to cover up her bodily charms; further it lessens the chances of prolonged or intimate exposure of the two sexes to each other, where no legal relation exists between them. It is in this context that the *Khalwah* (being in a secluded private place) is prohibited *even* if the *ḥijāb* is worn. It is also in this context that Muslim women are advised not to use too familiar or soft language when addressing strangers. Thus the physical *ḥijāb,* the manner of dress, does not exhaust the whole concept of *ḥijāb.* There seems to be a non-physical component of the *ḥijāb,* which is conveyed in a host of principles and directives regulating the behaviour, manners and conduct of a Muslim woman, when appearing in public. For instance, she is advised not to wear make-up or perfumes when going out in public. Her walk, look, manner and speech must also be consistent with the general intention of the *ḥijāb* as a barrier between the Muslim woman and the outside world.

Ḥijāb must not be viewed in isolation from the general scheme of things under which the whole issue of woman and her role is settled in Islam. The distinctive philosophy of Islam in this respect is that woman is a special partner of man who, though equal to him in human worth and religious responsibility, is to work and live under his leadership *(qiwāmah)*. Moreover, her role is different from that of man. She is, normally, more the mistress of the private aspect of life, the family, the home, the children. The domain of man is typically that of master of the public aspect, as well as being head of the family. Thus, an important meaning of *ḥijāb* is precisely its reinforcement of this distinction between the public and private sides of life in the Islamic organization of things. To undermine *Ḥijāb* is to obliterate this vital distinction and thus undermine the privacy of the Muslim home and family life by removing or weakening its private dimension. Assigning distinctive roles for man and woman in Islam is based on the conviction that their respective natures are different. Man is the stronger partner and therefore entrusted with *Qiwāmah* (general leadership) and with the custody of public life (assuming his role of the bread-winner). That man is generally and by nature more suited to the role of the bread-winner is advanced as one justification for his *Qiwāmah* over woman. A further reason for it is the fact that man has been favoured by God in being created stronger and more endowed with the appropriate progenities and aptitudes than woman. The woman is said to have been created and fashioned from the side (one of the ribs) of Adam. For this reason, she is generally less physical than man, and more prone to emotionalism.

In conclusion, the many narratives that we have presented in this essay demonstrate that the imposition of *ḥijāb,* though it was indeed directed to reinforce the general philosophy of Islam in relation to the status of woman in Muslim society, was never meant to act as a curfew upon the movement of Muslim women. Nor was it meant to work against their having a role in the public life of the Muslim society. The juristic weight of these narratives is enhanced by the fact that most of them also appear in the *aḥādīth* recorded in Bukhārī[24] and Muslim. They cannot therefore be brushed aside on the pretext that they are narratives of the *Sīrah* which rank third in regard to authority and degree of authenticity, after the Qur'ān and the *Ḥadīth*. With the exception of al-Wāqidī's *Kitāb al-Maghāzī,* which is generally agreed to contain some weak *aḥādīth,* the rest of the major *Sīrah* sources such as Ibn Hishām, Ibn Sa'd, aṭ-Ṭabārī and Ibn Kathīr are quite reliable, and are generally further confirmed by *al-Aḥādīth aṣ-Ṣaḥīḥah* of Bukhārī and Muslim. The discrepancies, where such are found, between these trustworthy *Sīrah* sources and the authentic sources of the *Aḥādīth* are neither widespread nor major.[25] This is certainly a great part of Allah's mercy and favours upon the Muslim *Ummah* and an honour for the Prophet of Islam that his life has been perfectly preserved in the most minute detail.

Notes and References

1. 'Islamist' is one of the terms used to designate Western academics specializing in the study of Islam. Other terms used are: Orientalist, which has a wider connotation covering all the Orient, of which Islam is just one aspect; Arabist, which is more useful for referring to those who specialize in the study of Arabic language and literature, including such disciplines as Arabic logic, philosophy and culture. The term 'Islamicist' is sometimes used but rather confusingly since it is also sometimes used to refer to Muslim activists involved in the movement for the revival of Islam in the present age.

2. W. Montgomery Watt, *Muhammad: Prophet and Statesman*. Oxford University Press, 1961, 1964, published as a Galaxy Book in 1974, New York, pp.231ff.

3. The term *Harem* is a more appropriate description of the sexual lives of some late Abbasid and Ottoman Sultans, who led a life of lust, comfort and luxury, enjoying many beautiful women of the city, with wine, singing, luxurious food and expensive perfumes and clothes. No such practice existed in the life of the Prophet Muḥammad nor in the lives of his Companions and successors.

4. *al-Muzzammil* 73: 1–4.

5. This study was originally undertaken in response to an invitation from the Selly Oak College, Birmingham, (U.K.) to read a seminar paper to their graduate students. A comprehensive study of the private life of the Prophet would easily occupy a lifetime and run into many, many volumes.

6. The Archangel Gabriel ordered the Prophet to reinstate Ḥafṣah because she was *ṣawwāmatun wa-qawwāmatun* (i.e. of much prayer and fasting). Ibn Sa'd, *Ṭabaqāt,* Vol. 8, p.84, published by Dār Ṣādir, Bayrout.

7. Afterwards, the Prophet's marriage to Umm Salamah proved a successful and an affectionate one. Umm Salamah had many of the qualities of Khadījah. Like her, she came from a noble Qurayshī family, being of Banū Makhzūm, and like her she was not without a good measure of beauty and radiance, despite her advanced age. Like Khadījah she had an engaging and affectionate character and was an excellent and congenial companion and associate. The Prophet liked staying longer in her apartment, a matter of constant irritation to 'Ā'ishah and Ḥafṣah. *Ibid.*, Vol. 8, pp.86–96.

8. *Ibid.*, Vol. 8, pp.116–20. Juwayrīyah was the daughter of the chief of Banū al-Muṣṭaliq (of Khuzā'ah). She fell captive after the defeat of her people, in the event of al-Muraysī'. She came to the Prophet seeking his help in restoring her freedom. He was moved by her plight and saw an opportunity to reconcile a sub-clan of a noble Arabian tribe, Khuzā'ah, which was, in the main, a faithful ally of the Muslims. Ibn Sa'd reports that as soon as news of the Prophet's marriage to her was known, more than a hundred families of Banū al-Muṣṭaliq were freed from captivity in one day. The in-laws of the Prophet could not be enslaved, the Muslims decided. Thus Juwayrīyah was a great blessing unto her people. When Juwayrīyah came to the Prophet's door she was met by 'Ā'ishah. Seeing her attractive looks, 'Ā'ishah tried her best to send her away without meeting the Prophet. But as the two women stood at the door, the Prophet chanced to look out of the house, and saw the ardent and eager Juwayriyah, refusing to be sent away. 'Ā'ishah later said that she tried to send her away lest the Prophet should see her and desire to marry her. Thus, there is no denying that her beauty was a factor in her marriage to the Prophet. Yet it was by no means the dominant one. He would have married her even if she had been less attractive and less youthful, as he had done many times before.

9. *Ibid.*, Vol. 8, pp. 63, 64ff. Also narrated by Bukhārī and other books of the *Sunnah*.

10. Ibn Sa'd gives the story of 'Umar's marriage to Umm Kulthūm bint 'Alī ibn Abī Ṭālib as follows:

> Said 'Umar: 'Give me Umm Kulthūm, your daughter, in marriage.'
> Replied 'Alī: 'But she is merely a child, O leader of the Faithful.'
> 'Never mind about that', replied 'Umar.

In another version, he is reported to have said: 'I wish to be joined with her, because of her prophetic lineage. I heard the Prophet saying that all lineage will be discontinued in the Hereafter, excepting my lineage, therefore I will to be joined with her.' Ibn Sa'd said that 'Alī ordered her to beautify herself and then gave her a mantle. He said: 'Take it to 'Umar and say to him that he can keep it if he likes it.' When she asked 'Umar about the mantle, he said: 'Blessed are you and your father; tell him that we have accepted and liked his mantle.' Umm Kulthūm was baffled by the behaviour of 'Umar, who showed no interest at all in the mantle, but kept his gaze fixed upon her. She told her father: 'He did not unfold the mantle, and looked at nothing except me.' Ibn Sa'd, Vol. 4, pp.463–4.

11. 'Urwah ibn az-Zubayr was 'Ā'ishah's nephew. He was perhaps the most brilliant of her students, especially in *Ḥadīth* and the interpretation of the Qur'ān.

12. The affair of the *Ifk* developed as the Prophet was coming home from the invasion of Banū al-Muṣṭaliq. 'Ā'ishah was left behind the caravans and had to be escorted home by the Companion Ṣafwān ibn al-Mu'aṭṭal. On seeing her enter Madinah, behind the main body of the Muslim army, being led by Ṣafwān ibn al-Mu'aṭṭal, the tongues of the hypocrites raged with slander. The accusation was very hard on 'Ā'ishah. However, she kept herself confined to herself, weeping out the day, and spending the night in sleepless anxiety and depression. Yet her hope in the mercy and justice of Allah never faded. It was this hope in Allah, this trust in Him, that sustained her and kept her alive.

13. Ibn Sa'd, Vol. 4, pp. 63, 64ff.

14. *Ṣaḥīḥ al-Bukhārī,* 'Bāb thiyāb al-Ḥarīr fi'l-manām'.

15. The episode of Zaynab's marriage to Zayd was designed to demonstrate that the practice of calling adopted sons by the names of their adoptive fathers was not sanctioned by Islam. Adopted sons are not like natural sons and therefore must not be accorded equal legal rights with those of natural sons. In particular, a natural father cannot marry the divorcee of his son. But this relation did not exist between Zayd and the Prophet Muḥammad, *ṣallā Allāhu 'alayhi wa sallam.* Thus came the Qur'ānic direction to the Prophet to marry Zaynab and abolish an unwarranted custom.

16. *al-Aḥzāb* 33: 37.

17. Ibn Sa'd, *Ṭabaqāt,* Vol. 1, pp. 364–6.

18. Zaynab, who was exceptionally attractive, turned towards the wall to evade the looks of the guests who were sharing the small room, which was to be her private apartment. The Prophet himself rose up and went out. Then he came back, but when he found that they were still there, he turned back. He did this more than once. But apparently those guests were not aware of the embarrassment they were causing to the Prophet, *ṣallā Allāhu 'alayhi wa sallam.*

19. *al-Aḥzāb* 33: 53. This is the famous verse in which *Ḥijāb* was ordained for the first time. As the occasion itself demanded, Allah wanted to make a clear distinction between the private and public life of Muslims.

20. *al-Muzzammil* 73: 1–8.

21. Some Muslim history sources (e.g. Imām Aḥmad) have it that 'Ā'ishah as she was marching towards the Battle of al-Jamal, which she commanded against 'Alī ibn Abī Ṭālib, passed through a village of Banū 'Āmir and dogs barked at her. She asked: 'What is the name of this place?' 'This is the well of al-Hawab of Banū 'Āmir.' She was tremendously saddened and distressed when she heard that. She said she was going back

to Madinah. When asked why, she said: 'I heard the Messenger of Allah saying: "How would it be when one of you will be barked at by the dogs of Hawab?" – meaning that would not be a good position.' Ibn Kathīr, Vol. 5–6, p. 211ff. Az-Zubayr ibn al-'Awwām played a major role in persuading her not to turn back, saying that, perhaps she would be able to bring about reconciliation between the Companions of the Prophet and thus end the conflict between 'Alī and Mu'āwiyah.

22. Ibn Sa'd gives many personal details about Umm 'Umārah, such as the different men to whom she was married (Zayd ibn 'Āṣim, Ghaziyyah ibn 'Amr), her sons and daughters from her various husbands, the many battles in which she participated, in addition to the Prophet's visits to her home, etc. Ibn Sa'd, Vol. 8, pp. 412–16.

23. Ibn Sa'd, Vol. 8, pp. 424–34.

24. The narratives which refer to the participation of women Companions of the Prophet are given in *Ṣaḥīḥ al-Bukhārī,* Vol. 4 *(Kitāb al-Maghāzī).*

25. Recent research in the *Sīrah* books has proved the general congruence of Ibn Hishām with the authentic *Aḥādīth.*

CHAPTER 4

The Socio-Economic Dimensions of the Prophet's State

1. Some Basic Concepts

Securing Madinah as a haven for the Prophet and his embattled Companions was a breakthrough of enormous magnitude for Islam. It was indicative of Allah's manifest design in favour of the Muslims, and His greatest mercy for His Prophet. Through the *Hijrah,* the fortunes of the Muslims were reversed; their lot being transformed from an oppressed and confined group in Makkah to the ruling elite of state and government in Madinah. The authority of the Prophet as the supreme ruler and Messenger of Allah was firmly established as soon as he arrived in Madinah, with all the Madinan clans vying with each other to welcome, honour and pay homage to him. The Jewish tribes of Madinah did the same, and agreed to enter into a pact with him which accorded them an autonomy in their affairs in all matters excepting matters relating to state sovereignty such as external relations, defence and the overall authority of Allah and His Messenger.

The new milieu of Madinah was very congenial to the Muslims, and very receptive to the ideas of Islam. Things had been stagnant for a long time, crippled by the unceasing petty feuds between the Aws and the Khazraj. The presence there of the Jewish colonies had been positive in many ways. Despite their deviations and misconceptions about their ethnic superiority over the Arabs, the Jews were grounded in teachings of Divine origin. They were in some respects, heirs of the great legacy of the Israelite Prophets, claiming, as they did, to be of the seed of Abraham. Because of their knowledge of the Torah, they spoke often of the imminent coming of the Prophet of Arabia. The Jews were also heirs to the great Semitic civilizations of Palestine and Mesopotamia. They had thus a more developed social consciousness and introduced many useful innovations in the art of living and working. Their moral values were originally derived from Divine Revelation; their culture was learned and sophisticated; their standard of living was considerably higher than that of their Arab neighbours. Moreover, they almost monopolized the internal commerce of the city and were the manpower of its industry. The Arabs were superior to them in numbers and military valour, but felt somewhat alienated by their exclusive Jewish culture and unable to compete favourably with them in commerce and industry, let alone in their knowledge of the Scripture and their mastery of ancient learning.

It would appear that the Madinan Jews initially tolerated the Prophet's supreme authority and entered into a binding legal pact with him only because they grossly underestimated him and his Companions. After all they were Arabs, like the Arabs of Yathrib: the Jews must have thought that they would have no difficulty in surpassing them, as they did the Yathribites, in all fields of life apart from political power. That inability to read the events correctly, and the even graver inability to recognize the intrinsic merit of men and ideas, was destined to bring them a great deal of misery and ill-fortune.

The *Hijrah* heralded a new and exciting era for Madinah. Events of the greatest magnitude were about to overtake it, and a mysterious outpouring of activity and advance in every sphere of life. Much to the dismay of its ill-wishers, the progress of Muslim power proceeded at an ever-greater rate with every new development, crisis or confrontation with hostile powers. The host of Muslims who migrated with the Prophet, *ṣallā Allāhu 'alayhi wa sallam,* were not ordinary men. They were, in modern idiom, 'hard-line' activists moulded and tested through their ordeals, the crucible, of the Makkan period. For thirteen years their resourceful Arab and Makkan stock had been reformed, their attitudes and individual character traits recast and made ready to bring about the Islamic transformation of human society. With the Qur'ān imprinted in their hearts, and imbued in their veins, nerves and bones, they had at their fingertips the full blueprint of the new order with its definite method, plan and strategy. Having been passively confined during those thirteen years, they were burning with the eagerness to see action in their new haven, to secure the pleasure of God and His Messenger by striving in the cause of spreading Islam to all.

We must recount, at this point, some of the new concepts and ideas that were stirring in their hearts and imaginations if we are to have any understanding of the forces that were about to be set on the march in the small and hitherto forgotten Arabian oasis of Yathrib.

1.1 Muḥammad the Man

According to Islam, Muḥammad, *ṣallā Allāhu 'alayhi wa sallam,* is not a supernatural being. He is *'abdan rasūlan,* a servant of God, appointed as a Messenger. He has to strive hard in the service of his Lord, as must all Muslims. Man, as also the *Jinn* for that matter, has been created to serve his Lord – that is the meaning and mission of man's life on this earth, and the most fundamental, cardinal obligation *(Taklīf).*

1.2 The *Khalīfatu Allāh* that is Man

To enable him to discharge his mission and to fulfil his obligation to his Lord, man is invested with the authority and powers of vicegerent of God on earth, *Khalīfatu Allāh fī al-Arḍ,* and if the Muslims are established on the earth, then it is their cardinal obligation to discharge their responsibility as vicegerents of God.[1]

1.3 The Basic Role of a Muslim

His mandate is to possess and develop the earth, to create conditions and circumstances conducive to pleasant and peaceful continuity of life on earth as affirmed in the Qur'ān.[2] It is affirmed in *az-Zabūr* as well as in the Qur'ān.[3] It is his duty and privilege to enjoy life, acknowledging the bounties and blessings of his Lord, without excess or extravagance. It is not required of him to deny himself all comforts, or to deny the good things of this life or to be ashamed of his flesh, his basic needs and instincts, or to view these as profane or impure. He is not required to reject the world. Rather he is exhorted to enjoy all of that within the limits of God's commandments – the *Ḥudūd Allāh.*

1.4 Supremacy of Islamic Law

Most of all, it is impressed upon his mind that the Islamic way of living, the Islamic shaping of society, cannot be carried out if Allah's *dīn,* and His law are not supreme on earth. Unless the Word of God is supreme and the power of the believers is upheld, the Islamic way of living and building human civilization will not be possible. So Muslims must first strive to do away with and relinquish the un-Islamic reality, demolish the old un-Islamic edifice and prepare and level the ground for the founding of the Islamic reality and civilization. Only if they do this, will Allah's promise in *az-Zabūr,* to establish them on earth, be fulfilled. This promise is also affirmed in the Qur'ān.[4]

1.5 Life-Affirming Vision

Insofar as Islam is life-affirming and world-affirming (though with certain moral reservations and restrictions), it is also highly value-conscious. Nothing should be unduly wasted. Those aspects of the pre-Islamic Arabian life which are positive and good should be adopted and incorporated without delay or hesitation into the new social order. This positive and progressive attitude on the part of the Muslims facilitated the process of transforming the Arabian society into an Islamic one and made it a lot easier and much more congenial for the Arabs to remould their national character in accordance with the precepts and new conceptions of Islam.

1.6 The Religion of Optimum Balance

A striking pervasive feature of Islam is its instinct for balance or equilibrium. Everything must be balanced, because this is constitutive of the natural order of things as God has created it. If the natural balance of things is tipped too much to one side, the resulting imbalance must be redressed, if peace, justice and truth are to be preserved for the pleasure of God and the well-being of man. Imbalance and disequilibrium constitute *fasād fī al-arḍ* (corruption on earth), which Islam does not tolerate as it is wasteful and harmful.

If those Muslims of *Muhājirīn* and *Anṣār* were moved into action, to the limit of their human capacity, heightened and developed to the full by a profound sense of commitment and obligation, then – to achieve the desired balance – they had to be rewarded by according them special social and religious status, and certain rights and privileges. Those rights and privileges act as counter-weights to the commitments, obligations and duties that are laid upon them – as a reward for the effort, the trials and hardships that the Muslims had had to go through and to suffer in the struggle to establish *Dīn Allāh fī al-arḍ* (the religion of God on earth).

1.7 The Dominating Spirit of the Qur'ān

It is not possible, within the scope of the present study, to enumerate the governing Qur'ānic principles that determine the shape, the quality and the rhythm of an Islamic society. These principles are so extensive that, in a real sense, they coincide with the whole Qur'ān itself – they cover the Makkan as well as the Madinan revelations. While the former were directed, among other things, to the building up and fostering of the Muslim personality, beliefs, attitudes, rites of religious worship – the inculcation of the basic Islamic conceptions and ideas – the latter were directed more to the realization of all these ideas in the societal domain and public life. But the two portions of the Qur'ān are, of course, inseparable. In what follows we shall attempt a cursory mention of a few of these governing Qur'ānic principles, together with a brief account of the Qur'ānic *sūrahs* that were revealed in the pre-Badr period of the history of Madinah.

1.8 The Early Madinan Qur'ānic Themes

There can be no doubt that the Qur'ānic revelation was the foremost and governing determinant in the inception and the subsequent shaping, of the Madinan society and state. The Qur'ān continued to pour into Madinah in a wondrous, rapid succession of long, melodious *sūrahs,* during the first period of the Prophet's stay therein.

According to Imām az-Zarkashī (Badr ad-dīn Muḥammad ibn 'Abdullāh, died in Cairo in 799 A.H.)[5] the Qur'ān as revealed in Madinah consists of the following *sūrahs,* arranged chronologically as follows:

I. *Sūrah al-Baqarah* is the first *sūrah* to be revealed to Muḥammad in Madinah after the *Hijrah* (with the exception of a few verses, e.g. the verses announcing the illegality of usury *(ribā)*).
II. Then *Sūrah al-Anfāl* (War-spoils).
III. Then *Sūrah Āl 'Imrān* (The House of 'Imrān).
IV. Then *Sūrah al-Aḥzāb* (The Confederate Forces).
V. Then *Sūrah al-Mumtaḥanah* (The Examined One).
VI. Then *Sūrah an-Nisā'* (The Women).
VII. Then *Sūrah az-Zalzalah* (The Earthquake).
VIII. Then *Sūrah al-Ḥadīd* (Iron).
IX. Then *Sūrah Muḥammad.*
X. Then *Sūrah ar-Ra'd* (The Thunderstorm).
XI. Then *Sūrah ar-Raḥmān* (The Compassionate).
XII. Then *Sūrah ad-Dahr* (Time or Man).
XIII. Then *Sūrah aṭ-Ṭalāq* (Divorce).
XIV. Then *Sūrah al-Bayyinah* (The Clear One).
XV. Then *Sūrah al-Ḥashr* (Exile or Summons).

XVI. Then *Sūrah an-Naṣr* (Victory).
XVII. Then *Sūrah an-Nūr* (The Light).
XVIII. Then *Sūrah al-Ḥajj* (Pilgrimage).
XIX. Then *Sūrah al-Munāfiqūn* (The Hypocrites).
XX. Then *Sūrah al-Mujādalah* (The Dispute).
XXI. Then *Sūrah al-Ḥujurāt* (The Living Quarters of the Prophet).
XXII. Then *Sūrah at-Taḥrīm* (The Banning).
XXIII. Then *Sūrah aṣ-Ṣaff* (The Rank).
XXIV. Then *Sūrah al-Jumu'ah* (The Congregational Prayer).
XXV. Then *Sūrah at-Taghābun* (Mutual Disillusion).
XXVI. Then *Sūrah al-Fatḥ* (Conquest).
XXVII. Then *Sūrah at-Tawbah* (Repentance).
XXVIII. The last *sūrah* to be revealed is, according to az-Zarkashī, *Sūrah al-Mā'idah* (The Table).

It is reported that the Prophet, *ṣallā Allāhu 'alayhi wa sallam,* recited *Sūrah al-Mā'idah* at the end of his Farewell Pilgrimage, and said: 'O People, the last of the Qur'ānic revelations is *Sūrah al-Mā'idah,* so make lawful what it makes lawful and make unlawful what it makes unlawful.'

Then az-Zarkashī gives a list of verses that were revealed in Makkah, after the *Hijrah* and for this reason are considered as Madinan verses.[6] Of these, he mentions verse 13 of *Sūrah al-Ḥujurāt,* revealed in Makkah on the very day of its opening (conquest or pacification). This is the famous egalitarian Qur'ānic verse which reads:

'O Mankind! Lo! We have created you of male and female, and have made you into nations and tribes that you may know one another. Surely, the noblest of you in the sight of Allah is the most God-fearing amongst you . . .'[7] It is significant that this verse was revealed on the very day the Quraysh were humbled and made powerless. In view of the fact that they took excessive pride in their ethnic and social class, there could hardly have been a better setting or occasion for this noble verse. Ibn Hishām[8] reports that the Prophet included this verse in his victory speech, at the door of the Ka'bah, when he declared amnesty for the captives of the Quraysh. Declared the Prophet, *ṣallā Allāhu 'alayhi wa sallam:*

Lā ilāha illā Allāhu waḥdah,
Lā sharīka lah
Ṣadaqa wa'dah
wa naṣara 'abdah
wa a'azza jundah
wa hazama al-Ahẓāba waḥdah

There is no God but Allah Alone
He has no partner or associate
He has made good His promise
He has made His servant victorious
And He has defeated the confederates alone.

Every claim of privilege or blood or property are abolished by me except the custody of the temple and the watering of the pilgrims.

O Quraysh, God has taken from you the haughtiness of paganism and its veneration of ancestors. Man springs from Adam and Adam sprang from dust.'

Then the Prophet recited verse 13 of *Sūrah al-Ḥujurāt* at a time and situation, when the vanquished Quraysh, with the sword of the Prophet at their necks, were fully attentive, making absolutely sure that they caught every word and syllable. Then came the momentous question and the answer to it:

What do you think I am about to do with you?
You are a noble brother and the son of a noble brother.
Go your ways, for you are now the freed ones.

The second verse revealed in Makkah, after the *Hijrah,* was the concluding verse of the Qur'ān, also included in another famous address of the Prophet (namely the Farewell (Pilgrimage) Address, at Minā, in the vicinity of Makkah).

This day have I perfected your religion for you and completed My favour unto you.
And have chosen for you as religion al-Islam.[9]

Al-Qaṣwā' (the Prophet's she-camel) was brought to the ground when this verse was revealed. Abū Bakr and 'Umar looked into each other's eyes, presently filled with tears, and then started to sob violently. Other Muslims looked on with bewilderment. Both Abū Bakr and 'Umar had understood, in a flash of insight, that the cessation of the Qur'ānic revelations meant that the Prophet's noble life, the fountain of live guidance and illumination, was drawing to a close. The Prophet had completed his Divine mission on this earth.

2. The Qur'ānic Phenomenon (*aẓ-Ẓāhirah al-Qur'āniyyah*)

To the uninitiated observer, the period from the Prophet's arrival in Madinah to the few months just before the Battle of Badr, may appear unusually calm and uneventful. Even a great scholar and leading Orientalist like the celebrated Montgomery Watt[10] seems to have overlooked, or failed to deduce, that changes and events of the highest seriousness and magnitude were taking place, almost by the hour, in the centre of the oasis of Madinah. True, those events were not spatio-temporal events in the ordinary sense of human history, if that is defined as an instantiation and exemplification of the material principle of causation. An event within such a process, materially construed, must be preceded by a long chain of other material events acting as its causes.

Clearly, the events that we are referring to, and events which were stirring and shaking and shaping things were not ordinarily causal, exclusively material, events. Even so they were taking place, there and then, and they were no less spatio-temporal than the daybreak or the falling of rain. Those events were occasions of the descent of *waḥī* or divine revelation. The Archangel Gabriel used to descend to the oasis at intervals, sometimes even daily – his coming made spatio-temporal connections. The Prophet's body used to sweat and shake violently and to show a massive increase of weight:

(i) Once the *waḥī* descended on the Prophet, *ṣallā Allāhu 'alayhi wa sallam,* while his head was resting on Umm al-Mu'minīn 'Ā'ishah. She later described this incident saying that the Prophet's head became so heavy that her thigh was almost crushed under its weight.

(ii) We have noted that al-Qaṣwā', the Prophet's she-camel, was brought to the ground when the Divine revelation descended upon him while he was delivering the Farewell (Pilgrimage) Address at Minā.

That occasions of *waḥī* constituted great events is not only attested by the fact that the Prophet himself used to await them with longing expectation, but also by the momentous changes that used to attend them and follow immediately in their wake. The Companions of the Prophet also used to follow the events of the coming of the Archangel Gabriel with great interest and anticipation.

Said 'Umar ibn al-Khaṭṭāb: 'I had a neighbour from the *Anṣār* of Banū Umayyah ibn Zayd, we agreed between us that one of us would stay with the Prophet the whole day to listen to the Qur'ānic *waḥī* and the news while the other attended to his normal work, the next day we would change our roles.'[11]

Even during the difficult period in Makkah, new converts to Islam used to reside with the Prophet for a number of days to listen to the Qur'ān and learn it, before departing to their respective clans and tribes to call them to Islam. Such was the case with Abū Dharr al-Ghifārī, aṭ-Ṭufail ibn 'Amr ad-Dawsī and Ḍimām ibn Tha'labah. As a result of the work of Abū Dharr, more than half of his tribe converted to Islam, while aṭ-Ṭufail had a tremendous success not only in winning the whole of the Yemeni tribe of Daws to Islam, but in inspiring them to such a degree of enthusiasm that they made the *Hijrah* to Madinah, never to return to Yemen. After the armistice of al-Ḥudaybiyyah, many deputations visited the Prophet at Madinah. They resided with the Prophet, who provided them with free lodging and food, and gave them long sessions of Qur'ānic lessons:

(i) Al-Bukhārī[12] narrated that Mālik ibn al-Ḥārith came to Madinah, with a delegation of his people. They stayed with their host, the Prophet, for twenty days. Then the Prophet thought they must be missing their families, and so gave them leave to go. He advised them to teach their people and lead them in prayer after his example; he appointed for them a *Mu'adhdhin.*

(ii) Banū 'Abd al-Qays[13] of Bahrain came to Madinah in two deputations on different occasions. They stayed with the Prophet, learned the Qur'ān and the prayer.

The Prophet said to Ashajj ibn 'Abd al-Qays: 'You have two qualities which Allah loves – *al-Ḥilm:* gentility, mild-temper, self-control; and *al-Anāh:* equanimity, patience, perseverance.'

So intense was the Companions' study of the Qur'ān, that it is little wonder that it so profoundly and pervasively affected their feelings and attitudes in life. The Qur'ān was for them a daily study, a manual of thought and conduct, hence their honorific title, 'the Qur'ānic generation'.[14]

2.1 The Two Fair Ones (*az-Zahrāwān*)

We have already quoted az-Zarkashī on *Sūrah al-Baqarah* (The Cow) being the first *sūrah* to be revealed in Madinah immediately after the *Hijrah. Sūrah Āl 'Imrān* (The House of 'Imrān) came third in the order of Qur'ānic revelation in Madinah, after *Sūrah al-Anfāl* (War-spoils) and before *Sūrah al-Aḥzāb* (The Confederates).

The Prophet, *ṣallā Allāhu 'alayhi wa sallam,* commended the oft-recitation of *Sūrah al-Baqarah* and *Sūrah Āl 'Imrān,* and called the two *sūrahs: az-Zahrāwān,* 'the two fair ones'.

Said the Prophet, *ṣallā Allāhu 'alayhi wa sallam:* 'Recite the two white ones *(az-Zahrāwān), Sūrah al-Baqarah* and *Sūrah Āl 'Imrān* for on the day of Resurrection, they will come as two clouds or as two shades or as if two flocks of birds arranged in ranks, pleading on behalf of those who recite them.'

Sūrah al-Baqarah is so preoccupied with argumentation and dialogue that one might suppose that to be the main theme of the whole *sūrah.* This is perhaps indicative not only of the large presence of Jews in Madinah, and the problematic nature of such a presence for the Muslims, but also of the inherent tension between the teaching of Islam and the dogmas of Judaism as known and practised by those Jews.

Given the pretentious claims of superiority cherished by those Jews, it is natural that the dialogue with them should be so lengthy and insistent.

2.2 **The Jewish Dilemma**

Imām Bukhārī reports[15] that when the Prophet reached Madinah the Jews hurried to meet him and be acquainted. There was 'Abdullāh ibn Salām, a leading rabbi amongst them, with three questions, that only a Prophet can answer:

(i) 'What are the portents of the hour (of Resurrection)?'
Answered the Prophet: 'A great fire that drives people from East to the West.'

(ii) 'What is the first food, people of paradise shall eat?'
Answered the Prophet (who is informed of the right answers by the Archangel Gabriel): 'They will eat the candate (extra) lobe of the fish liver.'

(iii) 'Why does a child draw the likeness of his father or of his mother?'
Said the Prophet: 'If a man's discharge surpasses (dominates) then the child will take the likeness of the father, but if the woman's discharge surpasses (dominates), then the offspring will take the likeness of the mother.'

Apparently, 'Abdullāh ibn Salām was satisfied with these answers, since he entered Islam, swearing that no one could know the right answers for these questions excepting a genuine Prophet. As for the generality of the Jews, however, they were in a dilemma. The Prophet was then the *de facto* ruler of Madinah with almost all the Arab clans – with the exception of the smallest clan of Aws al-Lāt (also called Aws-Manāt) – solidly behind him. It was wise for them not to oppose him, so they agreed to enter into a pact with him, the pact of *Ṣaḥīfah*. But it became increasingly difficult for them to reconcile their acute sense of ethnic and religious superiority with their subordinate position to the Arabian

Prophet, who, alas, to their growing dismay and discomfort was not of the seed of Israel or Jacob but rather of the seed of Ishmael, son of Hājar. Their frustration intensified with every new success and achievement that accrued to the Prophet, his Companions and Islam. Their room for manoeuvre *vis-à-vis* the Muslims was ever more restricted, and ultimately they found themselves opting for the extreme position of open confrontation and war with the Prophet, despite their legal covenant with him. By contrast, the Prophet had a great deal of room in which to act, if need be, to deal with their enmity and their plots. He left the widest options open to them – from conversion to Islam to the extreme opposite of that – waging war against Islam. His major strategy was to demand of the Jews that they fulfil their legal commitments, under the terms of the *Ṣaḥīfah* pact, to which they had agreed.

The Prophet's initial reaction to the presence of the Jews in Madinah was one of acceptance and indeed pleasure. He was eager to win their confidence, acceptance and even friendship. He did his best to reach out to them, personally as well as religiously and culturally. He visited their leading rabbis and chiefs, going to great pains to call upon them at their homes in their various colonies, out of the centre of Madinah. Imām Bukhārī reports that he even changed the traditional way he used to part his hair, adopting the Jewish fashion of dividing it across the middle of the head. He prayed towards Jerusalem, as they prayed, and fasted the Day of Atonement *('Āshūrā')*, as they fasted. In countless ways he tried to reach some degree of mutual understanding and co-operation with them, giving them the most generous and liberal terms in the pact of *Ṣaḥīfah*, as we saw earlier.

The Prophet must have been quite dismayed by the unexpectedly unfriendly and harsh rejection that he got from the Jews. Then the Qur'ān consoled him and educated him in their history and their cultural identity which they so jealously cultivated and transmitted from generation to generation. Revelation about the Jewish reality in Madinah, its history and cultural background, occupied a great portion of *Sūrah al-Baqarah* which takes its name from an incident in the Israelites' response to the Prophetic call of Moses.

Says Allah, *subḥānahū wa ta'ālā,* in the Qur'ān: ' . . . the Jews will never be pleased with you, nor will the Christians, till you follow their creed. Say: the Guidance of Allah is the (true) guidance. And if you should follow their desires, after the knowledge of that which has come to you, then you would have from Allah no protecting friend or helper.'[16]

This verse of *Sūrah al-Baqarah,* must have been revealed at a crucial moment, when the Prophet was doing his utmost to win the approval of the Jews. It put an abrupt stop to such endeavours, chastening the Prophet's hope of winning over the Jews. The verse marked the end of the first phase in the Prophet's relations with the Jews, the phase when relations were still cordial. The verse also contains an indirect warning to the Prophet not to compromise with or follow 'their desires for fear that he should thereby lose the right to hope for God's protection and help'.

A quick overview of *Sūrah al-Baqarah* will show how extensive the references are to the Jewish presence in Madinah, and the ingenuity of the Prophet in being able to govern a truly pluralist commonwealth in Madinah:

(i) Verses 6–20 refer directly to the Arab hypocrites, but as there was a pact between them and the Jews of Madinah, the latter are included indirectly.

(ii) Verses 40–120 were revealed on the Jews of Madinah, exposing their thinking and their real attitudes towards the Prophet and the Muslims.

(iii) Verse 84 could be taken to refer either to their Biblical covenant or to the covenant which they concluded with the Prophet and how they violated it later on: 'And when We made with you a covenant (saying): Shed not the blood of your people nor turn (a part) of your people out of your dwellings then you ratified (our covenant) and you were witnesses (thereto).'[17]

Verse 85 refers to the wars in which Jews fought Jews in Madinah, when various Jewish clans sided with opposing Arab clans; but if this is indeed a reference to the pre-Islamic wars, then verse 84 must be taken to refer to the Biblical covenant.

(iv) Verses 122–41 enumerate the many Divine favours to the Banū Isrā'īl and to their ancestors Abraham, Isaac and Jacob (Israel).

(v) Verses 142–50 deal with the change of the *Qiblah* from Jerusalem to Makkah. The passage tells of the jeering and controversy that raged on this issue, and the slanderous campaign which the Jews launched against the Prophet because of the change. The change of *Qiblah* was ushered in by a new and bitter phase in Muslim-Jewish relations. The goodwill period between the two communities was over. Following the change of *Qiblah*, verses were revealed criticizing the Prophet himself and certain of his Companions (Aws) for still harbouring an affection for the Jews, and for their lingering hopes of gaining their goodwill and co-operation.

Says Allah, *subḥānahū wa ta'ālā*, in the Qur'ān: Lo! You are those who love them (i.e. the Jews) though they love you not, and you believe in all the Scripture. When they meet you they say: We believe, but when they go apart, they bite the tips of their fingers at you, for rage.[18]

(vi) Verses 246–50 of *Sūrah al-Baqarah* also deal with Muslim-Jewish relations.

Thus the dominant theme of the longest *sūrah* of the Qur'ān is the Jewish question. This is very significant not only for the Muslims of the Prophet's generation, but for all Muslims in all times to come. As for the Prophet and his Companions, the *sūrah* foretold events to come, a prolonged and most bitter conflict destined to take place between the one-time allies of the *Ṣaḥīfah* covenant. If the Jews were culturally and religiously determined, indeed conditioned, by the teachings which they ascribed to the Torah, the Muslims were bound by the commands and exhortations of the Qur'ān. They were so preoccupied with the questions put by the Jews that many Qur'ānic verses were revealed to the Prophet discussing every facet of their history, cultural identity, and psychological make-up: 'Lo! This Qur'ān surely narrates unto the Children of Israel most of that concerning which they differ.'[19]

2.3 The Jews' Prayer Invoking the Name of Muḥammad (i.e. *Al-Istiftāḥ*)

The Qur'ān (verse 89 of *al-Baqarah*) reminds the Jews (of Khaybar) of the prayer, invoking the name of Muḥammad, which they used to make when they fought against the Arabs before the advent of Islam. The Qur'ān uses the word *yastaftiḥūn,* i.e. they prayed for victory by invoking that prayer: 'And when there came unto them a Scripture from Allah, confirming that in their possession, though before that they were asking for a signal triumph over those who disbelieved, and when there came unto them that which they knew (to be the Truth), they disbelieved therein. The curse of Allah is on disbelievers.'[20]

The two learned authors of *Tafsīr al-Jalālain,* commenting on that verse give details of the circumstances in which it was revealed:

The Jews of Khaybar were involved in a series of notorious wars with the neighbouring, powerful and war-like North Arabian tribe of Ghaṭfān. In these wars they used to invoke the following prayer *(Du'ā')* before plunging into battle with them:

O Lord, we ask Thee in the name and worth (love) of Muḥammad (or Aḥmad) the unlettered Prophet whom You have promised to bring forth unto us, that You make us victorious over our enemies.

On the authority of Ibn 'Abbās: when the Jews made use of that prayer, they became victorious over their Arabian adversaries.

When later on, they were engaged in war with the Aws and the Khazraj, they made use of that prayer again. They even used to threaten them by saying that the Prophet Aḥmad was going to appear and he would be on their side, and they would destroy their adversaries with his help and support. When the Prophet did appear, however, they disbelieved him. Ibn 'Abbās narrated that a Muslim delegation, viz. Mu'ādh ibn Jabal, Bishr ibn al-Barā' and Dāwūd ibn Salamah, went to the Jews and said: 'O Jews, fear Allah and become Muslims. You used to threaten us, when we were of the *Mushrikūn* (polytheists) by the imminent coming of Aḥmad, and you used to describe his physical appearance, viz. saying that in the Torah he was said to have wide and pensive black eyes, outlined by black ointment *(Kuḥl),* that he was of middle height, of black curly hair, and of very handsome looks (or countenance). Then when he did appear in actuality you rejected him and disbelieved in him.'

Sallām ibn Mishkam (of the Jews of an-Naḍīr) replied to the demands of the Muslim delegation, saying: 'He did not come to us with anything we knew, and he is not the Prophet we used to mention to you.'[21]

The significance of this verse 89, and of its reference to the Jewish practice of *al-Istiftāḥ,* is that:

(i) It confirms the idea that the coming of the Prophet Muḥammad was foretold in the Torah, so that if it is not there now, it must have been removed at some later period;

(ii) that the name of Muḥammad was well-known in Madinah and its environs as far north as Khaybar;

(iii) that the Jewish knowledge of the imminent coming of the Arabian Prophet helped to prepare the ground for the massive conversion of Madinah to Islam.

(iv) In view of the Jews' prior knowledge of the imminent advent of Muḥammad and of his physical and moral attributes, it is mystifying that they should reject him in the way they did, and that they should show such intense enmity and hatred towards his person, long before he began to respond to that hostility in kind, for it is confirmed that, initially, the Prophet was much attracted to them and strove hard to win their acceptance and approval.

Issue by issue, controversy between the Jews and the Prophet intensified and finally emerged as open conflict and outright war of survival; either the Prophet and the Muslims live and survive in Madinah or the Jews do. The Qur'ān reflects the passions involved in that conflict, one that the Prophet had tried very hard to avert and forestall, but which the Jewish sentiments of ethnic pride and supremacy imposed upon him had made inevitable. Not only does the dialogue with, and war of words against, the Jews, dominate the whole of *Sūrah al-Baqarah,* and to a similar extent *Sūrah Āl 'Imrān* (the two longest *sūrahs* of the Qur'ān), it is also referred to extensively throughout the Qur'ān.

2.4 **Reference to the Jews in the Qur'ān**

A computer survey of the Qur'ān[22] gives the following references to the Jews:

The word 'Jew' occurs 8 times:
— *Sūrah al-Baqarah* (The Cow), 113 (twice), 120
— *Sūrah al-Mā'idah* (The Table), 18, 51, 64, 82
— *Sūrah al-Tawbah* (Repentance), 30

The word 'Israel' occurs 42 times:
— *Sūrah al-Baqarah* (The Cow), 40, 47, 83, 122, 211, 246
— *Sūrah Āl 'Imrān* (The House of 'Imrān), 49, 93
— *Sūrah al-Mā'idah* (The Table), 12, 32, 70, 78, 110
— *Sūrah al-A'rāf* (The Heights), 105, 134, 137, 138
— *Sūrah Yūnus* (Jonah), 90, 93
— *Sūrah al-Isrā'* (Night Journey), 2, 4, 101, 104
— *Sūrah Ṭā Hā* (Ta-Ha), 47, 80, 94
— *Sūrah aṣh-Shu'arā'* (The Poets), 17, 22, 59, 197
— *Sūrah an-Naml* (The Ants), 76
— *Sūrah as-Sajdah* (The Prostration), 23
— *Sūrah Ghāfir* or *al-Mu'min* (The Believer), 53
— *Sūrah az-Zukhruf* (Ornaments), 59
— *Sūrah ad-Dukhān* (The Smoke), 30
— *Sūrah al-Jāthiyah* (Crouching), 16
— *Sūrah al-Aḥqāf* (The Sand Hill), 10
— *Sūrah aṣ-Ṣaff* (The Ranks), 6, 14

The Jews are also referred to by the phrase, *'al-ladhīna hādū'*, i.e. those who turned Jewish (or were of Jewish inclination), a term that may mean those born Jews as well as Jews by conversion. The phrase occurs 10 times:

— *Sūrah al-Baqarah* (The Cow), 62
— *Sūrah an-Nisā'* (Women), 46, 160
— *Sūrah al-Mā'idah* (The Table), 41, 44, 69
— *Sūrah al-An'ām* (The Cattle), 146
— *Sūrah an-Naḥl* (The Bees), 118
— *Sūrah al-Ḥajj* (Pilgrimage), 17
— *Sūrah al-Jumu'ah* (Friday Congregational Prayer), 6

The fourth way in which reference to the Jews is found in the Qur'ān is an indirect one. They are included in the general reference to the People of the Book (The Scripturists). The phrase *'Ahl al-Kitāb'* occurs 31 times in the Qur'ān as follows:

— *Sūrah al-Baqarah* (The Cow), 105, 109
— *Sūrah Āl 'Imrān* (The House of 'Imrān), 64, 65, 69, 70, 71, 72, 75, 98, 99, 110, 113, 199
— *Sūrah an-Nisā'* (Women), 123, 153, 159, 171
— *Sūrah al-Mā'idah* (The Table), 15, 19, 59, 65, 68, 77
— *Sūrah al-'Ankabūt* (The Spider), 46
— *Sūrah al-Ḥadīd* (Iron), 29
— *Sūrah al-Ḥashr* (Exile; The Gathering), 2, 11
— *Sūrah al-Bayyinah* (The Clear Proof), 1, 6

That the Jewish question is a major theme of the Qur'ān, and of *Sūrah al-Baqarah* in particular, reflects its dominance of the intellectual preoccupation of the Muslims in Madinah, in particular in the first years of the Prophet's stay there. The Jews were rich and powerful, enjoying a high standard of living through their virtual monopoly of commerce and finance. They were well established in the city, holding title to the greater part of its real estate, the business sector being within the quarter of Banū Qaynuqā', and near total control of the industry of household items and the manufacture of armour – they owned the trades of blacksmith and goldsmith. They also owned the best agricultural land in and around Madinah, and far out to the north of it in the valleys of Khaybar, Fadak and Taymā'. They also had a monopoly of knowledge and learning, being in possession of the Book of Moses, the Torah.

They boasted openly of their superiority in view of all these endowments, and above all they boasted of being of the seed of Abraham. To make things worse for the Arabs of Madinah, the Jews treated them with visible disdain and threatened that if the Arabian Prophet came, they would invoke his support and become victorious and dominant over them.[23]

Thus the Jewish presence in Madinah was a phenomenon to contend with. The cultural traits of these Jews, which the Qur'ān so fully portrays, could not allow them to remain in the background of events. They had well-developed channels for propaganda and information which they put to frequent use to make life most uncomfortable for the Prophet and the emerging Muslim community. What irritated them most was the political supremacy of the Prophet, and the fact that he had been the undisputed ruler of Madinah, since the day of his arrival. That position was secured by virtue of:

(i) the two 'Aqabah pledges, especially the second one, involving as it did the commitment, both of the Aws and the Khazraj, to defend him if attacked, by the Quraysh or others;

(ii) the overwhelming warmth of the welcome accorded to him by the whole Arab population of Yathrib, in particular by the powerful chiefs of the Aws and the Khazraj, including the chivalrous Usaid ibn Ḥuḍayr and Sa'd ibn Mu'ādh. The only exception was the hypocrite leader, 'Abdullāh ibn Ubayy of the Khazraj. However, it was generally recognized that Ibn Ubayy had personal and selfish motives for withholding full support. So complete was the authority of the Prophet, however, that not even Ibn Ubayy dared oppose him openly. That is why he became a 'hypocrite' – that is, claiming to be a Muslim and a supporter of the Prophet, whereas he really opposed him and wished him ill. The support of the leaders of the Aws and the Khazraj was not only political, they were sincere and ardent Muslims who regarded obedience to the Prophet as a religious duty;

(iii) last but not least, the provisions of the *Ṣaḥīfah* (document) made it very clear that in Madinah, all matters of conflict and disagreement be referred to the Prophet as the supreme judge of the city. The Jews were not an exception to the general acceptance and approval of this *Ṣaḥīfah*. The parties to it were called *'Ahl aṣ-Ṣaḥīfah'*, i.e. the People of the Document, and they included all the Jewish clans of Madinah, though the names of their tribes were not specifically mentioned. (The reasons for this were explained earlier; see above, p.186).

In legal documents, reference to the signatories, on whom the provisions are binding, must be as exact and unambiguous as possible. In this respect, the clan is a more definite entity than the tribe, hence the reference in the *Ṣaḥīfah* to the clans and sub-clans with which the Jews were associated.

In view of the very clear circumstances in which the *Ṣaḥīfah* was formulated and approved by 'the People of the Document', it is incomprehensible that Watt and others[24] should have tried to contrive all sorts of far-fetched explanations for the date, circumstances and origin of the *Ṣaḥīfah* other than the authentic ones, given by the best authorities of the *Sīrah*. Watt has relied in fact on unsubstantiated conjectures and obscure guesswork. Little wonder that the conclusions he draws are so wholly unconvincing, and in flagrant contradiction with established and acknowledged facts in all the trustworthy sources of Islamic history. For instance, Watt has declared emphatically that the Prophet's position in the initial Madinan period was precarious, he was 'merely one among a number of important men', and not the supreme authority.

In Watt's view, the *Ṣaḥīfah* was not written at one time, nor is it a consistent whole. He maintains that its first section was an incorporation of the second 'Aqabah Pledge, the later sections were not added until after the destruction of Banū Qurayẓah, in the fifth year after the *Hijrah*. Lacking evidence to support either of these claims, Watt has to struggle with the glaring facts that it is quite illogical to suppose that the

Ṣaḥīfah was written after the expulsion of the Jews of Banū Qaynuqā' and Banū an-Naḍīr and the destruction of Banū Qurayẓah because there were then simply no substantial number of Jews left in Madinah to have a pact with. What possible grounds can there have been for the *Ṣaḥīfah* at that time?

The *sūrah* paired with *Sūrah al-Baqarah, Sūrah Āl 'Imrān,* deals principally with the Arab Christians, chiefly those of Najrān in South Yemen. In contrast to the sharpness of tone prevailing in the dialogue with the Jews of Madinah in the former *sūrah,* the dialogue with the Christians, in the latter *sūrah* is markedly gentle and friendly. The explanation lies in the difference that existed in the nature and pretensions of the two groups. In contrast to the Jews of Madinah, the Christians were, as well as being of Arabic stock, by no means arrogant or pretentious. Their bearing was humble and courteous.

Ibn Hishām gives a colourful portrayal of their deputation as they entered the Prophet's Mosque, during the time of the noon prayer. The Prophet received them with full honour and requested of them to 'submit themselves to Allah'. They retorted that they had submitted before his advent (i.e. in being Christians). But he disputed this statement and questioned their creed about the nature of Christ.

> 'He is God' said one group because he raised the dead, etc.
> 'He is the Son of God' said another group because he had no natural father.
> 'He is the third person of the Trinity' said the third group.

When the Prophet rejected these three claims, they asked him:

> 'Who is his father then?' meaning Christ. The Prophet was silent. He did not answer that last question; apparently because he did not know the answer. But he told them that what barred them from the worship of the One, True God was their assertion that God has a son, and their worship of the Cross, and the eating of pork.

Then *Sūrah Āl 'Imrān* was revealed to the Prophet, telling the whole story of the life of Mary, and of the miraculous birth of Jesus Christ. That revelation makes up the first eighty verses of this noble *sūrah* paired with the earlier *Sūrah al-Baqarah*.

Perhaps more than any other *sūrahs* of the Qur'ān, these two Fair Ones, together with *Sūrah al-Anfāl* (War Spoils) established the ground and framework, the socio-religious foundations, of the Prophet's state in Madinah. Although visibly preoccupied with the People of the Book (Jews and Christians), that was not the most important nor the most pressing issue facing the nascent *Ummah* of Islam. A review of the main themes of the two Fair Ones reveals how far the Qur'ān shaped and directed the attitudes and ideas, the institutions and major organizations, in the Muslims' affairs. In fact, the Qur'ānic guidance in these three *sūrahs* and others that closely followed them constituted the very fabric of the new society. The Prophet's guidance and advice were sought about every detail of the daily life of the Muslims. The Qur'ān itself, together with the *Sunnah* of the Prophet, provided the most comprehensive practical directives on all matters, great and small, collective and individual. Nothing was allowed to drift aimlessly, unhelped. The Muslims' conduct from dawn to bedtime, was guided by the Qur'ān and by the practical example of the Prophet, his *Sunnah*, and so subject to exacting ideals and a rigorous discipline.

2.5 **The Socio-Economic Themes of the Two Fair Ones**

While the main preoccupation of the Prophet and his Companions during the first year after the *Hijrah* was the threat posed by the Quraysh of Makkah, the organization of the new society was an urgent and most important task. Everything depended on how the believers responded to the challenge of *Ummah*-building in accordance with the divine guidance. The Islamic social order commended by the Qur'ān was a strong challenge, a hard test of the new Muslims' commitment to their association in Islam which superseded their old association, whether ethnic or societal.

The Prophet, *ṣallā Allāhu 'alayhi wa sallam,* moved quickly to establish the institutions of the new society.

The new society was God-oriented. The very first task therefore was to establish a house for the worship of the One, True God, Allah, *subḥānahū wa ta'ālā.* With the Mosque in place, congregational prayer gathered the Muslims five times a day. In Makkah, the Muslims had performed *Ṣalāt* individually, secretly, in their homes. In Madinah, prayer was the most central part of the new socio-political order. The Muslims must be ready, and stand by, to answer the summons to congregational prayer fives times a day. The first prayer, the *Fajr* prayer, was said in the Prophet's Mosque, at day-break, before sunrise, while the last prayer was the *'Ishā'* prayer, said, again in the Prophet's Mosque, after sunset.

After prayers, the Prophet, as a rule, gave a lesson. If new Qur'ānic verses were revealed, they were read aloud by the Prophet and their meaning explained. If there was a new development, an event, a danger, some information, the congregation were made aware of it. If a task was to be done or a mission undertaken, they were alerted to it. Otherwise, they would be delighted to see the Prophet whom they loved more than they loved their kith and kin, and enjoy each other's company and the new freedom which they had secured by making Madinah an abode of Islam and *Salām* (peace).

The Prophet, *ṣallā Allāhu 'alayhi wa sallam,* was wedded to 'Ā'ishah soon after his arrival in Madinah, and he worked hard to construct the first private family house he had ever owned. In Makkah, he lived first in the house of Abū Ṭālib, and then moved to the house of Khadījah, after his marriage to her. 'Ā'ishah's house, and that of Sawdah, were built directly onto the eastern end of the Mosque. Both the Mosque and the Prophet's rooms were very simple structures indeed. The Mosque was modelled in simplicity after Prophet Moses' *'arīsh* (house/hut), and the family houses of the Prophet were very simple rooms, one room for each of his two wives, Sawdah and 'Ā'ishah.

The Emigrants *(Muhājirūn)* were poor, displaced refugees. The Prophet moved quickly to improve their situation. The practice of *al-Muwākhāt* was commended and widely accepted. In effect, each well-to-do *Anṣār* took into his household one of the poor Emigrants, to lodge and feed. However, the Emigrants were very dignified Quraysh whose sense of honour would not allow them to be dependent on others unnecessarily. They took to the markets and were soon active in trading, a profession in which they were by instinct very skilful. So, 'Abd ar-Raḥmān ibn Awf, Abū Bakr, 'Umar, Abū 'Ubaydah, 'Uthmān ibn 'Affān, az-Zubayr, Ṭalḥah and many others among the *Muhājirūn* were soon visible in the market place, previously a monopoly of the Jews of Madinah. Their appearance there and the consequent competition will have contributed to, even aggravated, the Jewish resentment of the Muslim presence in Madinah.

Indeed, so widespread was the preoccupation of the *Muhājirūn* with trade that the Qur'ān itself refers to it many times.

1. They are referred to as 'Men *(rijāl)* whom neither merchandise nor sales beguile from remembrance of Allah and constancy in *Ṣalāt,* and the offering of *Zakāt* – they fear a day when hearts and eyeballs will be overturned'.
2. On the day of Ḥudaybiyyah, the pledge of the Companions, under the tree, was described as *bay'ah.*
3. In several places in the Qur'ān, the Muslims' commitment to Islam and to Allah is also described as *bay'ah.*

Abū Hurayrah, the celebrated Companion of the Prophet and famous narrator of his sayings, alluded to the penchant of the Muslims for commerce, while explaining his ability to narrate a great number of the Prophet's sayings.

Said Abū Hurayrah:[25] 'The *Muhājirūn*' were busy, moving in the market place, *(Shaghalahum aṣ-Ṣafaq fī al-aswāq)* while the *Anṣār* attended their farms and orchards, but I was a poor man, who followed the Prophet around, and he used to feed me. That is why I was able to narrate and transmit so many *aḥādīth*. One day the Prophet said: 'Who would spread his mantle, and then fold it onto him, he will not forget what I say afterwards.'

Abū Hurayrah said that he did exactly as the Prophet ordered. After that, he said, he never forgot any *ḥadīth* which he heard from the Prophet.

The main themes of *Sūrah al-Baqarah* are as follows:

I. The Scripturists, especially the Jews, and exposition of their schemes, psychology and arguments.

II. The hypocrites and other ill-wishers of the Prophet and the Muslims.

III. The stories of Abraham, Ishmael, Isaac and Jacob with those of Moses and the Israelites.

IV. The story of Adam and the purpose of man's creation on earth and that of the rebellion of *Iblīs* (symbol of sin and evil). This incorporates the Islamic conception of life, of man and of the universe. It also gives the Islamic theory of evil.

V. Then the pillars of Islamic faith are prescribed:
   - formal prayer, *ṣalāt*.
   - payment of *Zakāt*, welfare tax.
   - Fasting in the month of Ramaḍān.
   - The Pilgrimage *(Ḥajj)* to Makkah.

The fifth pillar is the declaration with sincerity and understanding – *Lā ilāha illā Allāh, Muḥammad Rusūl Allah*'.

VI. The invitation to Muslims to spend of their wealth on the poor and dispossessed is widespread in both *Sūrah al-Baqarah* and *Sūrah Āl 'Imrān*. Hardly a single section is without mention of *infāq fī-Sabīl Allāh*. This is voluntary *Ṣadaqah* (or alms) distinct from *Zakāt*, which is obligatory.

One reason for the Qur'ānic insistence on the payment of *Zakāt* and the giving of *Ṣadaqah* (alms) is the central Islamic principle, mentioned in the Qur'ān, that wealth must not be a 'monopoly of the few' but shared and widely distributed.

Another reason was the need to improve the condition of the Muslim immigrant population of Madinah, who were typically poor and dispossessed. Later on, at the end of *Sūrah al-Baqarah, Ribā* (usury) was totally banned, after it had been condemned in the strictest possible terms. The reason for this is that Islam regards *Ribā* as a primary source of exploitation and a means of monopolizing wealth.

VII. Although the banning of *Ribā* was not fully implemented until after the conquest of Makkah in the eighth year of the *Hijrah,* and though the Qur'ānic verse outlawing *Ribā* was revealed much later than the opening verses of the *sūrah,* it fits in logically with a major and pervasive theme of the *sūrah* which commends *Anfāl* and the offering of interest-free loans *(qarḍ ḥasan).*

VIII. Verses 190–4 are the earliest Qur'ānic verses to legalize fighting a just war in self-defence. It must be remembered that fighting, even in self-defence, was forbidden in Makkah.[26] The rationale behind that was that in Makkah, the Muslims were a tiny minority with no means and no organization. They were no match for the might of the Quraysh. With the threat of an impending invasion of Madinah by the Quraysh, the Muslims had to be vigilant and combat-ready. This the Prophet achieved comprehensively – through congregational prayer, through economic solidarity, and night vigils for the remembrance of Allah. These were the most effective means possible of mobilizing the *Ummah,* and of generating an invincible spirit of striving and sacrifice, based on unfaltering love for Allah and His Messenger.

IX. The light of the Qur'ān, so gladly and wholeheartedly received, made of the Prophet's Companions spiritually enlightened men and women of the highest calibre. The drag of worldly pleasures and aspirations was so diminished in them, they became light in spirit, moving easily and readily in support of the Prophet and the lofty, though exacting, ideals of the new society. Little wonder then that the Prophet likened them to 'luminous stars'; in the Qur'ānic description of them, they took little sleep and were always God-conscious: 'The servants of the Beneficient are they who walk upon the earth lightly (modestly) and, when the fools (or the crude) address them, answer: "Peace!" And who spend the night before their Lord, prostrate and standing. And who say: "Our Lord! Avert from us the doom of hell, Lo! the doom thereof is anguish".'[27]

Turning to prayer and supplication was widespread and constant amongst them, an essential mode of life. The very opening verses of *Sūrah al-Baqarah* affirm that constancy in prayer was a cardinal feature of the life of those early Muslims. It is quite clear that the prayer referred to here is public or congregational prayer, because it is said of them collectively: *Alif Lām Mīm.* This is a scripture, whereof there is no doubt, a guidance unto those who are *muttaqūn* (pious), who believe in the unseen and establish *Ṣalāt* (prayer) and spend of that We have bestowed upon them. And who believe in that which is revealed unto you (Muḥammad) and that which is revealed before you, and are certain of the Hereafter.

Prayer, performed in the Prophet's Mosque five times every day, with the Prophet himself leading the prayer, was the major instrument for the moulding of the personalities of the new Muslims:

(a) It was the major means for the remembrance of Allah, in which long portions of the Qur'ān were recited, aloud in dawn, evening and night prayers, and silently in noon and mid-afternoon prayers.

(b) It was the major means of *Tazkiyyah,* making the Muslims better persons, nobler, purer, more God-conscious, refraining from shameful deeds, and righteous in their dealings and conduct.

(c) After prayer, especially *Fajr* (the dawn prayer) the Prophet held long teaching sessions, in which the Qur'ān was recited, and new Qur'ānic revelations made public and their meaning explained. So intensive and elaborate were these sessions, that they normally extended till the sun was high in the sky, and indeed, on one occasion, the Prophet, *ṣallā Allāhu 'alayhi wa sallam,* sat teaching from dawn prayer until noon prayer.

(d) Prayer helped to mobilize the Muslims and kept them near the Prophet – to receive his directives, to witness his general discharge of the affairs of state of the new Muslim community, then consisting of an alliance between Muslims and other groups.

Gathering for prayer five times daily, helped to keep the Muslims ever-vigilant, in touch with political developments hour by hour. In a society surrounded by hostile forces not only far away in Makkah, but also closer at home within the city itself, it was of the utmost importance that the populace should be in a constant state of vigilance and alertness. The small city state of Madinah was in danger of destruction not only by forces hostile to Islam as a new religion, but also by the powerful war-like bedouin tribes around Madinah. These tribes thrived on plunder and military raids.

The constant exhortation to *Infāq,* that well-to-do Muslims should spend of their wealth, is easily understood. Not only were the *Muhājirūn* poor, homeless and dispossessed, but also the financial cost of defending the city was enormous, and the state was, to begin with, almost without any sources of revenue.

X. It was of Allah's mercy to the Muslims that *Zakāt* was made an obligatory religious practice in Islam. The systematic organization of its collection by the state heralded a new economic order. *Zakāt* was not viewed only as a system of taxation intended to assist the poor, the typical recipients of *Zakāt* revenue, but also as a major indicator of a new economic philosophy.

XI. With *Zakāt* established as a pillar of worship in Islam, the value and importance of economic resources in the Islamic way of life was also established. To be able to pay *Zakāt,* a Muslim must be a person of means, of economic resources, he must be a well-to-do man. Contrary to the views of Abū Ḥāmid al-Ghazālī,[28] and fellow ascetics, poverty is not to be tolerated or aspired to, in an Islamic society. If anything, the duty of *Zakāt* is a powerful incentive, as well as a means, to combat poverty in Islam.[29]

XII. *Zakāt* is a powerful tool in spurring enterprise and investment. Money merely hoarded will be subject to the tax. *Zakāt* once it is distributed to the poor (who spend from it to secure their consumption needs) will contribute to the overall purchasing power of the community. Thus the society in which *Zakāt* is enforced will enjoy a wonderful balance between production and consumption.

XIII. *Zakāt,* important as it is, must not be regarded as constitutive of the Islamic economic system as a whole. It must be seen rather as a vital component within that whole. Complementary to *Zakāt* within such a system are profit-sharing (and joint ventures), the abolition of *Ribā* (usury), *qarḍ ḥasan* (lending without interest) and state expenditure (stipends, salaries, etc.).

The introduction of *Zakāt,* on a regular and organized basis by the Prophet from the sixth year of *Hijrah,*[30] went a good way to changing the living conditions of the Muslims of Madinah. It did a great deal to mitigate the harshness of life, and soften the consequences of the economic weakness the Muslims, especially the *Muhājirūn,* suffered in the initial period of the Madinan era. That the Muslims were hard-pressed to secure even the minimal food needs is quite clear in the basic *Sīrah* sources.

XIV. 'Ā'ishah made this point in a touching way. That at one time they passed three successive months without kindling a cooking fire in the house, because there was nothing to be cooked. They lived only on the 'two black' *(al-aswadayn)* dates and water. Later on, after the death of the Prophet, when life became much more comfortable, she would find tears come to her eyes every time an elaborate meal was prepared for her. She would be reminded of the austere life of the Prophet when he had often to go hungry for two or three days consecutively.

XV. The Prophet himself and other Companions, notably Mu'ādh ibn Jabal, had to resort to borrowing very extensively, quite often in order to secure necessary food provisions. Sometimes the borrowed money was used to prepare for *Jihād,* to buy armour or horses. The Qur'ān itself attests to the fact that borrowing was widespread. The longest verse of *Sūrah al-Baqarah* (verse 282) deals with the legal regulation of money-lending. The Jewish financial families played an important role as creditors. The Jews, enjoying a near-total monopoly in trade and commerce, must have recognized the usefulness of lending money in spurring trade, especially when they were assured of repayment. Though the Muslims resorted to borrowing for consumption, it would not be right to infer that they were living beyond their means. Though beyond their immediate means, they were already involved in extensive economic activities with good prospects of prompt returns. As for the *Muhājirūn,* they were generally involved in trading, coming as they did from the mercantile environment of Makkah – Abū Bakr, 'Umar, 'Uthmān, 'Alī, 'Abd ar-Raḥmān ibn 'Awf, Ṭalḥah, Az-Zubayr, among others. We have already mentioned Abū Hurayrah's reference to this activity among the Prophet's Companions.

So hard pressed were the Muslims in the initial period, that the Prophet had to borrow some money for his marriage to 'Ā'ishah. Abū Hurayrah said that he was one day driven by the pangs of hunger to the Prophet, to seek his help. On seeing that Abū Hurayrah had two stones around his waist, the Prophet lifted his mantle, and Abū Hurayrah saw three stones around his waist. But all of this was destined to change in a few years' time. The Muslim community of Madinah soon became prosperous – given their humble beginning, that in itself speaks greatly in favour of the new economic orientation.

The Prophet urged his Companions vigorously to work. Labour and enterprise were strongly favoured. The Prophet encouraged his Companions to take on business, especially in commerce and trade. In a well-known *ḥadīth* the Prophet says: 'Nine portions out of ten of people's earnings are in trade.' He liked to deal in fabrics and perfumes, when, before the start of his Prophetic mission, he was involved in trade.

While it is true that the Muslims' treasury *(Bayt al-Māl)* obtained considerable wealth from spoils of war (the *Ghanīmah*) with the Quraysh and its allies, and later from the rich Jewish tribes, the new wealth of the Muslims could not be attributed to booty alone. For one thing, waging war was itself very costly. Had it not been for the liberality of Abū Bakr, 'Uthmān, 'Abd ar-Raḥmān ibn 'Awf, Ṭalḥah, Sa'd ibn Abī Waqqāṣ and other well-to-do Muslims, these wars could not have been undertaken or sustained. The *Bayt al-Māl* itself bore a substantial portion of the cost of those expeditions. Even revenues from *Zakāt,* primarily to be allocated to the poor and the needy, had to be used for the purposes of *Jihād.*

The newly-found wealth of the Madinan society could be attributed to the following sources:

1. Revenues from *Zakāt* and *Jizyah* (defence tax), and other emergency taxes.
2. Revenues from *Ghanīmah* and *Khums.*
3. Revenues from commerce and trade.
4. Revenues from *Kharāj* and *'Ushr* (land taxes).
5. Revenues from *Ṣadaqah.*
6. Revenues from craftsmanship and the armour works.
7. Revenues from *Rikāz* (mineral wealth).

We must, however, look deeper if we are to reveal the real cause of the economic dynamism and vitality of the new society. No doubt, the threats and dangers of enemies within and without posed a great challenge and the instinct for survival, aroused to great heights in such circumstances, generated enormous creative energies. War, according to some views of the matter, has a tremendous mobilizing influence on the creativity of societies engaged in it, hence the maxim 'war is the mother of invention'. Modern Europe's economic power is unimaginable, this view goes, had it not been for the two world wars of this century. However, it remains difficult to explain the emergence of the wealth of the new Muslim society of Madinah simply in terms of 'war economy'. Whereas the Muslims' emerging economy experienced steady growth and expansion, a war economy is typically characterized by tensions, scarcity and instability. Even demands created by the necessities of war tend to be artificial and lapse as soon as the war is over.

In any case, it may be truer to say that, far from stimulating the economy, war may tend to exhaust it – the scarce resources which used to go into the service sector to meet basic needs, are channelled to fund military expenditure.

For these reasons the expansion of the Madinan economy, the creation of the new Muslim wealth, cannot be explained by the war-economy theory. It can only be explained by the intrinsic characteristics of the new economic order implemented by the Prophet.

The Prophet launched an uncompromising war against *Ribā,* widely practised in Madinah and Makkah before the advent of Islam. In Makkah, some wealthy Quraysh families, such as those of al-'Abbās ibn 'Abd al-Muṭṭalib (the Prophet's uncle) and Khālid ibn al-Walīd, and many others, used to run what could be likened to financial companies or banks whose sole activity was to lend money on interest. In the Islamic perspective, *ribā* is viewed as the very antithesis of *zakāt* and *ṣadaqah. Zakāt* and *ṣadaqah* are the economic foundation of a society based on co-operation, brotherhood, compassion and solidarity, whereas *ribā* is the economic foundation of a society based upon exploitation, injustice, competition and materialism. While *Zakāt* militates against concentrating the wealth of a nation in a few hands, and is an effective policy for discouraging hoarding of wealth, *ribā* does the opposite: it ultimately restricts the circulation of wealth, concentrating it in fewer and fewer hands, while the majority of the population become dispossessed and exploited.

The Prophet Muḥammad, *ṣallā Allāhu 'alayhi wa sallam,* personally organized and executed the campaign against *ribā.* Following the commandments of his Lord, he twice, and vehemently, condemned *ribā* in his Farewell (Pilgrimage) Address.

He declared, in his famous speeches, that henceforth all conventions and customs of *Jāhiliyyah* (pre-Islamic Arabia) were under his feet. In particular, the *ribā* (usury) of

Jāhiliyyah, including that of his uncle al-'Abbās, was to be abolished.

The Qur'ān itself condemns *ribā,* in the strictest language:

> O you who believe, fear Allah, and give up outstanding interest if you truly believe.
> But if you do not do so, then be warned of war from Allah, and His Messenger.[31]

Ribā is so abhorred in the Qur'ān because it is deemed to be the very antithesis of human fraternity and compassion. It is the major tool of exploitation and injustice, because, if practised widely and without restraints it gathers wealth out of the hands of the many and gives it into the power of the privileged few. In Islam, the guiding economic principle is that wealth must be circulated among the greatest possible number of people, so that everybody can participate to some degree in the economic life of the community and enjoy its fruits. The Prophet was ordered to distribute the booty of war *(al-Fay' wa al-Ghanīmah)* amongst the believers, especially the nearest of kin, the orphans, the poor and the wayfarers.

> So it (wealth) should not be a traffic merely amongst the rich of you . . .[32]

In a *ribā*-dominated economy, the wealthy can only become wealthier – no risk of a loss, since they get a guaranteed interest-rate on their money, come what may. If the investor incurs a loss, he must still pay all the interest plus the original capital that was loaned to him. It is, then, a simple arithmetical calculation that all wealth, and with it, power, gradually accumulates into the hands of the few – wealth to exploit even further, and power to oppress and dominate, to be corrupt and to spread corruption in the land and at sea.

Islam offers an alternative system to that of *Ribā.* It offers the system of profit-sharing, where the wealthy offer capital to the have-nots, not merely as a charity but as a joint venture: capital, perhaps also counsel and expertise come from the wealthy party; work, supervision and administration is offered by the dispossessed party. Eventually the profit is shared, according to terms agreed beforehand. If a loss is incurred, the wealthy party loses his capital, while the second party loses his labour, time and administration. Thus, there is a sufficient incentive for the joint venture to succeed given that the Islamic ethical values of honesty, hard work and sincerity are observed by both parties to the joint venture.

The Profit-sharing model provides for maximum employment and maximum investment, maximum participation in wealth creation and fairer distribution of its fruits.

Thus profit-sharing, which reflects the basic Islamic principle of *Muwākhāt* in societal organization, is the backbone of economic enterprise in Islam. *Zakāt* reinforces it, making up for natural disequalities in original capabilities, for disasters and misfortunes. It acts as a general principle of compassion, and as a specific means of providing for the underprivileged. *Zakāt* caters for their needs, providing them with new opportunities to start over again, by offering the possibility of full employment, and even capital as a gift.[33] The giving of *ṣadaqah,* different from *Zakāt,* further reinforces the economic system, and makes for even greater sharing of wealth in the Islamic community. Supporting this aim of wealth-sharing, the inheritance provisions in Islamic law divide the wealth of the deceased among his children and his parents. If the deceased had no children, his wealth is distributed among his next of kin. Finally, better-off Muslims are encouraged to help support their poor relatives.

'An uncle is in the place of a father and an aunt is in the place of a mother', declared the Prophet, *ṣallā Allāhu 'alayhi wa sallam,* when he was told that al-'Abbās did not pay *Zakāt.* He said he would pay in lieu of al-'Abbās and more than the required amount. Furthermore, a part of the true charity *(al-Birr)* is to give money to needy relatives. In the notorious affair of the *Ifk* (lie), Abū Bakr vowed not to continue paying charity to his cousin Misṭaḥ ibn Uthāthah, because he was one of those who helped spread the rumour concerning 'Ā'ishah, the Mother of the Faithful. But the Qur'ān commanded him not to observe that vow, but to forgive and forget, and to continue his financial obligation towards his cousin. All these practices and regulations ensure a maximum sharing in the common wealth of the community by all its members.

2.6 **The Family is Sacred**

Substantial portions of *Sūrahs al-Baqarah* and *Āl 'Imrān* deal with the personal law of the *Sharī'ah,* i.e. the legal provisions regulating family relationships in Muslim society. All aspects of family relations are carefully examined, and detailed, meticulous legislation laid down to place them on the most solid foundation. The family is the basic social unit and so received the fullest attention in the *sūrahs* revealed in the early years of the Prophet's stay in Madinah. They provide the conceptual as well as the legal framework for the emerging Muslim society.

I. There is strict legislation on *Nikāḥ* (wedlock). Wedlock is the surest means of securing the purity of lineage of the family. It is the only legitimate framework for family life in Islam. The laws of inheritance, to operate effectively, depend upon purity of genealogical descent. A child is entitled to inherit from his father only if he is of his blood and born in wedlock. Fornication *(zinā)* is considered sinful, because it violates the institution of marriage, hence the severity of punishment for it. In his Farewell Address, the Prophet devoted a whole paragraph to the importance and sanctity of the family in Islam.

II. Regulations pertaining to marriage proposal, marriage dowry, the rights of wives and husbands, polygamy, divorce, disagreement between wives and husbands, widowhood, remarriage of widows and divorcees, menstruation, breast-feeding, inheritance law, etc. are explained in some detail in *Sūrahs al-Baqarah* and *Āl 'Imrān.*

3. **The Conception of Woman (The Early Concept of *Ḥijāb*)**[34]

Whereas not all legislation concerning the status of woman is to be found in the early *sūrahs* of the Madinan era, what is mentioned is very significant. The essential role of the

Muslim woman is indicated in those early *sūrahs*. The themes omitted are as important as those discussed and elaborated upon. Almost all the issues discussed in relation to woman have to do with her role within the structure of the family. Nothing or very little is mentioned about her public role, assuming that she has a well-defined public role.

When woman is mentioned in a context related to public life, e.g. in the context of inheritance laws or that of giving testimony in the question of loans, then the impression is indirectly conveyed that her role there is secondary to that of man. For instance, the inheritance laws assign to her half of what is assigned to her male brother, the rationale being that a woman is not required to support a family, which responsibility falls upon man. This strongly gives the impression that woman is not a bread-winner – that is not her domain. It is the responsibility of the adult males of the family to be the bread-winners.

The same impression that the public domain is not the primary domain of the Muslim woman is also conveyed in the context of giving testimony, i.e. acting as a witness in writing out documents of debt accounts – who lent whom how much, and when. Two male witnesses are required for such a document; if only one male witness is available, he can be supported by two female witnesses – if one forgets, the second can remind her. In harmony with this tendency, there is a *ḥadīth* to the effect that the position of the supreme ruler of the Muslim state is not to be occupied by a woman: the Prophet said: 'The public affairs of people will not be well conducted if they take a woman as their supreme ruler.'[35]

Though the final form of the *Ḥijāb* was not given as law until the fifth year of the *Hijrah,* there is already indirect and moral *Ḥijāb* implicit in the prohibition that a man and woman should not be betrothed secretly. If a widowed woman has not completed her term of confinement *(al-'Iddah),* the man is advised not to propose to her in person, but to make his intentions known to her guardian. Should he bring up the topic in her presence, he should be discreet and the words he utters must be indirect and polite. He should not propose to her in a direct way.[36]

Moreover, the Qur'ān clearly stipulates that close and

intimate relations can only exist between a wife and her husband, as far as relations between the two sexes are concerned: 'It is made lawful for you to go unto your wives on the night of the fast. They are raiment for you and you are raiment for them.'[37]

One Ramaḍān night the Prophet was observing *I'tikāf* (retreat and religious seclusion) when he was visited by his wife Ṣafiyyah bint Ḥuyay ibn al-Akhṭab. He went out with her to see her to her home, near the house of Usāmah ibn Zayd. On the way, he met two of his *Anṣārī* Companions. When they saw the Prophet, they hurried their pace, and moved out of the way, feeling shy to embarrass the Prophet because he was in the company of his wife. The Prophet called out loudly to them: 'Why are you hurrying?' or 'Do not hurry.' 'This is only Ṣafiyyah bint Ḥuyay.'

This is an authentic and significant *ḥadīth*.[38] The incident clearly belongs to the early Madinan period, before the ordinance of *Ḥijāb*. While it is very clear that the basic role of the Muslim women belonged to the family domain, they still had a significant, though secondary, role, in the public domain. The outgoing, extrovert temperament of Umm al-Mu'minīn, Ṣafiyah bint Ḥuyay ibn Akhṭab, and indeed a good number of the Prophet's wives, is indicative of that. When the Prophet used to be secluded for *I'tikāf*, in the Mosque, Ṣafiyyah was a frequent visitor. Of course, no sex was involved, as it is not permitted during the period of *I'tikāf*. But Ṣafiyyah had felt a longing to see and converse with the Prophet, so she used to visit him, even during the night. If we bear in mind that Ṣafiyyah's house was on the outskirts of Madinah, within the apartments of Usāmah ibn Zayd, the extrovert disposition was by no means a peculiarity of hers.

3.1 The Role of the Prophet's Wives

I. 'Ā'ishah's role in disseminating knowledge of the Qur'ān, *Sunnah* and *Fiqh* is well known. Despite her tender years, she is counted third among the *Ḥāfiẓ* of the Qur'ān, one-third among the authorities of Islamic law.

II. Zaynab bint Jaḥsh was called Umm al-Masākīn, the Mother of the Poor. She had an important role in the field of social work.

III. Umm al-Mu'minīn, Ḥafṣah bint 'Umar ibn al-Khaṭṭāb, was an activist, a devout ascetic and the keeper of the records and scrolls of the Qur'ān, before these were edited by the third Rightly-Guided Caliph, 'Uthmān ibn 'Affān.

IV. The role of Khadījah, *raḍiya Allāhu 'anhā,* in the Makkan period is too well known to be in need of further comment.

V. Umm Ḥabībah bint Abī Sufyān was the daughter of Abū Sufyān ibn Ḥarb, the head of the Quraysh opposition until the opening of Makkah. But she accepted Islam and made the minor *Hijrah* to Abyssinia. There is also the famous incident when, after she was married to the Prophet and her father visited her, she refused to permit him to sit on the Prophet's bed. Her understanding of Islam was strikingly movement-oriented and of the highest purity.

3.2 **Unique Relationship with Some Outstanding Muslim Women**

VI. Some Muslim women were related to the Prophet in a unique way because of a special relationship. From these women, Ibn Sa'd[39] mentions Lubābah al-Kubrā, mother of al-Faḍl, and wife of the Prophet's uncle, al-'Abbās. The Prophet had a special affection for her. He used to visit her quite often and she used to cleanse his hair and put ointment of *Kuḥl* in his eyes. When doing this, he used to put his head in her lap, though she was not *maḥram* to him. Zayd ibn 'Alī ibn al-Ḥusain ibn 'Alī, *raḍiya Allāhu 'anhum,* said that she was the only woman with whom the Prophet acted in this manner. Later on, Umm al-Faḍl became the milk-nurse of al-Ḥusain ibn 'Alī, the Prophet's grandson.

VII. A shining example of an honourable role for the Muslim woman in the public domain is that of Umm

'Umārah. Her story is indeed significant, because it obtained both the approval and the pleasure of the Prophet.

(a) Umm 'Umārah witnessed and took part in the second 'Aqabah Pledge and was thus one of the first Muslims of Madinah. The instrumentality of that pledge in making Madinah *Dār al-Hijrah* (the land of *Hijrah*) is well known in Islamic history.

(b) Umm 'Umārah (Nusaybah bint Ka'b of Banū an-Najjār, the maternal uncles of the Prophet) took part in the fighting at Uḥud, al-Ḥudaybiyyah, Khaybar, Ḥunayn, and at the Battle of al-Yamāmah during the Apostasy Wars.

(c) She lost her hand in the fighting during the Battle of al-Yamāmah.

(d) But the high point of her life was, no doubt, reached at the Battle of Uḥud when the fighting turned against the Muslims, many of whom fled, leaving the Prophet exposed to his Quraysh enemies. Not only was Nusaybah bint Ka'b one of the few Muslims who held their ground around the Prophet, but she intercepted and fought with Ibn Qami'ah who tried to kill the Prophet. He struck her neck with his sword, causing a deep wound which took a whole year to heal. Altogether she received thirteen wounds during the Battle of Uḥud.

The Prophet was so pleased with the performance of Nusaybah, her husband Ghaziyyah ibn 'Amr and her two sons, that he prayed to Allah that they be his companions in Paradise.[40]

VIII. Another shining example of the women Companions of the Prophet, who played a major role in the public life of early Islam, is Umm Sulaim bint Milḥān ibn Khālid[41] from Banū an-Najjār. Umm Sulaim was the mother of Anas ibn Mālik, the personal attendant of the Prophet. She was young when she participated in the Battle of Uḥud, giving water to the thirsty and treating the wounded. However, she did not take part in the fighting as did Umm 'Umārah. When Mālik ibn an-Naḍr died, she married Abū Ṭalḥah Zayd ibn Sahl. Actually Abū Ṭalḥah was a *Mushrik* when he proposed to her. He became a Muslim at her suggestion and persuasion. She participated in the Battle of Ḥunayn, though she was pregnant with her son 'Abdullāh ibn Abī Ṭalḥah (which indicates that she was still on the young side). When she went out to the battlefield, she was armed with a *Khanjar* (dagger) which she carefully tied around her waist. The Prophet saw it and smiled in approval.

Anas ibn Mālik narrated that the Prophet, *ṣallā Allāhu 'alayhi wa sallam,* visited his mother. She used to offer him food which she made especially for him. The Prophet would eat and pray, rest, sometimes even take his siesta in her home. That was indeed a special relationship with this resourceful woman of Banū an-Najjār, his maternal uncles. Umm Sulaim was not an old woman at that time; because the Prophet used to entertain and play with her children (specially Abū 'Umair whom the Prophet used to admire).[42]

Said Umm Sulaim: 'The Prophet used to rest in my house in the mid-noon. I used to spread a *Naṭu'* (a rug made of skins or leaves of date trees) and he used to sleep on it, and as he used to sweat excessively, I used to collect his sweat and mix it with my *suk* (a special perfume).' One day, as the Prophet slept in her room, she scooped the sweat from his body. He awoke and asked: 'What are you doing Umm Sulaim?' She answered: 'I am collecting this *Barakah* (blessing) that is oozing from you.'

Later Muslim authorities may wonder about the nature of this very special relationship which bound the Prophet, *ṣallā Allāhu 'alayhi wa sallam,* to Umm Sulaim. But the following circumstances may afford an explanation:

(a) First of all, the Prophet enjoyed a special relationship with all Muslims, male or female, young or old, slave or free man. This relationship was owed to him in his capacity as the Messenger of Allah, *subḥānahu wa ta'ālā.* The Qur'ān itself has stipulated this special relationship: 'The Prophet is more caring (responsible) for the believers than their selves, and his wives are (as) their mothers.'[43]

(b) Secondly, both Umm Umārah and Umm Sulaim were from Banū an-Najjār, who were the maternal uncles of the Prophet. The exact blood relationship is not specified in our sources, but it is quite possible that it was a very close one.

(c) Moreover, Umm Sulaim seems to have held a public office in the Prophet's household, the 'manager' of his home affairs, because, for one thing, her son Anas was the personal attendant-cum-secretary of the Prophet, and secondly, she almost always travelled with the Prophet's wives. The Prophet used to advise Anjashah, his guide who was entrusted with the caravan of his wives, to be gentle in his handling of the she-camel of Umm Sulaim and he used to advise him to do the same with his wives: 'O Anjashah, be gentle in your handling of these glass cylinders' – meaning the women: *(Yā Anjashah rifqan bil Qawārīr).*

Further evidence is provided by the fact that when the Prophet went on a pilgrimage, he looked for Umm Sulaim and did not find her. He enquired about her absence and later demanded an explanation from her concerning her absence. He obviously expected her to be in the company of his wives on a regular basis, which could only be the case if she was in his permanent service.

Whatever the precise nature of the office, it is clear that both Umm 'Umārah and Umm Sulaim held some important public office in the service of the Prophet and of the Muslim state. Nusaybah (Umm 'Umārah) had something of the role of an officer of high rank in the medical corps of the Muslim army, while Umm Sulaim was more like the manager of the Prophet's household. This interpretation concerning the status of Umm Sulaim seems quite natural in view of the fact that the Prophet actually had in his service a number of functionaries.

3.3 **Men and Women in the Private Service of the Prophet**

(i) 'Abdullāh ibn Mas'ūd, Anas ibn Mālik, Bilāl ibn Rabāḥ, Rabāḥ (a black youth), Abū Mūsā al-Ash'arī (occasionally), Rabī'ah ibn Ka'b al-Aslamī (he used to sleep outside his door at night: a night guard), Hind and Asmā' bint al-Ḥārith (from Banū Aslam), these were more like maids of the Prophet.

Rabī'ah ibn Ka'b was also the Prophet's attendant and companion on his travels. He used to attend to the personal needs of the Prophet. It is this Rabī'ah ibn Ka'b who reportedly said that he served the Prophet for five years and never received a single complaint ('He never asked me why I did what I did, or why I omitted what I omitted').[44] Anas ibn Mālik is also reported to have said something to the same effect.

(ii) Other personal functionaries of the Prophet included Anjashah, responsible for the upkeep of the Prophet's horses and camels. Hudhayfah ibn al-Yamān was his *Kātib as-Sirr* (personal scribe). Abū Bakr, personal advisor, friend, father-in-law, principal minister and in charge of protocol (telling emissaries what to wear in the presence of the Prophet and how to greet him, once they were allowed in). 'Umar was the second minister. Other functionaries of the Prophet included his regional rulers, judges, *Zakāt* collectors, the people of *Shūrā* (consultation), the heads of the armies, the scribes of the *Waḥī*, etc.

Thus it is not unnatural to suppose that some of these official and personal functionaries were in fact women. It must be borne in mind that the female element was never absent, in the initial stage of Islam, both in the Makkan period, and the early Madinan period, before the imposition of *Ḥijāb*. Thus it is safe to conclude that both Umm 'Umārah and Umm Sulaim were holding either public offices or were in his service as personal functionaries. But to be a functionary of the Prophet was also a public office of a special nature.

To complete the picture of the public role of the women Companions of the Prophet, we need to add two more considerations: (a) their involvement in trade and business; and (b) the degree of mixing between the two sexes, at least in the initial Madinan period before the ordinance of the *Ḥijāb (Sūrah al-Aḥzāb)*.

Khadījah's involvement in trade is well-known. She did not give it up after she became a Muslim. Al-Kattānī al-Fāsī in his book *at-Tarātīb al-Idāriyyah*[45] mentions that 'Umar ibn al-Khaṭṭāb gave both 'Ā'ishah and Ḥafṣah, wives of the Prophet, plots of agricultural land, in the vicinity of Khaybar. They accepted the gift, and supervised cultivation of their lands.

As regards the degree of mixing between the two sexes, in the pre-*Ḥijāb* period, it occurred in a public context, on a number of occasions:

(i) Women participated in the two long *hijrahs* to Abyssinia;
(ii) in the two 'Aqabah pledges;
(iii) in the major *Hijrah* to Madinah.
(iv) Women used to attend the lessons of the Prophet and also congregational prayer in the mosque, sitting behind the rows of men. They also participated in the *'Īd* congregational prayers.
(v) Women used to receive guests (strangers) in their homes and dine with them from the same food pot. 'Umar once dined with the Prophet and 'Ā'ishah, and ate from the same pot. When his hand touched that of 'Ā'ishah during the meal, the dish being common, he was visibly embarrassed, and prayed to Allah for a revelation restricting the mixing of the two sexes. Soon afterwards, the Qur'ān verses ordaining *Ḥijāb* were revealed.

The incident of the Companion of the Prophet who put out the light so that his guest would eat his full, while he and his wife only pretended to be eating, the food being hardly enough for more than one person, is well-known. But this incident clearly belonged to the pre-*Ḥijāb* period.

The ordinance of *Ḥijāb* changed all that. After the verses of *Sūrah al-Aḥzāb* the Prophet's wives were secluded from the public eye. They could only be addressed from behind a curtain. When they ventured out in public, they were totally covered, even their faces were covered if a stranger came in sight. Whether such *ḥijāb* was meant to be binding on all Muslim women or meant as a special prerogative of the Prophet's wives is a controversial matter among contemporary Muslims. The conservatively-minded say it is a universal ruling, whereas the liberally-minded say that *Ḥijāb* in the full sense of covering everything, the face included, is only a prerogative of the Prophet's wives. But even the liberally-minded accept a minor version of *Ḥijāb* which covers everything, excepting the face and the hands. This minor *Ḥijāb* must be such that it is neither transparent, nor tight as to show the contours of the body. Imām Mālik ibn Anas favoured the lesser *ḥijāb,* for all Muslim women, whereas Ibn Ḥanbal favoured the complete *ḥijāb.*[46]

Exactly to what extent Muslim women participated in public life after the ordinance of *Ḥijāb* is uncertain. Exhaustive research must be done of all domains of the *Sīrah* in the wider sense which includes not only the Qur'ān, the *Ḥadīth* and the *Sunnah,* the specialized *Sīrah* books, but must also include the more modern books of the *Sīrah,* the books of Islamic and Arabic history, the books of *Dalā'il an-Nubūwah* (proofs of prophethood) and the books of *Shamā'il* (character traits of the Prophet), and the books of *Āthār*[47] (life histories of the Prophet's Companions). This research is urgent if an authentic and coherent picture is to be obtained.

It is most important to be able to infer the rules that governed the conduct of Muslim women in the private and public domains, after the ordinance of the *Ḥijāb.* The permissible conduct before *Ḥijāb* has little or no legislative value since the verses of *Ḥijāb* have abrogated legislation in the pre-*Ḥijāb* period, either totally or partially, depending on how universally the *Ḥijāb* verses are interpreted.

3.4 **Madinah: A Community of Faith**

As the Prophet arrived in Yathrib, mounted on his she-camel al-Qaṣwā', his mood, though joyful, was sombre yet serene, profoundly humble and grateful to Allah, most High and Exalted. He recounted, silently, Allah's blessing for him:

— He had been born an orphan, yet now he was the ruler of a city.
— He had been born in an age of ignorance, yet now he was the Messenger of guidance.
— He had been poor and in need of a supporter, yet now he was rich, both in material and spiritual terms.

Quite naturally, being the considerate and compassionate man he was, the Prophet's first thoughts as ruler of the community turned to the destitute, the poor, the uprooted, the strangers.

As the Yathribite crowds cheered him, and greeted warmly his coming to the city, he issued his first decree. It was a simple, but most profound statement:

> 'You are all brothers unto one another. No stranger exists in this community. So greet you each other. Spread greetings to whoever you meet, because whoever you meet, is, from this day onwards, a brother of yours. He is no stranger, because Madinah is now the city of one extended family of believers in Allah and His Messenger, and assuredly believers are brethren unto each other.'

Madinah was to be one extended neighbourhood. So the Prophet shouted at the top of his voice to the cheering, welcoming crowds: 'Spread salutations of peace! *Afshū as-Salām! Afshū as-Salam!'* Then, he added: *'Wa aṭ'imū aṭ-Ṭa'ām!* (Feed with food!). *Wa aṭ'imū aṭ-Ṭa'ām!'*

The classic Arabian generosity was reinforced and confirmed by the Prophet, on the very day of his arrival in Madinah. Generosity had a long tradition, a most profound root, in Arabian society. Prophet Abraham was legendary in his generosity. This trait was inherited by Ismā'īl, his son by Hāgar, who was destined to be the father of the Arabized Arabs of the Quraysh *(al-'Arab al-Musta'ribah)*. Traditions had it that Ismā'īl, when he grew up in the valley of Bakkah (old name for Makkah) first got married to an Arabian woman from Jurhum (a Yamanite tribe). But she was niggardly, so Abraham was not offered any hospitality by her when he visited his son in Bakkah, who happened to be outside the home. Abraham commanded him to divorce her on account of her lack of generosity. Ismā'īl did so and remarried from another Arabian tribe (Khuzā'ah). The generosity of Abraham is praised in the Qur'ān. When he had guests (who were actually Angels in disguise) he slaughtered a fat calf as a gesture of welcoming hospitality towards them.

The new Muslim society in Madinah was to be founded

on the values of brotherhood, peace, goodwill and generosity. When people eat together, their hearts come closer, acquaintance and mutual trust develop between them, and they learn to share a very valuable commodity, food. Given the scarcity of food in a city already strained by the influx of Muslim immigrants from Makkah, and indeed from elsewhere in Arabia, the wisdom of the Prophet in emphasizing the sharing of food could not be lost on any intelligent person. Then the Prophet added: 'Honour the ties of kinship and pray in the night hours when men sleep. *(Wa ṣilū al-arḥām, wa ṣallū wa an-nāsu niyām).* If you do this, you will enter paradise in peace.' The universal brotherhood between believers with no blood ties, naturally extends to believers within the same family bound by kinship, in addition to the ties of faith. The family becomes thus the basic entity in this universal fraternity. If every extended family is based on a solid foundation of compassion and solidarity so will be the whole of the community.

The fourth provision of this famous inaugural speech of the Prophet spelt out the spiritual orientation of the new Muslim community. It states in unmistakable terms that it was a community intended to be, above all else, God-oriented – striving in order to seek God's pleasure and approval, and the reward of Paradise in the Hereafter. The city of Madinah was founded as a city of God and His Messenger, and it lived up to this expectation. A sublime, spiritualized society developed there whose overriding concern was the realization of Allah's word on His earth, and whose objective was to make His commandments rule supreme.

The moral and spiritual values expressed in the inaugural speech were later reinforced and carefully implemented in the Prophet's personal life as well as in the public life of the city he ruled. There was never duplicity in his conduct, nor in his dealings. What he preached, he implemented at the first available opportunity. Political power was thus a valuable instrument to achieve and implement those spiritual and moral values. In his conduct of state affairs, the Prophet never assumed the pretensions of a king or a prince, he continued to live and act as a spiritual leader, a moral teacher, as the Prophet of God, with a Message to deliver from Him.

Said the Prophet, *ṣallā Allāhu ʿalayhi wa sallam*: 'Surely I was sent to perfect the moral virtues . . .' His life-style continued to be frugal, austere, even ascetic, shunning the pomp and glitter of this world, even when he was the absolute ruler of the whole of Arabia from the boundaries of Syria in the north, to the southern Arabian States of Bahrain, Ḥaḍramaut and Yaman (Arabia Felix). He lived in very humble rooms, having nothing or very little to eat sometimes for days on end. Towards his Companions, he was most easy and congenial, never imposing nor oppressive. He was more like a father in his kindness and leniency towards them than a ruler. The Qur'ān itself portrays him so in the well-known verse: 'It was by the mercy of Allah that you were lenient with them (O Muḥammad), for if you had been stern and fierce of heart, they would have dispersed from around you. So pardon them and ask forgiveness for them,[48] and consult with them on the conduct of affairs.'

The Prophet took great pains to educate his Companions to be proud, dignified men, and yet most humble servants of their Lord, and the most compassionate amongst themselves. He taught them to be equal, as the tooth of the comb, with no discrimination of any sort between them. Elevation to rank was to be only on the basis of *taqwā* (God-fearing) and the achievement of righteous and useful deeds. The criterion for social and political preferment were fair and objective: the Prophet used to tell his Companions: 'Let those who sit nearest to me be of:

1. The people of *Sābiqah* (the first to accept Islam).
2. Then the people of *Hijrah.*
3. Then the people of *Jihād* (who witnessed the various battles, those who witnessed Badr being the first category).
4. Then those with knowledge, and those more advanced in age (men of experience).'

It is no wonder that the Quraysh as well as those who had a very humble start (being former slaves) were able to achieve the highest distinctions in Islam. The egalitarian principle continued to rule supreme. Rank did not figure, nor was expressed, in any special protocol – except in a most oblique, subdued way. The Prophet gave the best example in this respect, refusing to be acknowledged by a special protocol. He ordered his Companions not to stand up when he appeared in public. He hated to be distinguished from his Companions in dress, or even in his place of audience. If they worked he joined with them in the same work. When it was time to eat, he ate with them; even in recreation and games he played as one of them. Yet they loved and revered him as they did not love or revere their own fathers and mothers. Said ʻAmr ibn al-ʻĀṣ, that though he once hated the Prophet so intensely, before he became a Muslim, he came to love and respect him so much, that he never, even once, was able to look him fully in the face, so that the Prophet passed away and he was not able to describe his noble countenance.

The Prophet stated that his mission was essentially spiritual and moral. When he assumed full state power, his utmost and foremost concern remained to call people to the service of their Lord, and to lead a life, though vigorous and affirming, yet God-oriented and of the highest moral excellence. In Makkah his mission had been clearly, passionately and unswervingly well disseminated. Then, when time and opportunity presented themselves in Madinah it was very clearly and steadily implemented and accomplished. The Qur'ān itself attests to this:

'Truly you are of immense moral stature.'[49]

'There has come unto you a Messenger from among yourselves, who is grieved if you are ever over-burdened, full of concern for you, for the believers, he is full of compassion, merciful.'[50]

With this brief epilogue, we bring this study to a close. In a forthcoming publication, *Inshā' Allāh,* we will deal with peace and war in the life of the Prophet. The task of writing a comprehensive study of the *Sīrah* seems, at this point, quite an impossible one. We will strive, as long as we live, with the help and guidance of Allah, *subḥānahū wa taʻālā,* to continue working on it as time and circumstances allow.

We pray to Allah for forgiveness and of His mercy to endow us, *wa nuṣallī wa nusallim 'alā sayyidinā Muḥammad ṣallā Allāhu 'alayhi wa sallam.* The last of our prayers is – All thanks are due to Allah Alone, the Lord of the Heavens and the Earth, Lord of Mankind.

Notes and References

1. *al-Ḥajj* 22: 41.
2. *al-Anbiyā'* 21: 105.
3. The words *'min ba'd adh-Dhikr'* is a reference to the original version of the Scripture lodged in the *al-Lawḥ al-Maḥfūẓ,* the Preserved Tablet, which is also referred to as *Umm al-Kitāb* (the Mother of the Book).
4. *al-An'ām* 6: 165.
5. See: Imām az-Zarkashī (Badr ad-dīn Muḥammad ibn 'Abdullāh: *Al-Burhān fī 'Ulūm al-Qur'ān)* (4 vols.) edited and annotated by Muḥammad Abū al-Faḍl Ibrāhīm, Dār Iḥyā' al-Kutub al-'Arabiyyah, owned by 'Īsā al-Bābī al-Ḥalabī and Co., Cairo, 1957. Vol. 1, pp. 194ff.
6. *Ibid.,* Vol. 1, pp. 195ff.
7. *al-Ḥujurāt* 49: 13.
8. Ibn Hishām, Vol. 4, p. 553. Translated by A. Guillaume, Oxford University Press, Sixth impression, 1980 (Karachi).
9. *al-Mā'idah* 5: 3.
10. See: W. Montgomery Watt, *Muhammad, Prophet and Statesman,* Oxford University Press, American Version (1978). Says Watt: 'Altogether, then, Muhammad's position in these months was still precarious . . . The community was established in Madina, but it was far from being firmly established . . . Life in the oasis was still conducted mainly on the basis of previous customs . . . The ideas of the Qur'ān were thus by no means the only factor determining the course of life in Madina' (pp. 100–1).
11. *Fatḥ al-Bārī fī Ṣaḥīḥ al-Bukhārī,* Vol. 1, p. 195.
12. *Ṣaḥīḥ al-Bukhārī* (as-Sindī Commentary, Vol. 4, p. 41).
13. Narrated by Muslim.
14. Sayyid Quṭb, *Milestones (Ma'ālim fī aṭ-Ṭarīq),* Cairo, 1965.
15. *Ṣaḥīḥ al-Bukhārī,* Vol. 5, pp. 190ff., edited by M. Muhsin Khan, Crescent Publishing House, Turkey.
16. *al-Baqarah* 2: 120.

17. *Ibid.*, 2: 84.

18. *Āl 'Imrān* 3: 119.

19. *an-Naml* 27: 76.

20. *al-Baqarah* 2: 89.

21. *Tafsīr al-Jalālain, Sūrah al-Baqarah,* verse 89, footnote to pages 20, 21, 22ff. Dār al-Ma'rifah, Bayrout.

22. I am grateful to the authorities and the staff at the computer section at the Islamic Foundation (Leicester) for the help and service they rendered me by preparing lists of references for a number of words and entries from their computerized Qur'ān.

23. We have the witness of the wife of the Prophet, Ṣafiyyah bint Ḥuyay ibn Akhṭab (leader of the Jews of Banū an-Naḍīr) that her father and uncle, after they came back from visiting the Prophet, had a curious dialogue, which she overheard, to the effect that they recognized Muḥammad as the future Prophet foretold in the Torah. Nevertheless, they determined to oppose him out of spite and hatred because he was not of the seed of Israel (Jacob). See Ibn Hishām's account of the biography of Ṣafiyyah bint Ḥuyay ibn Akhṭab.

24. W. Montgomery Watt, *Muhammad at Medina,* pp. 227, 228ff., Oxford University Press, 1981. See also: (a) R.B. Serjeant, 'The Constitution of Madina', *Islamic Quarterly,* Vol. 8 (January–June 1964), pp. 3–16; also his article on a similar theme in *BSOAS,* 41 (1978), pp. 1–42; (b) Barakat Ahmad, *Muhammad and the Jews,* Vikas Publishing House Ltd., New Delhi (India), 1979, pp. 39ff. Ahmad does little more than quote the Orientalists' sources with absolute and unquestioning approval.

25. Ibn Ḥajar, *Tahdhīb al-Tahdhīb,* Hyderabad, 1327 A.H., Vol. 12, p. 265.

26. Before the *Hijrah,* fighting, even in self-defence was not permissible for the Muslims, because, being few in number, scattered, and stateless, they were no match for the overwhelming power of the Quraysh. To what extent Muslims living as persecuted minorities may choose this as a norm depends on the extent to which their situation is parallel to that of the early Muslims of Makkah. The total number of Muslims in Makkah cannot have exceeded more than a few hundred, given that the total number of Muslims participating in the Battle of Badr was little more than three hundred men.

27. *al-Furqān* 25: 63, 65.

28. See: al-Ghazālī, *Iḥyā' 'Ulūm ad-Dīn,* Kitāb az-Zuhd wa at-Tawakkul (The book of the Revival of Religious Sciences).

29. See: Yūsuf al-Qarḍāwī: *az-Zakāt.*

30. *Zakāt,* as a religious obligation, was not instituted in Madinah, it was done in the early Makkan period. Thus an early reference to *Zakāt* is to be found in *Sūrah al-Muzzammil* (73: 20). *Sūrah al-Muzzammil* was perhaps the third *sūrah* to be revealed in Makkah. However, well-to-do Muslims continued to pay *Zakāt* on an individual basis. Insofar as the Muslims were poor in the first stages of their history, only a few individuals were in a position to pay *Zakāt.* Then the circumstances of persecution and the *Hijrah* effectively mitigated against a regular payment of *Zakāt.* Al-Baladhurī suggested that the regular collection of *Zakāt* started in the year 6 *Hijrah,* when the Prophet sent 'Alā' ibn al-Ḥaḍramī to Bahrain to collect *Zakāt* (*aṭ-Ṭabarī,* 1, 1601; 3, 117, 148). Then Mu'ādh ibn Jabal was sent to Yemen. Other delegates and tax collectors were sent to almost all the regions in which Muslims lived in a majority. The Prophet briefed them extensively on the regulations of *Zakāt,* teaching them himself, on all matters pertaining to *Zakāt.* Sometimes, he had those instructions on *Zakāt* written out in detail and then he handed them the scrolls on which these were written.

31. *al-Baqarah* 2: 278, 279.

32. *al-Ḥashr* 59: 7.

33. According to Yusūf al-Qarḍāwī (in his book *az-Zakāt*), the ultimate aim of *Zakāt* is to eliminate poverty. So, if the funds of *Zakāt* permit, the poor recipients of *Zakāt* should receive not only a small amount of money to relieve their immediate suffering, but should be given enough to take them beyond the limits of poverty and thus provide full employment for them, so that, in future, they would not qualify to receive *Zakāt.*

34. The word *Ḥijāb* signifies the rules of the *Sharī'ah* which stipulate the conditions and the kind of dress which a Muslim woman has to observe if she goes outside the home, or when she mixes with non-*Maḥram,* persons not related to her by a sacred bond, like husband, parents, brothers and sisters, uncles, aunts, etc. The male non-*Maḥram* are those persons to whom a woman could legally be joined in marriage.

35. This *ḥadīth* is found only in the *Musnad* of Imām Aḥmad ibn Ḥanbal.

36. *al-Baqarah* 2: 235.

37. *Ibid.,* 2: 187.

38. This *ḥadīth* is narrated on the authority of 'Ā'ishah by both Bukhārī and Muslim.

39. Ibn Sa'd, Vol. 8, p. 278, Dār Ṣādir, Bayrout (this volume is devoted to the study of women Companions of the Prophet).

40. *Ibid.,* p. 410ff.

41. *Ibid.,* p. 424ff.

42. *Ibid.*

43. *al-Aḥzāb* 33: 6.

44. Al-Shaikh 'Abd al-Ḥay al-Kattānī: *Niẓām al-Ḥukūmah an-Nabawīyah.* Also called *at-Tarātīb al-Idāriyyah,* 2 vols. (Arabic), Vol. One, p. 20ff. Fāss (Morocco), n.d.

45. *Ibid.*, Vol. 2, pp. 44–5ff.

46. See: Zakaria Bashier, *Muslim Women in the Midst of Change,* The Islamic Foundation, Leicester, 1978, 1985.

47. The books of *Āthār* (or life stories of the Companions of the Prophet) are an important source of the sociological dimension of the early Islamic society of Madinah. The most important among these *Āthār* books are the following:

(a) *Muṣannaf 'Abd ar-Razzāq.*
(b) *Muṣannaf ibn Abī Shaybah.*
(c) *Sunan Sa'īd ibn Manṣūr.*
(d) *Sharḥ Ma'ānī al-Āthār* by aṭ-Ṭaḥāwī.
(e) Ibn Sa'd, *At-Ṭabaqāt al-Kubrā,* Vol. 8 (on women Companions of the Prophet).

48. *Āl 'Imrān* 3: 159.

49. *al-Qalam* 68: 4.

50. *at-Tawbah* 9: 128.

Index